Non-Governmental Orphan Relief in China

Based on field studies and in-depth interviews across rural and urban China, this book presents a socio-legal analysis of non-state organised care for some of China's most vulnerable children.

The first full-length book to examine non-state organised care of modern China's "lonely children" (*gu'er*), this book describes the context in which abandonment occurs and the care provided to children unlikely to be adopted because of their disability. It also explores the various faith groups and humanitarian workers providing this care in private orphanages and foster homes in response to perceived deficiencies in the state orphanage system, in the context of a broader societal shift from "welfare statism" to "welfare pluralism". Formal law and policy has not always kept pace with this shift. This study demonstrates that, in practice, state regulation of these unauthorised care providers has mostly centred on local-level negotiations, hidden rules, and discretion, with mixed outcomes for children. However, there has also been a recent shift towards tighter state control and clearer laws, policies, and standards.

This timely research sheds light on the life paths and stories of today's "lonely children" and the changing terrain of civil society, humanitarianism, policy-making, and state power in modern China. As such, this book will appeal to students and scholars of Asian and Chinese studies, law and society, NGOs, and comparative social and child welfare.

Anna High is lecturer in law at the University of Otago, New Zealand. Her primary research interests are Chinese Law and Criminal Law.

Routledge Contemporary China Series

199 Illicit Industries and China's Shadow Economy
Challenges and Prospects for Global Governance and Human Security
Edited Victor Teo and Sungwon Yoon

200 Re-engineering Affordable Care Policy in China
Is Marketization a Solution?
Peter Nan-shong Lee

201 The Land Question in China
Agrarian Capitalism, Industrious Revolution, and East Asian Development
Shaohua Zhan

202 Radio and Social Transformation in China
Wei Lei

203 Internet Video Culture in China
YouTube, Youku, and the Space in Between
Marc L. Moskowitz

204 Securitization of the Umbrella Movement in Hong Kong
The Rise of a Patriotocratic System
Cora Y.T. Hui

205 Non-Governmental Orphan Relief in China
Law, Policy, and Practice
Anna High

206 Living in the Shadows of China's HIV/AIDS Epidemics
Sex, Drugs and Bad Blood
Shelley Torcetti

For more information about this series, please visit: www.routledge.com/Routledge-Contemporary-China-Series/book-series/SE0768

Non-Governmental Orphan Relief in China

Law, Policy, and Practice

Anna High

Routledge
Taylor & Francis Group
LONDON AND NEW YORK

First published 2020
by Routledge
2 Park Square, Milton Park, Abingdon, Oxon OX14 4RN

and by Routledge
52 Vanderbilt Avenue, New York, NY 10017

Routledge is an imprint of the Taylor & Francis Group, an informa business

First issued in paperback 2021

British Library Cataloguing-in-Publication Data
A catalogue record for this book is available from the British Library

Library of Congress Cataloging-in-Publication Data
Names: High, Anna, author.
Title: Non-governmental orphan relief in China : law, policy, and practice / Anna High.
Description: Abingdon, Oxon ; New York, NY : Routledge, 2020. |
Series: Routledge contemporary China series | Includes bibliographical references and index.
Identifiers: LCCN 2019016217 (print) | LCCN 2019018254 (ebook) |
ISBN 9780429447150 (Ebook) | ISBN 9780429823855 (Adobe Reader) |
ISBN 9780429823848 (ePub) | ISBN 9780429823831 (Mobipocket Encrypted) | ISBN 9781138331686 (hardback)
Subjects: LCSH: Orphans–Services for–China. | Orphans–Government policy–China. | Orphans–Legal status, laws, etc.–China. |
Non-governmental organizations–China. | Non-governmental organizations–Law and legislation–China.
Classification: LCC HV1317 (ebook) | LCC HV1317 .H54 2020 (print) |
DDC 362.730951–dc23
LC record available at https://lccn.loc.gov/2019016217

ISBN: 978-1-138-33168-6 (hbk)
ISBN: 978-1-03-209139-6 (pbk)
ISBN: 978-0-429-44715-0 (ebk)

Typeset in Times New Roman
by Wearset Ltd, Boldon, Tyne and Wear

Contents

Acknowledgements

This research depended entirely on the willingness of volunteers and caregivers working at dozens of orphanages, foster homes, and other not-for-profit organisations to invite me into their lives and share their stories with me. I am continually humbled by the extraordinary devotion and resilience of these friends in China who have committed to caring for some of China's most vulnerable.

I am profoundly grateful to my supervisors at the University of Oxford, Professor Fernanda Pirie and Professor Rachel Murphy, for their encouragement and supervision throughout my graduate studies. I benefitted enormously, and in many ways, from being their student. Thanks also to my DPhil examiners, Dr Tobias Kelly and Professor Anna Lora-Wainwright, for their helpful feedback, and to Professor Terence Halliday of the American Bar Foundation, for reading my thesis with generosity and encouraging me to write this book. At the University of Otago, the ideas in this project continued to be shaped with the support of Emeritus Professor Stuart Anderson, a constant source of wisdom and insight. I am also grateful to the many other friends and colleagues who have provided advice and assistance along the way, including Ann Marie Blanchard, Jesse Wall, Mark Henaghan, Nicola Peart, Rex Ahdar, Leslie Wang, Amanda Gilbertson, Lili Song, Drew Snoddy, and Jonathon Yeldon.

China has become such an important part of my personal and professional life thanks largely to two wonderful Mandarin teachers, Pei-Lien Hsueh and Paul Valese, who have between them instilled in thousands of students a love for Chinese language and culture. China can be an exhausting fieldwork site, and gathering data on my most recent trip in 2017 was made more challenging by having my baby daughter in tow. This would not have been possible without the help of our dear friend Stephanie Homan, who gave up her summer to travel with us, taking wonderful care of Margaret and providing us both with immeasurable support. My sincere thanks also to the many generous friends who have helped in different ways on various trips to China over the course of this project, including Johnson Tan, Joe Boyle, Karim Issa, Caitlin Mullins, Katie Truss, Peng Han, and Carl and Sachi Hinze. I am also very grateful to have had the help of three outstanding research assistants, Ambrosia O'Connor in China and the US, and Feifei Zhou and Hannah Pedgrift in New Zealand, each talented scholars in their own right.

Financial support for research and writing was provided by the Rhodes Trust, Magdalen College Oxford, the Mustard Seed Foundation, the Henry Luce Foundation/American Council of Learned Societies Program in China Studies, the Association for Asian Studies, the University of Otago Faculty of Law, the University of Otago Humanities Division, and Mr Johnson Tan. Earlier versions of parts of this book have previously appeared in "'It's Grace and Favor, It's Not Law': Extra-Legal Regulation of Foreign Foster Homes in China," *University of Pennsylvania Asian Law Review* (2017) 12: 357–405; "Grassroots NGO Regulation and China's Local Legal Culture," *Socio-Legal Review* (2013) 9, no. 2: 1–50; and "China's Orphan Welfare System: Laws, Policies and Filled Gaps," *University of Pennsylvania East Asia Law Review* (2013) 8, no. 1: 126–76. Thank you to the publishers for permission to use these materials.

Finally, I am constantly grateful to Ryan, Margaret, and Fred High, and to my family and friends, for their unconditional love and support.

1 Introduction

"Small government, big society" and the negotiated emergence of private orphan relief in modern China

St Martin's Home for Children with Disabilities[1] occupies a compound of ageing double-storey concrete buildings set between two large cornfields on the outskirts of a small county in Hebei, China. It was founded in 1993 by Sister Chen, a quiet, diminutive Catholic nun who is now in her seventies. Prior to establishing St Martin's, Sister Chen was working as a nurse in her diocese's community clinic. One day, a young boy around ten years old was brought to the clinic by a local villager, who said he had found the boy "thrown away" (*reng*) in a nearby rubbish dump. The boy was intellectually disabled and had been found naked, emaciated, and eating from the garbage with a dangerously high fever. The sisters of the clinic bathed and fed him, treated his fever, and found a local Catholic family willing to take him into their home as an informal foster child. Not long after, another abandoned child, this time an infant only a few weeks old, was left at the sisters' residence. Once more, the child was treated and then sent to live with the same generous foster family. The family was soon caring for four abandoned children, in addition to their own biological children. The plight of these children and the overburdened family weighed heavily on Sister Chen's mind. She began to feel that although she had followed her spiritual calling to be a nun, she was not living a sufficiently loving life. She sought counsel from her priest, who encouraged her to follow where this feeling was leading her: to set up an orphanage for the abandoned children of her community. Convinced of God's call to this new vocation, Sister Chen borrowed 300,000 *yuan*[2] from a parishioner to rent and renovate facilities and began to collect donations of supplies and money from local supporters of her cause. In time, as more and more people came to hear about Sister Chen's work, St Martin's grew from caring for just a few foundlings to over one hundred children at any one time, spread out among the orphanage grounds and local foster families. These children came to St Martin's from all over the county, some abandoned by the roadside, some in hospital corridors, still others left furtively on St Martin's doorstep. Since Sister Chen set up St Martin's, and as more state funding for vulnerable children has become available, a state orphanage has been built in her county; but when that first ten-year-old boy was brought to the nuns, there were very few options for orphaned or abandoned children in the area. And so, St Martin's came to be—an organic, grassroots response to a pressing local need. Most of the children in

Sister Chen's care had never known a home other than St Martin's, or experienced family other than with the children, nuns, and volunteers of the orphanage. As an unofficial and unregistered orphanage, with no ties to the system of state-run orphanages through which formal adoptions are processed, St Martin's children were not on the waiting lists for either national or international adoption. It was also extremely difficult to find local foster families for the St Martin's children because they almost all had severe mental or physical disabilities requiring costly specialised care.

I first stayed at St Martin's in the summer of 2010, one of dozens of orphanages and foster homes I visited in the course of researching the stories of non-state organisations devoted to the care of orphaned and abandoned children in China. There were around forty-five children living at St Martin's at the time, each assigned to one of eight *jiating* (family groups) of five to six children. At St Martin's, I spent most of my time with *jiating* number six, a group of older girls who shared a dormitory room on the second floor. This was a clean and bright space decorated with paper flowers, colourful bedding, and a big mirror which the girls used as they styled each other's hair. There was lots of laughter in *jiating* six. Like most sisters, the girls both looked out for each other and annoyed and teased each other. They had a variety of disabilities and medical conditions, from intellectual impairments to dwarfism to spina bifida, but they were all relatively self-sufficient. Their room was somewhat of an oasis at St Martin's. In other rooms, the bleaker side of orphanage life was evident as teams of dedicated and cheerful, but clearly exhausted, nuns, *gongren* (paid workers), and *yigong* (volunteers) cared around the clock for many severely incapacitated and sick children. Some of these children were so painfully thin that every bone showed clearly through their skin. Others spent hours at a time tied to their beds; according to the sisters, this was done so that they could not fling themselves out and be injured. Every morning at 5:30 a.m. and every evening at 7 p.m., the sisters, volunteers, and as many children as could walk or wheel their way would gather into a simple ground floor chapel for Catholic prayers and mass. On Sundays, these were led by a visiting priest, and the children would change into new clothes for the week to mark the occasion. After evening mass, the older children and younger volunteers would head out to the courtyard to bounce on a rusty trampoline, snack on tomatoes and kumquats from the large adjoining kitchen orchard, or climb onto the roof of a small annexe to watch the sun set.

Sister Chen was not one to complain. In all of our conversations, she would emphasise her gratitude for the many donors and volunteers who had supported her work in the years since St Martin's first opened its doors and for God's provision. It was also plain that she and the other sisters had overcome many difficulties in caring for hundreds of charges over the years with at times very limited funding. If pressed, Sister Chen would recall with quiet dignity the exhaustion of the home's earliest years, when the orphanage had no kitchen and the nuns had to cook each meal on an open fire, when there was no money to spare and they had to wash torn and threadbare cloth diapers by hand multiple times a day to be worn over and over, and when every waking moment was spent thinking of how the children could be fed and clothed and kept warm in the bitingly cold winters. Frostbite was common. By the time of my visits, St Martin's was warm in winter and well supported by donations from the local Catholic community, as the general standard of living in the area had improved. There was also enough money to employ a small team of young Christian women from nearby villages to ease the workload of the sisters. But still St Martin's had the look of a place where the sisters were doing what they could with the little they had. Despite repeated requests, the orphanage had never received more than token financial support from its local Civil Affairs bureau (the government department responsible, among other things, for child welfare) and had not been able to register as an approved care provider or non-governmental organisation (NGO). Its care practices and standards were not regulated, and its accounts were not subject to the scrutiny that registered institutions and NGOs receive. On the other hand, Sister Chen described her work as permitted (*pifu*) by local Civil Affairs officials, who had shown tacit approval over the years by giving token gifts at Chinese New Year, providing documents to facilitate adoption on the few occasions when a local family had been found for a St Martin's child, and even occasionally bringing children to be cared for at St Martin's.

The evening scene at St Martin's was very similar to one that played out at Good News Training Centre, on the outskirts of a city the next province over. Like St Martin's, Good News was founded to help address the special needs of abandoned children, and there was a strong sense of kinship and community among the caregivers, volunteers, and children who called Good News home. Good News was founded not by Chinese Catholics but by a European Protestant couple, Alain and Brigitte. Unlike the children of St Martin's, the children at Good News were registered as orphans. They had formerly resided in state-run orphanages across China, but due to being blind or visually impaired, they had been brought into Good News' care to receive specialist care. At Good News, they learned and lived with other blind children, receiving occupational therapy and instruction in braille, in addition to mainstream education. Alain and Brigitte began their work many years ago, on a smaller scale and in a different location, by visiting orphanages in person and negotiating for children whose special needs could be better served off-site to be released to their care. Good News was one of scores of "foster homes" across China that partnered directly with state orphanages in this way. These foster homes—as the term is used in this book—differed from traditional foster families that bring one or two children into an existing family unit. China's orphan foster homes employed salaried caregivers to provide congregate care to a larger number of children than would usually live in one household. They also differed from private orphanages in that their children were formally in the guardianship of the state but had been fostered from state orphanages. Most of China's most prominent and established foster homes were set up by foreigners, but I also visited foster homes set up and run by Chinese nationals. All were run by Christians who had chosen to respond to the biblical call to "look after orphans ... in their distress"[3] by assisting state orphanages in their enormous task. This was done by taking children from state orphanages off-site, often for years at a time, and providing them with specialist medical care and education, opportunities that have historically not always been available in the state welfare system. In many cases, this specialist care ultimately improved the child's chances of being placed for domestic or international adoption.

Like St Martin's, Good News had a large kitchen garden, but with raised beds to allow blind children to try their hands at sowing and growing. Good News was generously funded by deep international pockets, and its most recent location was in a large, newly renovated rental house in an upmarket private country estate. In summer, the children would go for walks around the estate to pick fruit from nearby organic orchards, listen to the estate's resident peacocks, and pet the dairy goats that grazed in a neighbour's field. They lived in dormitories designed to emulate family groups, each with a housemother, becoming brother and sister to each other. The inflow of euros, US dollars, and Chinese *yuan* from loyal international and local supporters was evident in the quality of the facilities and care practices. Through many years of working with blind children from across China, and with the support of volunteer experts from across the globe, Good News had developed cutting edge occupational and educational programmes to teach their children independence and self-sufficiency.

Caring for China's "lonely children"

The English term "orphan" is experienced by some as pejorative and objectifying, defining a child solely by her parental status. It is also narrow, implying a child's parents have both passed away. In China, the children cared for in orphanages and foster homes like St Martin's and Good News are not necessarily "true orphans"; most still have one or both parents living but have been abandoned by their birth parents and extended family for a wide range of reasons. The Chinese word for orphan is *gu'er*. Taken literally, the term *gu'er* is broad enough to accommodate these various life experiences—*er* meaning "child" and *gu* meaning "solitary", "isolated", or "alone". As used in this book, "lonely child", or *gu'er*, is a simple and poignant way to refer to children who are no longer cared for by their parents. This can be due to death, abandonment, or other life circumstances—a child orphaned by illness, a child whose widowed father is sent to prison, or a child with complex medical needs his parents cannot afford to treat, who is left in a hospital corridor out of desperation. This is a vulnerable population in need of special provision, protection, and care.

Across China, tens of thousands of *gu'er* are living in the care of orphanages set up by the government. Since the 1990s, when reports of systemic abuse and shockingly high mortality rates emerged from a number of state-run orphanages, these institutions have received increased attention and funding to improve caregiving standards and outcomes for their resident children. Although a great deal of progress has been made, there have been ongoing gaps and deficiencies in state-provided orphan welfare in China. State orphanages are generally only located in large urban centres and are often unable to provide optimal care for their charges, the vast majority of whom have special medical needs or disabilities. In response to these problems, hundreds of humanitarian workers, both Chinese and foreign, have organised a range of voluntary groups, charities, and caregiving facilities to provide supplementary welfare for China's lonely children.

Based on longitudinal ethnographic research, this book tracks the changing scope of a spectrum of civic engagement with orphan relief in China. This is not an exhaustive survey of the sector. Rather, the stories presented are chosen to illustrate the diverse lived experiences of *gu'er* and their caregivers across China, while pointing to the shared concerns and challenges of orphanages and foster homes as they negotiate changing laws, policies, and practices. The organisations surveyed for this study ranged from rural grassroots Catholic and Protestant orphanages, taking in children directly and without much state involvement, to foster homes like Good News, providing long-term off-site care to children from provinces across China, to multimillion-dollar onsite partnerships between American mission groups and state orphanages. These non-profit enterprises comprised an alternative and often unacknowledged system of care for one of China's most vulnerable populations. While they varied greatly in size and scope, these organisations had in common that they existed, until recently, in a legal grey zone and were generally not formally authorised or supervised by the state (unregistered). This book introduces the changing state policies and laws on NGOs and child welfare that have regulated the sector on paper over time, but my focus is on the more interesting question of how those laws and policies have actually played out in practice, in different locations and at different times. My research shows a local welfare system in which formal, restrictive laws have frequently been sidelined, with unauthorised welfare providers permitted to play an important, but fragmented and underutilised, role in providing care for some of China's loneliest children.

Modern civic engagement with orphan welfare: responding to gaps and scandals

After the founding of the People's Republic of China (PRC) in 1949, state welfare programmes were a key aspect of establishing the newly ruling Communist Party's legitimacy as the party of and for the people. To this end, most private orphanages across China were either closed or appropriated by the state, and over time the government came to monopolise institutional care for orphaned and abandoned children.[4] These state-run orphanages, known as "welfare institutions" in Chinese (*fuliyuan*), were generally only established in urban areas. In rural areas, rather than take direct responsibility for *gu'er*, the state primarily relied on local agricultural communes (*renmin gongshe*) and informal kinship networks to ensure *gu'er* welfare.[5] However, when China entered the reform era in the 1980s, the system of rural communes was effectively dismantled. Vulnerable groups—such as *gu'er*, the elderly, and persons with disabilities—became more reliant on traditional family networks to meet their welfare needs.[6] At the same time, factors such as rural-urban migration, high rural poverty rates, and strict birth-planning policies all served to weaken those kinship networks and drive child abandonment, resulting in an increased need for coordinated *gu'er* welfare services in areas unserved by state welfare institutions. In response to rural *gu'er* needs, and in the absence of state-provided alternative care, orphanages like St Martin's emerged over time at the grassroot level across China. This type of private *gu'er* relief developed organically and typically without state oversight or support. Hundreds of thousands of children have been cared for in China's private orphanages, organisations that varied greatly in size, quality of care, and funding. For the most part, their resident children were not included in official state surveys of *gu'er*, as they were not affiliated or registered with the state system of welfare. This also meant they were not usually on state adoption waiting lists.[7]

In addition to this grassroots gap-filling, a great deal of civic engagement has occurred over the years in response to perceived deficiencies within the state system. These problems were brought into the international spotlight in the mid-1990s by a series of dramatic Western exposés (most notably, the British documentary *The Dying Rooms* and a Human Rights Watch/Asia report, *Death by Default*) that highlighted appalling conditions and mortality rates in a number of Chinese state orphanages. Even today, images of sick babies dying lonely deaths in overcrowded institutions dominate popular conceptions of orphan welfare in China. But there is a more hopeful, less visible story to be told. Volunteerism is on the rise in China, and today many state orphanages, even in remote areas, are assisted on a regular basis by groups of university students, churchgoers, and expatriates. International adoption has brought an influx of funding from foreign adoption agencies, and government programmes have been put in place to improve institutional facilities and medical care. And outside of orphanage walls, scores of specialist foster homes such as Good News were set up in recent decades by both Chinese and foreign humanitarian groups. These orphanage alternatives had different specialties, structures, and care models but a common mission: to provide high-quality medical care and family-style upbringings to children who were still in the legal guardianship of the state. China's foster homes ranged from small-scale operations, in which a dozen children were cared for by a handful of volunteers and paid *ayis* (nannies, literally "aunties") in a rented hospital wing or suburban home, to large institutions caring for hundreds of children at any one time in palatial, purpose-built facilities. Many of the homes had expertise in providing care for a particular condition, such as cerebral palsy, or a particular type of medical intervention, such as heart surgery. The children resident in foster homes were fostered out by state orphanage directors on the basis of trust and good *guanxi* (connections, relationships) but remained in the legal guardianship of the state orphanage. Unlike local foster families, which are increasingly relied on by some state orphanages, the foster homes introduced in this book were caring for children from many different, distant provinces, with little to no formal oversight by state authorities.

Welfare pluralism with one eye closed

This new landscape of non-governmental orphan relief reflected trends in the Chinese nonprofit sector more generally. When the PRC was founded, the new socialist regime largely staked its moral authority on its ability to provide for the basic needs of the people through the work unit (*danwei*) and commune (*gongshe*) systems. Welfare was seen as the prerogative of the state. Accordingly, in the tumultuous first few decades of the PRC (1949–1978), most independent social organisations, including charities, were subject to takeover or dissolution, as the state sought to establish total control over social resources and activities.[8] However, as post-Mao China entered the modern reform era and moved away from the commune/work unit system and towards a more open market economy, the state began to experience tremendous welfare pressure. Social service responsibilities were decentralised to underfunded local governments, which were frequently unable to meet the welfare needs of local vulnerable and marginalised populations. Accordingly, the nonprofit and voluntary sector gradually began to be revived, a tacit acknowledgement of state welfare deficiencies.[9] In the 1990s, the Chinese government promoted the slogan "small government and big society" as it implemented various policies and programmes aimed at increasing non-governmental welfare and charitable projects.[10] The Chinese welfare system began to transform, moving away from a secretive state monopoly and towards a more transparent and mixed (public/private) system.[11] This policy shift has been described as a move from welfare statism to welfare pluralism, with more openness on the part of the state to facilitating private/non-governmental financial support of welfare programmes and initiatives.[12] As Linda Wong elaborated at the time,

> [t]he retreat of the state has occurred in provision, funding and regulation ... greater pluralism in welfare has undoubtedly emerged... In the 1980s, privately run services were almost non-existent. In the current decade [1990s], amenities operated by individuals, like nurseries, old people's homes, facilities for the handicapped, have made their appearance. Many non-government organisations have likewise operated with overt state blessing. Even the old demons, missionary groups from the West, have joined in the fray.... Under Mao, charity had a bad reputation. Now, the verdict on philanthropy is overturned.[13]

As is often the case given China's rapid pace of development, formal law and policy has not always kept pace with this shift to welfare pluralism in practice. There are millions of unregistered nonprofit groups providing grassroot social services across China, including non-governmental orphanages, foster homes, and other orphan relief services. These groups were long permitted to play a role in welfare provision without being subject to formal regulation by the state. Oversight tended to happen instead at the local level, on an informal and discretionary basis, commonly described as the "one eye open, one eye closed" approach to "illegal" activities by unauthorised groups.

This informal approach to local oversight of civil society created space and flexibility for unregistered organisations to care for children in need. Such care arrangements were tolerated by local officials and in some cases encouraged and informally supported—but, unsurprisingly, only for so long as nothing went wrong. A tragic example of something going wrong occurred in 2013 in Lankao county, Henan province. For many years, a local street vendor named Yuan Lihai had been running an unofficial orphanage from her home in Lankao, with the knowledge and apparent blessing of the county government. Her community was not serviced by a state orphanage, and by 2013 she had eighteen *gu'er* and young adults in her care. Her mission ended abruptly when a fire broke out while she was away from home. Six children, aged from seven months to five years, and one young adult were killed.

Official state media reports were quick to describe Yuan's orphanage as illegal, but it also seems that prior to the fire, her work had been accepted and even encouraged at the local level, including by state agencies, as a legitimate humanitarian response to children in need. She had received favourable media coverage in the past, and the county government had publicly praised her actions. It was only after the fire that the orphanage was denounced as illegal. Six local officials lost their jobs for tolerating the "illegally run" orphanage and thereby failing in their duty of supervision. It is not known whether better state supervision, support, or intervention could have prevented the fire at Yuan's orphanage or lowered the death toll, especially given the state's poor track record in providing quality *gu'er* care. But it did become clear after the fire that state entitlements, such as orphan subsidies and access to regulated adoption, were not reaching the unregistered *gu'er* in Yuan's care prior to the fire. Further, the tragedy showed that while the "one eye closed" approach could accommodate cooperation between local government and ostensibly prohibited social services, it could also result in a problematic supervision gap. As Professor Shang, a leading expert in *gu'er* relief in China, had argued years earlier, the state had been missing from this field as regulator, hesitant to establish formal relations with private welfare providers, and vulnerable children were at risk as a result.[14]

The nonregulation of unauthorised orphanages and foster homes also created uncertainty for both state and social actors, as seen in the aftermath of Lankao. Foster homes across China felt the ripple effects of the fire when Henan province responded to the tragedy by clamping down on inter-provincial foster care. Many foster homes, including Good News, experienced pressure from various provinces to return *gu'er* to their home state-run institutions. Private orphanages also reported that in the years following the Lankao fire, state regulation and oversight of their activities stepped up, at least in some locations. As this book explores, these sorts of reactive, abrupt policy changes had long been an inevitable part of life for orphan relief organisations working in a legal grey zone. As one of my research participants described it, even prior to the Lankao fire, "illegal" grassroots orphanages and foster homes were living between "lines that are moving constantly—it's a moving target. What is acceptable one day is not OK the next. You don't know where the line is so it's easy to cross it" (*Alana, founder/director of Red Thread Foster Home, 2009*). Importantly, their survival had always been contingent not only on top-down policy changes but also on local negotiations with paternalistic state actors. These negotiations tended to be governed by hidden rules and demonstrated a local legal culture in which flexibility, *guanxi* (personal networks), *renqing* (human empathy and obligations), and individualised justice were arguably more important in practice than abstract, general, and certain rules.

In the chapters and case studies that follow, I explore the changing nature of state oversight of non-governmental orphanages and foster homes in China. What did the transition to welfare pluralism look like at the level of local *gu'er* relief? How did these local organisations interact and negotiate with state actors and society and cultivate legitimacy, despite their "illegality", and what could these local processes tell us about the nature of regulation and law/policy-making in modern China? What were the power dynamics, rules, and processes that impacted the scope and limits of their work with *gu'er*? How have recent developments in Chinese charity and foreign NGO law impacted the ability of the voluntary sector to contribute to improving quality of life for China's *gu'er*? And looking forward, what are the rights-based duties of the Chinese state to facilitate, coordinate, and oversee these types of contributions?

China's complicated relationship with the third sector

The emergence of organised social assistance for *gu'er* in China has taken place in a sociopolitical context that is often antagonistic towards the third sector (voluntary, as opposed to state or private, associations). Given the welfare pressures facing the state, welfare pluralism is now seen as indispensable to China's economic and social development. At the same time, the Chinese state has frequently treated the third sector with suspicion, viewing non-governmental groups and associations as threatening for the civic organisation and possible political agendas they represent. As Yuwen Li has noted,

> [t]he government has exhibited undeniably contradictory ideas about NGOs. On the one hand, there is some degree of recognition that NGOs provide social services that governmental bodies cannot do or cannot do well ... On the other hand, the fear and suspicion that some NGOs may challenge governmental policy and undermine political stability, has resulted in the government strictly controlling the establishment and operation of NGOs.[15]

This perceived tension between the emergence of organised social engagement and the preservation of China's communist political ideology is reflected linguistically: the literal translation of "non-governmental organisation" (*fei guanfang zuzhi* or *fei zhengfu zuzhi*) could also be taken to mean "anti-government organisation" (*fei* meaning both "non-" and "anti-"). The tension is also reflected in a restrictive and controlling legal regime governing charities and NGOs, which is widely considered China's "most serious and fundamental barrier to [NGO] development".[16] Nonprofit and voluntary groups can register as one of three main types of NGO: "social organisations" (*shehui tuanti*), "social service organisations" (*shehui fuwu jigou*, previously *minban feiqiye danwei*), or "foundations" (*jijinhui*). In order to register, an organisation must first secure the support of a relevant government agency to act as an organisation's "professional supervising unit" (PSU). PSUs are known colloquially as *popo*, or "mothers-in-law", due to their close oversight of organisational activities and operations. The PSU system means that registered NGOs in China tend not to be as autonomous from the state as in democratic contexts but instead are effectively absorbed into the penumbra of government bureaucracy. At the same time, these types of theoretical restrictions on NGO activity are frequently ineffective in practice, in that the vast majority of Chinese nonprofit voluntary organisations are unregistered, operating in "various quasi-legal states", and not subject to formal *popo* oversight.[17]

Accordingly, China's third sector consists of a continuum of associational structures, ranging from state-dominated registered NGOs to relatively autonomous unregistered groups.[18] This makes it difficult to generalise about state-society relations in China, and there is ongoing debate as to whether China has a realm of associational activity that amounts to "civil society".[19] Indeed, "civil society" is a contested concept. In a narrow political sense, civil society denotes a state-society relationship premised on democratic norms of civil rights and oppositional representation. In other words, the term can be used normatively to refer to the "conditions of liberty".[20] This book instead uses a broader, sociological conception of "civil society" as referring to organised civic participation in the public realm,[21] while recognising that in China there is a great deal of divergence within this associational realm in terms of autonomy from and opposition to the state, and civil organisations may over time "constitute both a challenge to the state and a supporter of shared goals with the state".[22] To explore this divergence, I adopt what Bin Xu refers to as a "complex coexistence" approach to understanding civil society in China, which stresses the complex, changing, and contingent nature of local state-society relations.[23]

Those complex, contradictory feelings towards civil society are also compounded in the field of orphan relief by the number of faith-based and foreign-funded organisations at play. *Gu'er* relief efforts are not exclusively motivated by religious altruism but faith-based work represents a significant piece of the puzzle. China's private[24] orphanages are mostly run by faith-based groups;[25] similarly, my research found that the majority of foreign NGOs providing foster care services for *gu'er* in China were founded by Christians and funded by international churches.[26] Religious groups have long been regarded with special suspicion and mistrust by Chinese authorities given their organising power and allegiance to a higher moral authority than the Communist Party. As a result, Christians in China face a unique set of political and social constraints that impact their ability to provide *gu'er* welfare. Similarly, foreign-funded social work in China tends to be very closely monitored and has historically been seen as unwarranted, demeaning, "welfarist" intervention in China's internal affairs. Foreign involvement in orphan welfare is particularly politically sensitive due to the international shaming China has received since the 1990s for its orphanage standards and due also to China's humbling status as a sending, rather than receiving, country for international adoption. Orphan relief services also by their very existence draw attention to the issue of child abandonment in China, a phenomenon the Chinese government has a vested interest in underemphasising due to its connection to controversial birth-planning policies. In all, questions of "who looks after our children", and the proper role of religious and foreign groups in orphan relief, are inherently emotive and politically charged in the Chinese context.

The case studies that follow shed light on Chinese civil society by looking in detail at a group of unregistered grassroots organisations, rather than focusing on registered NGOs at the state-dominated end of the spectrum. Chinese NGO scholars estimate that there are millions of unregistered nonprofit and voluntary groups in China. But being unregistered does not mean social groups are simply left alone by the state. Rather, at this local state-society interface, state control of social organisations is often veiled and informal. Strict NGO laws, vague child welfare policies, and top-down scepticism towards third sector orphan welfare have been contextualised and adapted to local needs and local politics, such that the "legal rules are only a small piece of the complex".[27] This has created space for informal, unregistered homes to play a quiet but significant role in orphan relief.

By moving in this way beyond a focus on a legal/illegal dichotomy, my research suggests that legitimacy has often been more important than legality when it comes to NGOs in China and their interactions with state and society. The concepts of legitimacy and legality are closely related, with the former often being used in a particular sense to mean "conformable to law", the more general sense being "conformable to rules or standards".[28] Similarly, in Chinese there are two terms for legitimacy—*hefa* and *heli*, literally "complying with law" and "complying with reason", respectively. For most private orphanages and foster homes in China, compliance with legal rules was not an easily achievable, or necessarily desirable, objective, due in part to an ambiguous and shifting regulatory context. Rather, there was much more emphasis in this field of activity on achieving other types of legitimacy in the eyes of society and the state—by providing a useful service, conforming to unspoken rules against evangelism and human rights activism, and avoiding an overtly politicised agenda. It was legitimacy—more than legality—that created opportunities to contribute to orphan welfare. My research brings to light the factors underpinning legitimacy that determined who could play what role in supplementing the state welfare system, adding to our understanding of locally negotiated welfare pluralism and the legitimacy-centred nature of civil society in China generally.

"Lonely child" rights and state duties

On my first visit to St Martin's in 2010, as I spent time in *jiating* number six, I got to know Lina, a twelve-year-old girl who spent almost all of her time on the floor of her room. Lina was a very sharp and observant girl, with a dry sense of humour and a keen interest in learning about my background and how I came to be staying at her home that summer. Lina was born with spina bifida and had a gaping wound at the base of her spine and a slightly enlarged head as a result. She had never seen a map of the world and had never met a *laowai* (foreigner) who could speak to her in Chinese, so she took great interest in questioning me about the world outside of China. Lina shared the *jiating* dormitory with her "sisters", five other girls and teenagers with various physical and intellectual disabilities. Lina was the clear boss and *jiejie* (older sister) of her room, ruling from her nest of towels and blankets in the prime TV-watching position. Although she had a workable, old wheelchair that allowed her to get from the second floor dormitory and down an outside ramp to the chapel and courtyard, Lina wasn't able to attend school, as the local schools could not accommodate her wheelchair or her personal hygiene needs. Instead, volunteers from the local university would come to St Martin's during their summer holidays to teach Lina and some of the other St Martin's children to read and write.

Over the years, some of Sister Chen's children had been adopted by local Catholic families, but finding a local family for Lina was always unlikely, given her medical needs. Research shows that *gu'er* in rural areas who are relatively healthy and developmentally typical are often taken in by informal kinship networks or domestic adoption but that this is much less likely for those with special needs.[29] Unlike state-run orphanages, St Martin's was not associated with the China Centre of Adoption Affairs, the agency exclusively responsible for foreign adoptions, so Lina was never on the international adoption waiting list. But Sister Chen and the other nuns at St Martin's had gone to great lengths to provide as safe and nurturing a home as possible for Lina and her "brothers and sisters". It is not my place to speculate on how Lina's life might have differed if instead of growing up at St Martin's, she had been matched with a family of her own through adoption. For those children that do find a "forever family", joining their new family means leaving the place and people they have always known as home and embarking on a radically different life journey.

I witnessed one such farewell firsthand in 2010 at Good News, when I attended an adoption party for Tessa. Tessa was fourteen years old, congenitally blind, and had been living at Good News for six years before being matched with adoptive parents from America. I spoke to Tessa briefly over lunch before the adoption party began, just after she had met her mother and father in person for the first time. She told me she felt "quite good but so nervous I can't speak. I'm so nervous I can't say anything to them". After lunch, the party began. The children of Good News formed an honour guard at the doorway into the playroom, waving balloons, blowing whistles, and banging toy drums to welcome Tessa and her parents as they processed in. The newly formed family sat in a place of honour at the centre of the room, in front of a projector screen which was showing a touching display of photos from Tessa's time years at Good News. Then came a video in which the other children of Good News said their farewells: "Goodbye, my sister, don't forget about us. We will miss you". Finally, when the emotions of meeting her parents and hearing the messages of love on the video seemed about to overwhelm Tessa, the children came one at a time to kneel in front of her and say goodbye one last time in person. I could keenly feel the intensity of this rite of transition from one family to another.

The very different life paths of Lina and Tessa each highlighted the important role played by non-governmental orphan relief organisations in protecting and advancing the interests and human rights of children. Children who have been deprived of their (birth) family environments have the right to special protection and assistance from the state.[30] Orphaned and abandoned children are also more likely to experience impeded access to basic entitlements such as health care, education, and identity. In China, the state response to *gu'er* vulnerability mainly takes the form of providing institutional care in state-run orphanages. But the consensus of child development experts and the intercountry adoption community is that institutional care should be a subsidiary measure of last resort, given how destructive it can be for children who have already suffered the trauma of losing their birth family and identity. Moreover, the suitability of Chinese state orphanage care has been called into question based on numerous reports and eyewitness accounts of underfunding, lack of training, medical care, and, in some cases, outright abuse and fatal neglect. The foster homes I visited, including Good News, were playing a quiet but important role in addressing those deficiencies, improving *gu'er* access to first-world resources and services, and trying to emulate a family environment as far as possible for children who may otherwise have been institutionalised (family-style care is important for addressing the attachment difficulties experienced by many *gu'er*). Foster home care also typically increased a child's chances of finding an adoption placement, due to the work that foster homes could do to definitively diagnose medical conditions, put in place clear treatment plans, and advocate their children to prospective families abroad. Non-governmental groups that were permitted to partner with state orphanages were in this way able to contribute to the protection and promotion of the human rights of *gu'er*.

This book illustrates that the flow of third-sector resources and services to state orphanage *gu'er* through the foster home model was happening in an unequal, uncoordinated, and fragmented way. In the absence of central oversight or facilitation, foster homes tended to strike up caregiving agreements with accessible state orphanages by building good *guanxi* (relationships) through personal introductions and recommendations. Foster homes depended on those directors being willing to entrust children to their care and on local officials turning a blind eye to the unorthodox nature of such arrangements. Some state orphanages were unwilling to associate with outside organisations, meaning their children did not have access to those imported resources and services. Others were steered by open-minded directors willing to take on the political risk of fostering children out to external, foreign-funded homes. Accordingly, the distribution of non-government resources and services to *gu'er* across China was unequal. It was also fragmented and inefficient, based not on which children had the greatest needs, but on which orphanages were geographically and politically accessible. This resulted in unequal care for *gu'er* depending on which province they called home, mirroring the stratification that has resulted from the long-standing rural-urban duality of Chinese welfare generally.[31] This stratification was even more pronounced when it came to private orphanages like St Martin's. These grassroots, community-based orphanages varied dramatically in terms of the quality of care provided but had in common a lack of state financial or policy support for their work. Moreover, due to their isolation from the state orphanages and international adoption system, their children typically had limited adoption prospects and did not benefit from access to NGO-orphanage partnerships such as foster home initiatives. In exploring these aspects of non-governmental *gu'er* relief, this book will highlight the importance of welfare pluralism being actively promoted and coordinated by the state, with clear frameworks and standards in place to encourage and govern high-quality third-sector initiatives. Such measures are necessary in light of the state's duty to protect and promote the rights of *gu'er* to health care, education, family, and noninstitutional upbringings.

Changing attitudes to philanthropy and the localisation of humanitarian work

When I left China in 2010, I promised Lina that I would keep in touch, and I sent her a package containing stickers, a world map, and some photos I had printed of the two of us from our time together. I never heard back and assumed the package had been lost in the mail. When I returned to China in 2017, I returned to St Martin's. Sister Chen welcomed me warmly and we toured the grounds. The orchard—brimming with grape vines, eggplants, corn, and flowers—was now surrounded by chicken coops and a goat pen. Colourful bunting had been stretched across the courtyard. The trampoline was still there, and the annexe had been upgraded to accommodate a new canteen for the children, so they no longer had to eat in their dormitories. We visited the chapel, where we had attended mass together daily. Sister Chen showed me around the old dormitory rooms, which had been turned into dedicated spaces for physical therapy, occupational therapy, and schoolwork. The children now lived in a new wheelchair-friendly extension behind the main building. There I ran into Lina, now a young woman of nineteen. We were both shy at first, and I wasn't sure if she even remembered me. But then she went to her room and came back with a photo of the two of us from seven years earlier—the package had arrived after all. We were only able to chat briefly, but like millions of young Chinese, Lina has a smartphone now and uses WeChat, China's major social-messaging platform, to keep in touch with friends, so we are able to check in with each other every now and then from half a world away.

As Lina was growing up, donations to St Martin's were steadily increasing. Supporters of the orphanage had paid for Lina to study computer science at a school that catered to students with special needs. She still lived at St Martin's with her sisters and Sister Chen, but the grounds had been modernised, so the petite girl who used to rule the roost from her bedroom floor could now move freely around in a much more modern wheelchair. Much of this change in St Martin's financial position could be attributed to the increasing online connectedness of Chinese society. Most notably, WeChat had become ubiquitous in China both as a messaging and commerce platform, which made it easier for supporters of St Martin's to stay up to date with the home's needs and to respond to those needs with instant fund transfers or by signing up to volunteer; by 2017, Sister Chen had more volunteers and church groups and school groups visiting than ever to support her work and help out in practical ways. On the day of my last visit, a group of young adults had travelled from a large church over an hour away to put on a cabaret performance for the children; Lina had a front-row seat. Those hard, early years of St Martin's, when Sister Chen struggled to find coal to ward off frostbite, or sufficient food and clothing for her scores of children, seemed even further removed in 2017 than when I had first heard her story in 2010.

As China's third sector has emerged, a broader social shift has been taking place in terms of attitudes to charity and philanthropy. Chinese culture has historically been suspicious of non-governmental charitable efforts. There are a number of historical layers to this apathetic discourse surrounding the concept of charity. Beneficence, philanthropy, and "assistance of the weak" (*fu lao zhu can jiu gu ji kun*) are long-standing traditions of Confucian China.[32] But given the Confucian emphasis on duties within the family network, private giving within personal kinship networks traditionally took moral priority over arm's length, public-sphere charity in China.[33] And in the new PRC, charity was explicitly cast as a maligned Western concept. The Communist Party decried charitable organisations as "tools used by the ruling class to cheat people and poison their minds" and initially suspended their operations.[34] As recently as 1991, the *Encyclopaedia of China* defined "charity" as

> [t]he provision of monetary, material or other practical forms of assistance to the poor or the weak out of compassion, pity or religious considerations ... It has a heavy religious and superstitious colour. Its purpose is to get rewards for good deeds ... it is only a temporary and passive assistance to a minority of people ... and its social effect is doubtful.[35]

The concept of charity has been "rehabilitated" as politically correct in the intervening years.[36] China observers have pointed to the Sichuan earthquake relief effort of 2008 as a watershed moment due to the outpouring of domestic civil donations, increased volunteerism, and the willing receipt of even international relief funds that ensued (2008 is sometimes referred to as *gongmin shehui yuannian*, or "year of the emergence of civil society", for this reason). Even before the earthquake, charities were beginning to regain space and legitimacy from as early as the 1990s as China transitioned to a socialist market economy, albeit in a field dominated by government-organised bodies.[37] Many of my research participants reported an increasing openness, in recent decades, on the part of local communities, donors, and officials to the idea of voluntary, nonprofit philanthropy.

For St Martin's, this had translated to increased and more immediately accessible funding, expansion opportunities, and improvements in care practices. For homes like Good News, that were established with foreign funds and had historically relied almost exclusively on the generosity of overseas donors to meet operating costs, an increasing proportion of funding needs were being met by domestic donors. In fact, as civic engagement with welfare initiatives increased within China, many orphan relief organisations that were established by foreigners were deliberately pursuing a strategy of localisation, with a long-term vision of relying exclusively on domestic donations and handing over management to local leadership. At the same time, the importing of first-world caregiving practices and medical resources continued, based on the volunteering, training, and supervision efforts of experts from both within and outside China.

This pivot to domestic donations and management was also seen by many organisations as a necessary strategy for long-term survival, given the increasingly restrictive political climate in China today for foreign-funded NGO work. In January 2017, the new Foreign NGO Management Law came into effect.[38] The law requires overseas NGOs that are active in China—this would include China-based orphanages and foster homes funded by overseas charities and foundations—to find an official Chinese sponsor and register with the police ministry (Chinese NGOs, by comparison, are required to register with the Ministry of Civil Affairs). It also gave the police broad search, seizure, and detention powers over noncompliant organisations. Given that most of the foreign-run foster homes in China were still at least partly dependent on donations channelled through foreign charities, the law appeared to formalise police oversight of the sector. A long-standing debate over how and when foreign nonprofits could be registered in China seemed to have been resolved, at least on paper, in favour of authoritarian restrictions and high hurdles to foreign nonprofit activity. As discussed in Chapter 6, the future of China's private *gu'er* relief sector became more uncertain than ever in light of this new legislation and related restrictive legislative and policy developments.

Fieldwork and methods

This book is primarily based on participant observation and interviews conducted in twenty-five non-state orphanages, foster homes, and similar *gu'er* relief organisations in Hebei, Henan, Shaanxi, Beijing, and Shanghai. Following two short-term volunteer placements at an established Beijing foster home in 2005 and 2007, the majority of this research took place in the summers of 2009, 2010, and 2017. In 2009 and 2010, approximately half of my time was spent living at various orphanages and foster homes, helping out with childcare, administrative work, and English lessons, which allowed me to work closely with Chinese and foreign caregivers and gain a better understanding of daily life for the resident children. On my return in 2017, I was able to introduce a longitudinal aspect to my research and consider what had changed in the field in the intervening years. These changes could be attributed to many sociopolitical factors, the most important of which were a change in Chinese leadership, the Lankao fire, and the enactment of new central laws and policies on charities, foreign-funded NGOs, and foster care. I supplemented this ethnographic fieldwork with over twenty formal, recorded interviews, each ranging from one to two hours, with child-related NGO staff members and Chinese and Western volunteers. Data from these case studies and other sources was combined to form a theoretically meaningful "extended case study".[39] I obtained informed oral consent for each interview and conducted the majority on a condition of anonymity; accordingly, I have used pseudonyms to refer to my research subjects, both individuals and organisations. I translated Chinese interviews to English freely rather than literally, with regard to linguistic nuance and emphasis. I also studied news coverage, state documents, and legislative instruments relevant to child welfare specifically and NGO law and practice in general.

Like all researchers doing fieldwork in China, I had to rely heavily on mutual trust built on networks and relationships (*guanxi*). In building these relationships, I was mindful of being both an insider and an outsider in the field. I was seen as an insider, particularly by expatriates in China, for at least three reasons—my apparent appreciation of and respect for Chinese culture, as evidenced by a lifetime of studying the Chinese language; my Christian faith, which was shared by the vast majority of research participants; and our shared commitment to child welfare. There were also times when I felt I was being received primarily as an outsider, as a visibly non-Chinese researcher with a privileged, first-world background. On all three research trips, there were people I requested to interview who declined. These factors could not be controlled away but instead needed to be incorporated as I interpreted my findings and constructed this narrative.[40] In writing this manuscript, I have tried to be reflexive, accounting for the impact of my presence, agenda, and personal preferences on data collection and interpretation.

As a foreign graduate student researching a politically sensitive topic, it was very difficult to gain access to government representatives to hear their views on unregistered private welfare providers and the broader situation of *gu'er* in China. I was able to meet with a retired senior-level official from the central Ministry of Civil Affairs (the agency with ultimate responsibility for social welfare, including state orphanages and other welfare institutions) and conducted telephone interviews with representatives of two branches of the Ministry, the Charity and Donation Information Centre and the NGO Service Centre. However, the bulk of my data came from a civil, rather than state, perspective, a factor that I have been mindful of in describing the social field and drawing conclusions. A related point is the sheer geographic and political size of China, which makes it unwise to generalise about "state" and "government" priorities, concerns, and objectives. Rather than focusing on broad metanarratives of globalisation, modernisation, and economic development, this book aims to add texture and nuance to those questions by examining sociolegal processes and social policy questions as they were playing out at a local level, with particular emphasis on the experiences and expectations of citizens in society.

The chapters to follow

Using a number of in-depth case studies, the chapters that follow help paint a fuller picture of orphan relief in modern China by introducing a largely hidden sector of alternative care. They also illustrate the various ways state and social actors interact in the context of ambiguous and rapidly changing laws and policies. Chapter 2 provides a broader context for *gu'er* welfare initiatives, by discussing the demographics and life experiences of *gu'er*, including the two main risk factors for abandonment (sex and disability) and the creation of new families through adoption. I also review the formal state response to *gu'er*, including significant policy initiatives aimed at improving quality of life in state institutions, and ongoing concerns about the state's programme of institutional care.

There has been enormous progress in terms of China's orphan welfare policies and programmes in recent decades. However, in many rural areas, communities have continued to rely on unregistered, grassroots orphanages to care for relinquished children in the absence of state-provided alternatives. In Chapter 3, I examine the ad hoc emergence of organisations such as St Martin's in response to rural childhood vulnerability, including their ambiguous legal status; the evolving nature of their relationship with local and central authorities; and the challenges faced by workers in the field such as Sister Chen in accessing resources and services prior to the Lankao fire. Chapter 4 undertakes a similar ethnographic analysis of foster homes, such as Good News, providing off-site care for children who would otherwise reside in state institutions. Both of these chapters are based primarily on fieldwork carried out in 2009 and 2010. My analysis is not intended to condemn medical and caregiving practices within state-run institutions, or to portray an overly sympathetic view of non-state contributions to *gu'er* welfare, but rather to improve our understanding of the lives of the children who found themselves taken in by these largely invisible alternative systems of care.

Chapter 5 considers the impact of recent law and policy developments on non-state orphanages and foster homes, beginning with the 2013 Lankao fire. It is based primarily on fieldwork carried out in 2017, by which time the sector as a whole was facing a great deal of uncertainty. Many private orphanages had been shut down post-Lankao; others had been appropriated into the system of state-funded welfare, while still others had not noticed any significant changes in terms of their role or their relationships with state actors. As for foster homes, my research participants were facing even more challenges and uncertainty. With the enactment of China's 2016 Charity Law [*Cishan Fa*] and 2017 Foreign NGO Management Law [*Jingwai Fei Zhengfu Zuzhi Jingnei Huodong Guanli Fa*], unregistered charities and NGOs generally were facing increased political pressure, particularly those receiving funds from foreign NGOs. In the wake of Lankao and other scandals, some provinces had withdrawn children from cross-country foster care, and there were rumours of a central crackdown to come. In response to these developments, many foster homes were adopting strategies of localisation, and closer state collaboration, as a hedge against the uncertain political climate.

These strategies have since proven extremely important, as Chinese authorities have continued to revise and rewrite the rules for private orphan relief in the interim. Despite their best efforts, many foster homes have been forced to shut down or restructure in the face of these changes.

In Chapter 6, I reflect on the implications of the story of private orphan relief in China for our understanding of Chinese civil society, welfare pluralism, law- and policy-making, and legal culture. I also look forward, to the future of private orphan relief in China, which continues to be in a state of flux at the time of writing. Taken together, these chapters illustrate the pressing need for the Chinese state to actively promote and coordinate welfare pluralism in the field of *gu'er* relief, in line with its duty to use maximum available resources to protect and promote the basic rights and entitlements of vulnerable children.

Notes

1 To preserve confidentiality, pseudonyms have been used throughout this book to refer to the individuals and organisations who have participated in my research.
2 Approximately 50,000 US dollars.
3 Jas 1:27 (NIV).
4 Xiaoyuan Shang, "Looking for a Better Way to Care for Children: Cooperation between the State and Civil Society in China," *Social Service Review* 76, no. 2 (June 2002), 205.
5 Xiaoyuan Shang, Xiaoming Wu, and Yue Wu, "Welfare Provision for Vulnerable Children: The Missing Role of the State," *The China Quarterly* 181 (March 2005), 126. Another important feature of rural welfare in China's socialist welfare system was the customary community-based practice of *wubao* or "five guarantees". *Wubao*, which survived the subsequent dismantling of rural agricultural communes, is a locally resourced programme that provides free food, clothes, fuel, health care, and education for vulnerable populations. However, in many parts of rural China, *wubao* is an ineffective safety net, as some local governments and communities do not have sufficient funding to ensure *wubao* is reliably resourced and available to all those who are entitled: Shang, Wu, and Wu, "Welfare Provision for Vulnerable Children," 128.
6 Shang, Wu, and Wu, "Welfare Provision for Vulnerable Children," 126.
7 As discussed in Chapter 5, the governance of private orphanages changed dramatically, at least in some locations, following the Lankao fire of 2013.
8 Qiusha Ma, "The Governance of NGOs in China since 1978: How Much Autonomy?" *Nonprofit and Voluntary Sector Quarterly* 31, no. 3 (September 2002), 308; Liu Peifeng, "Development of Charities in China since the Reform and Opening Up," in *NGOs in China and Europe: Comparisons and Contrasts*, ed. Yuwen Li (Farnham: Ashgate, 2011), 73.
9 Shawn Shieh and Jonathan Schwartz, "State and Society Responses to China's Social Welfare Needs: An Introduction to the Debate," in *State and Society Responses to Social Welfare Needs in China: Serving the People*, eds. Jonathan Schwartz and Shawn Shieh (Abingdon: Routledge, 2009), 11–12; Renee Yuen-Jan Hsia and Lynn T. White III, "Working amid Corporatism and Confusion: Foreign NGOs in China," *Nonprofit and Voluntary Sector Quarterly* 31, no. 3 (September 2002), 334.
10 Ma, "The Governance of NGOs in China since 1978," 306.
11 Kay Ann Johnson, *Wanting a Daughter, Needing a Son: Abandonment, Adoption, and Orphanage Care in China*, ed. Amy Klatzkin (St Paul, NM: Yeong & Yeong, 2004), 188.
12 Shang, "Looking for a Better Way to Care for Children," 2002.

13 Linda Wong, *Marginalization and Social Welfare in China* (London: LSE/Routledge, 1998), 155.
14 Shang, Wu, and Wu, "Welfare Provision for Vulnerable Children," 2005.
15 Yuwen Li, "Introduction: Challenges and Opportunities for NGOs in Different Parts of the World," in *NGOs in China and Europe: Comparisons and Contrasts*, ed. Yuwen Li (Farnham: Ashgate, 2011), 2. See also Ma, "The Governance of NGOs in China since 1978," 2002; Zengke He, "Institutional Barriers to the Development of Civil Society in China," in *China's Opening Society: The Non-State Sector and Governance*, eds. Zheng Yongnian and Joseph Fewsmith (Abingdon: Routledge, 2008).
16 Li, "Challenges and Opportunities for NGOs," 2. Ashley and He have noted that, tellingly, the promulgation of new restrictions on NGOs in China has often occurred soon after domestic and international political movements such as the Tiananmen Square student protests of 1989, the Falun Gong protests in 1999, and the Colour Revolutions in Eastern Europe between 2003 and 2005: Jillian S. Ashley and Pengyu He, "Opening One Eye and Closing the Other: The Legal and Regulatory Environment for 'Grassroots' NGOs in China Today," *Boston University International Law Journal* 26, no. 1 (Fall 2008).
17 Ashley and He, "Opening One Eye and Closing the Other," 32.
18 Vivienne Shue, "State Power and Social Organization in China," in *State Power and Social Forces: Domination and Transformation in the Third World*, eds. Joel S. Migdal, Atul Kohli, and Vivienne Shue (Cambridge: Cambridge University Press, 1994), 77–78.
19 This is reflected in the fact that there are at least four different terms for civil society in China: *shimin shehui* (city people's society), *minjian shehui* (people-based society), *gongmin shehui* (citizen's society), and *wenming shehui* (civilised society): Richard Madsen, *China's Catholics: Tragedy and Hope in an Emerging Civil Society* (Berkeley: University of California Press, 1998), 131–34.
20 Ernest Gellner, *Conditions of Liberty: Civil Society and Its Rivals* (London: Hamish Hamilton, 1994). Some scholars question whether this model of civil society is applicable in China, given the many "corporatist" features of the state's approach to the third sector (for example, tightly controlling NGOs and developing a state-sanctioned alternative, namely government-organised NGOs): Bin Xu, *The Politics of Compassion: The Sichuan Earthquake and Civic Engagement in China* (Stanford: Stanford University Press, 2017), 17–18.
21 Gordon White, Jude A. Howell, and Xiaoyuan Shang, *In Search of Civil Society: Market Reform and Social Change in Contemporary China* (Oxford: Clarendon Press, 1996), 3–4.
22 Schwartz and Shieh, *State and Society*, 10.
23 Xu, *The Politics of Compassion*, 18.
24 I use the term "private" to distinguish these orphanages from state-run orphanages; none of the private orphanages presented in this book are profit-making.
25 Xinde Review, *Chinese Non-Government Child Adoption Seminar* [*Zhongguo minjian ertong yangyu yantaohui*] (Shijiazhuang: *Xinde wenhua yanjiusuo* [Xinde Cultural Institute], 2014), 1 (on file with author).
26 As this book will make clear, it is difficult to know how many private organisations are working with *gu'er* in China at any one time. Keyser has noted, and my research confirms, that the "various structural and legal challenges faced by many of these organizations discourage them from making themselves widely known." Catherine H. Keyser, "The Role of the State and NGOs in Caring for At-Risk Children: The Case of Orphan Care," in *State and Society Responses to Social Welfare Needs in China: Serving the People*, eds. Jonathan Schwartz and Shawn Shieh (Abingdon: Routledge, 2009), 48.
27 Sally Falk Moore, "Law and Social Change: The Semi-Autonomous Social Field as an Appropriate Subject of Study," *Law and Society Review* 7, no. 4 (Summer 1973), 720.

28 See, for example, Suchman's definition of legitimacy, widely adopted in Western organisational theory scholarship: "Legitimacy is a generalized perception or assumption that the actions of an entity are desirable, proper, or appropriate within some socially constructed system of norms, values, beliefs, and definitions." Mark C. Suchman, "Managing Legitimacy: Strategic and Institutional Approaches," *Academy of Management Review* 20, no. 3 (July 1995), 574.

29 Kay Ann Johnson, *China's Hidden Children: Abandonment, Adoption, and the Human Costs of the One-Child Policy* (Chicago: University of Chicago Press, 2016).

30 Convention on the Rights of the Child art 20, 20 Nov., 1989, 1577 U.N.T.S. 3. Available at www.refworld.org/docid/3ae6b38f0.html (retrieved 17 January 2019).

31 For discussion of the institutionalised inequality of state welfare provision in China, which is characterised by a "strong pro-urban bias in terms of level of support", see Tony Saich, "The Politics of Welfare Policy: Towards Social Citizenship?" in *Handbook of Welfare in China*, eds. Beatriz Carrillo, Johanna Hood, and Paul Kadetz (Cheltenham: Edward Elgar, 2017), 83.

32 See Alfred H.Y. Lin, "Warlord, Social Welfare and Philanthropy: The Case of Guangzhou Under Chen Jitang, 1929–1936," *Modern China* 30, no. 2 (April 2004), 152–53, outlining the cultural practice of alms-giving to widows, orphans, the childless, and the poor in the imperial period and the "mixed economy" of welfare (voluntary and state action intertwined) which developed in the Ming and Qing dynasties.

33 This is reflected in the notion of "utilitarian familism", discussed in Chapter 2 at [38]. Interestingly, I occasionally encountered echoes of this historical preference for an in-network, private concept of charity in the field. Sister Chen, of St Martin's, held the view that it would be inappropriate to solicit donations from strangers because that would be an imposition—she preferred to receive support from people who knew her well and trusted her, in other words, on the basis of an established relationship, or *guanxi*. Similarly, the manager of Still Waters, a Chinese foster home, indicated a preference for donations to come from "so-called relatives—people who have a relationship with us and know the kids—like extended family. If we're not family, if we don't have a relationship, why do you want to give me the money? ... It's not just about getting money from anyone" (*Grace, Still Waters Foster Home, 2017*). For a discussion of the rules of *guanxi* and the notion of charity in premodern China, see Carolyn L. Hsu, "'Rehabilitating Charity' in China: The Case of Project Hope and the Rise of Non-Profit Organizations," *Journal of Civil Society* 4, no. 2 (September 2008), 84–86.

34 Liu, "Development of Charities in China," 73.

35 Liu, "Development of Charities in China," 77n12.

36 Hsu, "'Rehabilitating Charity' in China," 2008; Elaine Jeffreys, "Entrepreneurs, Celebrities and Charitable Foundations: Elite Philanthropy in China," in *Handbook of Welfare in China*, eds. Beatriz Carrilo, Johanna Hood, and Paul Kadetz (Cheltenham: Edward Elgar, 2017), 320.

37 Liu, "Development of Charities in China," 2011; Hsu, "'Rehabilitating Charity,'" 2008.

38 Law on the Management of Foreign NGO Domestic Activities [*Jingwai Fei Zhengfu Zuzhi Jingnei Huodong Guanli Fa*] 2017 (People's Republic of China).

39 Michael Burawoy, "The Extended Case Method," *Sociological Theory* 16, no. 1 (March 1998).

40 Mario Luis Small, "How Many Cases Do I Need? On Science and the Logic of Case Selection in Field-Based Research," *Ethnography* 10, no. 1 (2009).

Bibliography

Ashley, Jillian S., and Pengyu He. "Opening One Eye and Closing the Other: The Legal and Regulatory Environment for 'Grassroots' NGOs in China Today." *Boston University International Law Journal* 26, no. 1 (Fall 2008): 29–96.

Burawoy, Michael. "The Extended Case Method." *Sociological Theory* 16, no. 1 (March 1998): 4–33.

Gao, Bingzhong. "The Question of Legitimacy of Social Organizations." *China Social Sciences* 2 (2000). Translated in Han Junkui, "International NGOs in China: Current Situation, Impacts and Response of the Chinese Government." In *NGOs in China and Europe: Comparisons and Contrasts*, edited by Yuwen Li, 23–52. Farnham: Ashgate, 2011.

Gellner, Ernest. *Conditions of Liberty: Civil Society and Its Rivals*. London: Hamish Hamilton, 1994.

He, Zengke. "Institutional Barriers to the Development of Civil Society in China." In *China's Opening Society: The Non-State Sector and Governance*, edited by Zheng Yongnian and Joseph Fewsmith, 161–73. Abingdon: Routledge, 2008.

High, Anna Jane. "China's Orphan Welfare System: Laws, Policies and Filled Gaps." *University of Pennsylvania East Asia Law Review* 8, no. 2 (2013): 127–76.

High, Anna Jane. "Grassroots NGO Regulation and China's Local Legal Culture." *Socio-Legal Review* 9, no. 2 (2013): 1–50.

High, Anna Jane. "'It's Grace and Favor, It's Not Law': Extra-Legal Regulation of Foreign Foster Homes in China." *University of Pennsylvania Asian Law Review* 12, no. 3 (Spring 2017): 357–405.

Hsia, Renee Yuen-Jan, and Lynn T. White III. "Working amid Corporatism and Confusion: Foreign NGOs in China." *Nonprofit and Voluntary Sector Quarterly* 31, no. 3 (September 2002): 329–51.

Hsu, Carolyn L. "'Rehabilitating Charity' in China: The Case of Project Hope and the Rise of Non-Profit Organizations." *Journal of Civil Society* 4, no. 2 (September 2008): 81–96.

Jeffreys, Elaine. "Entrepreneurs, Celebrities and Charitable Foundations: Elite Philanthropy in China." In *Handbook of Welfare in China*, edited by Beatriz Carrillo, Johanna Hood, and Paul Kadetz, 317–37. Cheltenham: Edward Elgar, 2017.

Johnson, Kay Ann. *China's Hidden Children: Abandonment, Adoption, and the Human Costs of the One-Child Policy*. Chicago: University of Chicago Press, 2016.

Johnson, Kay Ann. *Wanting a Daughter, Needing a Son: Abandonment, Adoption, and Orphanage Care in China*. Edited by Amy Klatzkin. St. Paul, MN: Yeong & Yeong, 2004.

Keyser, Catherine H. "The Role of the State and NGOs in Caring for At-Risk Children: The Case of Orphan Care." In *State and Society Responses to Social Welfare Needs in China; Serving the People*, edited by Jonathan Schwartz and Shawn Shieh, 45–65. Abingdon: Routledge, 2009.

Li, Yuwen. "Introduction: Challenges and Opportunities for NGOs in Different Parts of the World." In *NGOs in China and Europe: Comparisons and Contrasts*, edited by Yuwen Li, 1–20. Farnham: Ashgate, 2011.

Lin, Alfred H. Y. "Warlord, Social Welfare and Philanthropy: The Case of Guangzhou Under Chen Jitang, 1929–1936." *Modern China* 30, no. 2 (April 2004): 151–98.

Liu, Peifeng. "Development of Charities in China since the Reform and Opening Up." In *NGOs in China and Europe: Comparisons and Contrasts*, edited by Yuwen Li, 71–94. Farnham: Ashgate, 2011.

Ma, Qiusha. "The Governance of NGOs in China since 1978: How Much Autonomy?". *Nonprofit and Voluntary Sector Quarterly* 31, no. 3 (September 2002): 305–28.

Madsen, Richard. *China's Catholics: Tragedy and Hope in an Emerging Civil Society*. Berkeley: University of California Press, 1998.

Moore, Sally Falk. "Law and Social Change: The Semi-Autonomous Social Field as an Appropriate Subject of Study." *Law and Society Review* 7, no. 4 (Summer 1973): 719–46.

Saich, Tony. "The Politics of Welfare Policy: Towards Social Citizenship?" In *Handbook of Welfare in China*, edited by Beatriz Carrillo, Johanna Hood, and Paul Kadetz, 81–97. Cheltenham: Edward Elgar, 2017.

Shieh, Shawn, and Jonathan Schwartz. "State and Society Responses to China's Social Welfare Needs: An Introduction to the Debate." In *State and Society Responses to Social Welfare Needs in China: Serving the People*, edited by Jonathan Schwartz and Shawn Shieh, 3–21. Abingdon: Routledge, 2009.

Shang, Xiaoyuan. "Looking for a Better Way to Care for Children: Cooperation between the State and Civil Society in China." *Social Service Review* 76, no. 2 (June 2002): 203–28.

Shang, Xiaoyuan, Xiaoming Wu, and Yue Wu. "Welfare Provision for Vulnerable Children: The Missing Role of the State." *The China Quarterly* 181 (March 2005): 122–36.

Shue, Vivienne. "State Power and Social Organization in China." In *State Power and Social Forces: Domination and Transformation in the Third World*, edited by Joel S. Migdal, Atul Kohli, and Vivienne Shue, 65–88. Cambridge: Cambridge University Press, 1994.

Small, Mario Luis. "How Many Cases Do I Need? On Science and the Logic of Case Selection in Field-Based Research." *Ethnography* 10, no. 1 (2009): 5–38.

Suchman, Mark C. "Managing Legitimacy: Strategic and Institutional Approaches." *Academy of Management Review* 20, no. 3 (July 1995): 571–610.

White, Gordon, Jude A. Howell, and Xiaoyuan Shang. *In Search of Civil Society: Market Reform and Social Change in Contemporary China*. Oxford: Clarendon Press, 1996.

Wong, Linda. *Marginalization and Social Welfare in China*. London: LSE/Routledge, 1998.

Xinde Review. *Chinese Non-Government Child Adoption Seminar* [*Zhongguo minjian ertong yangyu yantaohui*]. Shijiazhuang: *Xinde wenhua yanjiusuo* [Xinde Cultural Institute], 2014 (on file with author).

Xu, Bin. *The Politics of Compassion: The Sichuan Earthquake and Civic Engagement in China*. Stanford: Stanford University Press, 2017.

2 Demographics of childhood vulnerability

Abandonment, adoption, and the state response

I first visited Compassion Family Life House, situated in a leafy, affluent housing estate not far from Beijing, in 2009. The foster home, which was founded by an evangelical American couple in 2003, specialised in caring for infants, children, and teenagers with brittle bone disease from state orphanages around China. Although Compassion's founders had no experience in the treatment of brittle bone disease when they set up their home, they quickly developed hands-on expertise and became well known throughout China for the effective specialist medical and occupational treatment they were able to provide. One of the teenagers I met at Compassion was Rose, an eighteen-year-old who had come to the foster home from a state orphanage in Henan province. During my next visit to China in 2010, Rose was interviewed by filmmakers from a nearby expatriate church, a long-time supporter of Compassion's work with *gu'er*. This is her story, as told to the filmmakers in her own words:

> My name is Rose. I am from Henan and I am eighteen years old. I lived in a village with my parents and older sister. We were very happy children. Our parents cared for us. But one day, when I was four years old, my older sister accidentally poured boiling water over my head. I was in so much pain and started crying. Papa heard me and ran over to see what had happened. He took me to the doctor, who said to put toothpaste over the burns. My sister helped me apply the toothpaste, but it only helped a little. I had terrible wounds. Papa was so angry with my sister that he beat her. She was so regretful and felt so sorry for what had happened to me. Not only was I scarred, my family were too poor to send me to school. So, one day, Papa brought me to the door of the local [state] orphanage. A kind *ayi* took me in, and I started my life there.
>
> My *ayi* was really very kind to me. The other children were also good. But they could be so strong-willed and sometimes rough, sometimes bossy. We often had our differences. My scalp was burned, and it left such a scar emotionally. I didn't like to talk. From the time I arrived, I stopped talking much. The children started bullying me. The *ayis* were really kind to me, so the other kids bullied me. That was my life, every day. After each meal, we played ballgames together, but I was just no good, and they started excluding

> me. I started playing on my own. I would watch the workers in the vegetable garden. I would spend time on the roof. It was so high. I was scared. Every day, my life was like this. I had no goals, I had no interests.
>
> ... When I was ten, I began my new life with the family at [Compassion]. I found being here so surreal. I kept my distance from the other children. I didn't hang out with them or talk with them much. I only spoke to reply to their questions and sometimes not even then. But they really wanted to make friends with me.
>
> ... My roommate has taught me a lot of things in my years here. I've learned how to bathe, how to wash my clothes and clean my shoes, how to play the piano. I've learned how to take care of myself. I'm really grateful to [my roommate] Catherine, she is like a blood sister to me. I've felt the warmth of love here, and I feel very blessed.

There is, of course, much more to Rose's life than this short explanation of how she came to be living first at the state orphanage and then at Compassion. But her story of losing her biological family is helpful in pointing to the types of social and economic forces that impact the lives of orphaned and abandoned children in modern China. Like many *gu'er*, Rose had special medical needs and physical disabilities. Her parents were still living but had relinquished her to the care of the state, a decision apparently impacted by both economic constraints and Rose's medical needs. After losing her birth family, Rose experienced both kindness and isolation at a state orphanage. She subsequently went on to forge new bonds of kinship when at the age of ten she was diagnosed with brittle bones disease and sent to Compassion to receive specialist care. At Compassion, Rose began studying English and geography in earnest with the goal of becoming a tour guide. Unlike in the institutional setting of the state orphanage, Rose experienced Compassion as a family, describing it as "a family full of love, like angels ... they treat me like I'm their own child. It's like sunlight".

At another Christian foster home near Beijing, New Grace Foster Home, directors David and Martha Dale likewise emphasised that the children in their care needed to be treated with individualised love and affection, something that in their experience was frequently lacking in crowded state orphanages. In the beginning, this took the form of a traditional family-based care arrangement. Their first two fostered *gu'er* were babies who lived alongside the Hill's biological children in the family's small fifth-floor village apartment (one of these babies went on to become their daughter through adoption). Over time, they brought more and more *gu'er* with special needs to live in their apartment and eventually relocated to larger premises. The Hills moved their immediate family into a private home and their scores of fostered children into a custom-designed "healing home" next door. There, the children's daily needs were met by a team of hardworking local villagers. These *ayis* were expected to treat the children as their own and were trained in the importance of emulating a warm, nurturing, and affectionate family environment with the children. Each child was primarily cared for by two *ayis* who worked in shifts, to encourage the forming of emotional bonds between child and foster "mama". On my last visit to New Grace in 2017, seventeen years after the Dales had brought their first child home from the state orphanage, Martha was no longer changing nappies and reading bedtime stories for each of the hundreds of children in her care, but she had somehow found the time to hand-sew a quilt for every child who had passed through the foster home, and she could still recall them all by name. Their pictures lined the hallways, and visiting volunteers would put together scrapbooks for each child, to be passed on to adopting parents as a record of their earliest years with the New Grace family. Each child had his or her own towel, clothing, toothbrush, and bed—small things intentionally done to ensure each child had a sense of individual identity and belonging.

There was always a sense of excitement at New Grace when news came that a child had been matched with an adopting family and would soon be on his or her way to a permanent home. It was not unusual to see photos of a smiling American family pinned to a playroom wall, sent months ahead of a scheduled "gotcha day"[1] along with letters, presents, and other mementos. These care packages were helpful for the nannies in preparing the matched child mentally and emotionally for the enormous, life-changing transition from New Grace to his or her "forever family" and from China to a new country, transitions that often involved a great sense of loss and grief. The photos were also a daily reminder for the nannies that they would soon need to say goodbye to a child after many months or years of bonding and love. For children who had not yet been matched but were old enough to have some understanding of family and adoption, these photos could be a source of confusion and longing. Most of the *gu'er* at New Grace left as infants or toddlers for their adopted families, but over the years there were also children who were not matched until they were much older. Josiah was five when we met, at least eighteen months older than most of the children at New Grace at the time. In his years at New Grace, he had seen many of his younger "brothers" and "sisters" receive family photos and eventually leave to begin new lives, most commonly in America. His yearning for a journey to a family of his own came through every time we went outside to draw chalk figures on the baking concrete steps of the foster home that summer, and he would request a drawing of a big aeroplane. His favourite thing to do was to pretend to hop in the aeroplane and fly to America to meet his family. He would often ask me if I knew who they were, and when I said I was so sorry, but I didn't, he would ask when he would get to see them in a picture. Despite the love of his *ayis*, the Dales, and his New Grace family, Josiah recognised that the children of New Grace were waiting for something different, fathers and mothers of their own. Josiah was both a deeply loved child and yet still lonely.

Children separated from family in a familial culture

In traditional Chinese culture, the basic building block of society is not the individual but the family. The interests of the family are prioritised over those of the individual, and identity is embedded in kinship. This cultural norm of familialism, which has influenced Chinese society from imperial to modern times, is rooted in the Confucian tradition, an enduring ethical system in which social harmony and individual moral virtue are seen as deriving from the fulfilment of hierarchical relational duties. Of these duties, the most central are the son's duty of filial piety towards the father and the father's corresponding duty of benevolent responsibility towards the son. China's strongly familial culture comes through in the term for a child who has been orphaned, *gu'er*, literally "isolated child". A child who is *gu* is solitary and alone and therefore isolated from both identity and responsibility; the family-less child in a family-centric culture. This is a status that is inherently objectifying and stigmatising, casting a child without a family as the socially abnormal "unfortunate other"[2] based on unspoken assumptions about her personal history and her parents' choices.

The meaning of *gu'er* in official law and policy has changed over time as the Party-State has become more willing to acknowledge the problem of abandonment, from a narrow focus on "true" orphans (children whose parents are both deceased) under the age of fourteen[3] to a broader focus on children under the age of eighteen who have lost their parents through death or abandonment and are "unsupported by others".[4] This definition is somewhat vague, but it does not appear to include other groups of children living apart from their immediate families, such as victims of child trafficking, vagrant minors, and children in the long-term care of grandparents or extended relatives (this latter group includes children whose parents are serving prison sentences,[5] as well as the "left behind" children of China's enormous migrant worker population). Although these populations can overlap and face similar vulnerabilities to *gu'er*, the focus of this book is children who have been orphaned or abandoned, and entered into the care of state or private orphanages, not having been taken in by relatives or adopted into a traditional family setting. I use the term *gu'er* to describe the population in the care of China's state and private orphanages in an attempt to avoid the pejorative connotations of loaded English terms such as "orphan" and "abandoned"; regardless of whether the Chinese or English term is used, it is not my intention to reproduce stigma or to define and objectify children based on their family status.

The most recent government survey of this population, carried out in 2016, reported that there were eighty-eight thousand children supported by state orphanages across China, and my research indicates there are many thousands more living in hundreds of private orphanages.[6] The majority of these children have some sort of disability or special medical need—although healthy children are sometimes abandoned or orphaned, they are more likely to quickly find a new home through adoption or foster care. The mission and role of state and private orphanages can only be understood in the context of the broader social, cultural, and economic forces that shape the lives of their resident children. This chapter sets out to understand the patterns of relinquishment that cause children in modern China to lose their birth parents, the types of possible pathways to new forms of caregiving and kinship open to children who have been orphaned or abandoned, and the state response to children who await new families or independence. What factors explain which children find new forms of kinship and caregiving? Which children are more likely to be left behind in more institutional settings, and what do those state institutions look like? Who are the lonely children?

Relinquishment risk factors: sex and disability

The majority of children in Chinese orphanages have one or both parents living but have been abandoned.[7] It is difficult to precisely measure child relinquishment rates in China, partly because a large number of abandoned children are taken in by informal adoptive families or private orphanages without ever coming to the attention of state authorities. Professor Shang, a leading expert on childhood vulnerability in modern China, has estimated a national abandonment rate of between ten thousand and twenty thousand children annually.[8] There was an apparent surge in abandonment rates in the late 1990s and early 2000s, with a corresponding sharp increase in state orphanage populations.[9] In 2017, media reports in the wake of the Lankao fire put the abandonment rate at one hundred thousand children per year.[10]

Sex and disability are the two most prominent factors impacting the demographics of abandonment in China today. The heightened vulnerability of both girls and children with disabilities to parental relinquishment is reflected in the inclusion of anti-abandonment provisions in the Law on the Protection of Women's Rights and Interests ([*Funü Quanyi Baozhang Fa*] 1992) and the Law on the Protection of Disabled Persons ([*Canjiren Baozhang Fa*] 1990). The Marriage Law ([*Hunyin Fa*] 2001), the Adoption Law ([*Shouyang Fa*] 1991), and the Protection of Minors Law ([*Weichengnianren Baohu Fa*] 1991) also prohibit abandonment. However, criminal prosecution for parental abandonment of a minor has historically been extremely rare.[11]

Terms such as "relinquished" and "abandoned" are loaded terms that may imply a child was simply unwanted by her birth parents. In the Western[12] imagination, China is frequently cast as a strongly male-preferring culture that cruelly undervalues girls, resulting in rampant female infanticide and heartless abandonment, a place where boys are cherished and girls are easily discarded, leading to overcrowded orphanages full of unwanted baby girls. But Kay Johnson's seminal ethnographic research on Chinese parents who relinquish infants and families who take in such foundlings challenges the "unwanted baby girl" narrative which so often dominates discourse about Chinese orphanages, instead telling a much more nuanced and painful story.[13] Similarly, there is also more to the story of relinquished children with disabilities than "unwanted imperfect children". Although abandonment implies a voluntary decision, there are multiple coercive structural conditions that impact this type of parental decision and contribute to sexist and ableist abandonment patterns, most notably restrictive birth-control policies and inadequate systems of elder care and disability welfare in rural areas. The causal connection between abandonment and these broader structural constraints has at times resulted in discursive silence around the issue of child relinquishment, as drawing attention to the former is seen as an implicit criticism of the latter.[14] The connection is reinforced by Johnson's finding that when abandoning families are punished by the authorities, in most cases the punishment consists of a fine coupled with sterilisation of the birthmother. The implication is that the state's concern over abandonment is centred on maintaining tight control over fertility rates, rather than on child protection or welfare.[15]

"Raise sons for support, but a boy and a girl complete a family"

China has long self-identified as a child-loving culture and a society that prioritises the welfare and happiness of children.[16] Although Confucianism emphasises the ascending duties of the subordinate son to the superior father, the father is also charged with duties of benevolence and compassion towards the son, as reflected in the idiom *zun lao ai you*, or "respect the elderly and love the young". But China is also a traditionally patrilineal culture, in which ancestral veneration, support of elderly parents, and continuation of the family line are considered the duties of adult sons, rather than adult daughters who marry into other families. Accordingly, especially in relatively impoverished areas where other forms of social security for the elderly were lacking, sons were historically of more practical importance to families than daughters, who were seen as "temporary" children requiring more investment from their parents than they would be able to return.[17] This is reflected in traditional sayings such as *duo zi duo fu*, "more sons, more fortune", and *yang'er fang lao*, "raise sons for support in old age" (this phrase also translates simply as "filial piety"). This so-called "son preference" has endured for centuries in China and could have deadly consequences for daughters; female infanticide was common in imperial China, and China has long had a strongly skewed sex ratio as a result.[18]

Under the Communist Party, and with the advent of work units and communes, the welfare safety net for Chinese citizens initially improved. However, rural communes were dismantled in the post-Mao reform era, and the development of a replacement system of social welfare for vulnerable citizens such as the elderly has been slow and piecemeal.[19] As a result, many people in China are heavily dependent on kinship networks for support in old age, and childless elders are a particularly vulnerable group. This is reflected in the Elder Care Law, which provides that the primary support persons (*shangyang ren*) for the elderly—with responsibility for providing financial, physical, and emotional care—are their adult children.[20] And in practice, due to continuing patrilineal traditions, it is healthy male, rather than female, offspring who are primarily relied on by rural parents for elder care.

These economic constraints have intersected with restrictive birth-planning policies to reproduce entrenched discrimination against female offspring. In the modern reform era, the Party-State introduced a series of increasingly restrictive birth-control measures aimed at lowering the national fertility rate as part of the nation's modernisation and development strategy. These initially consisted of voluntary, incentive-based propaganda campaigns, such as the 1970s *wan–xi–shao* (later–longer–fewer) campaign that incentivised later marriage, longer gaps between children, and fewer children overall. In the 1980s, the infamously intrusive and coercive one-child policy was introduced. Under this policy, urban couples were limited to one child. In most rural areas, the policy was modified in the late 1980s to a "1.5-child policy", meaning parents whose firstborn child was female were permitted a second birth after a certain mandated break between children (the 1.5-child policy was phased out in 2015 to allow two children per couple).[21] The enforcement of these policies varied enormously from region to region, depending on local political climate and economic conditions. Enforcement also varied over time, with periodic tightening and loosening of the state's grip on reproductive freedom. Given China's strong pro-natal culture, the restrictions were fiercely and creatively resisted by many families; nonetheless, in areas and at times of rigorous enforcement, there were many reports of cruel and arbitrary measures such as forced sterilisation and abortion.[22] Johnson's research into "out-of-plan" children has also revealed extreme cases in which children were removed from their birth or adoptive families and placed for international adoption.[23]

The overall effect of China's birth restrictions has been remarkable, not only in terms of the national fertility rate but also on the status of daughters in the Chinese family. In particular, the 1.5-child, or "one son or two children", policy implicitly assigned female offspring a lower functional value than males, entrenching gender discrimination within families and society (the same can be said for exceptions to the policy for parents of children with disabilities).[24] Strict enforcement of birth control policies also resulted in mass female abortion, high rates of child abandonment generally, and higher rates of child abandonment for girls than boys. Sex discrimination was not an intended consequence of birth-planning restrictions, and waves of propaganda campaigns attempted to combat emerging patterns of female abortion, infanticide and abandonment, and the resultant population sex imbalance. As Palmer has noted, "[p]erhaps the most persistent public image of children in post-Mao China ... has been that of the idealised single-child family in which a poster depicts a young daughter lovingly held by the affectionate hands of her doting parents".[25] But despite these iconic pro-daughter campaigns, the heightened vulnerability of girls to abandonment persisted, causing a disproportionate representation of girls in orphanages. This in turn has contributed to a strong and enduring international impression that China is full of unwanted abandoned baby girls.

The "unwanted baby girl" narrative has been propagated by Western pro-transnational-adoption accounts of Chinese orphanages as dumping grounds for girls heartlessly discarded by their families and in turn their nation. It is also a narrative that Johnson and her colleagues have refuted. Based on in-depth interviews with over 350 parents who had permanently relinquished children through abandonment, Johnson found strong evidence of a two child–two gender ideal. This is reflected in the phrase *ernü shuang quan*, "a boy and a girl complete a family" and has been noted by other ethnographers of contemporary Chinese culture.[26] While 90 per cent of the abandoned children in Johnson's sample were female, almost all were also second- or third-born daughters in sonless families.

The implication is that the rise of daughter abandonment is not a simple matter of "son preference"; instead, Johnson's research paints a more nuanced picture of abandonment as an anguished and coerced response to the intersection of strict birth-planning constraints and inadequate social welfare for sonless parents in a patrilocal culture.

The status of children with disabilities in a suzhi-*driven world*

Once when I was chatting with Lina at St Martin's, she asked me whether other countries have *canjiren* (people with disabilities). When I said that there are *canjiren* all over the world, she thought for a moment and then guessed that China must have the most because "*zheli you yibai lingwu canying*"—"here we have 105 disabled babies". The children at St Martin's all had some sort of special medical need or disability. These included cerebral palsy, Downs syndrome, intellectual impairment, club feet, missing limbs, spina bifida, and congenital heart disorders. Sister Chen believed that most of these children were not true orphans but had been relinquished by their parents for reasons relating to their disabilities:

> Why are they abandoned? The main thing is their bodily defects. Because you know, in rural villages, if you have a disabled child like this, parents would have to spend a lot of money [on health care]. And they're not able to go to work. So, they have no choice. It's not that they are willing and content with throwing their child away. That's not the mentality. It causes them great hardship, but they are compelled by their circumstances.
>
> You know, very often, clothes and money are left at our door—the parents know their children are here, but they do not dare to come and visit and see their child themselves. In their hearts, they must suffer greatly. We have had mothers who came back because of the deep regret they have felt.
>
> *(Sister Chen, St Martin's Home for Children with Disabilities, 2010)*

Like Sister Chen, Chinese child welfare experts have emphasised that disability is often a crucial factor in determining whether to abandon a child.[27] As birth-planning restrictions have eased since the 2000s and relinquishment rates for healthy infant girls have declined, birth defects and special medical needs are now more significant factors than sex when it comes to categorising children in Chinese *gu'er* institutions.[28] There are multiple social, cultural, and economic constraints that underpin the decision to give up a child with special needs. As discussed above, due to inadequate social welfare coverage in rural areas, impoverished rural parents are more likely to be dependent on their children to support them in their old age. As is the case with daughters, who are seen as belonging to other families and unlikely to be a reliable source of support for their parents, medically needy children may be seen as less able to fulfil future duties of elder care.[29]

Such beliefs about the prospects and potential of children with disabilities are shaped by the broader cultural discourse surrounding disability in general, which is at times very stigmatising. In Chinese culture, childhood disability or disease is traditionally seen as retribution for parental moral failure.[30] For parents of "imperfect" children in a family-centric culture, this results in public loss of face and shame. Further, as Eleanor Holroyd has argued, in traditional Confucian culture, with its emphasis on reciprocity and relational obligations over individual rights, children with disabilities are frequently presumed unable to carry out their "right and proper" obligations—most notably, to carry on the ancestral line and to care for their parents in old age—and so are seen as disturbances to family and social harmony:

> Chinese children who have disabilities represent disruptions to the flow of exchanges, in that giving good things to ill children might not make life meaningful in the usual cultural sense understood by a Chinese parent. Thus the "natural" progression of patterns of reciprocity that flow over into ancestry and birth is neither immediate, in the form of gratitude, nor generalised, in the form of delayed care, with debts never able to be reclaimed.[31]

Kohrman has similarly described a deep, intrinsic nexus between disability and moral duty in traditional Chinese culture, arguing that the emphasis placed on visible difference in modern China is linked to the Confucian emphasis on the preservation of one's body as an aspect of filial duty.[32]

This duty-based understanding of the body is rooted in the idea of *suzhi*, a deeply embedded cultural concept that has impacted the status and treatment of children with "imperfect" bodies in China for centuries. Literally "essentialised quality", *suzhi* is an amorphous concept that defies easy translation but is usually described as encompassing the physical, mental, and moral characteristics or status of a person. The concept of population *suzhi* came to prominence in the Republican era, when the poor physical quality of the population was blamed for China's perceived national "backwardness" and improvement of *suzhi* was represented as essential for national survival; accordingly, persons with disabilities (imperfect or "low [physical] quality" bodies) were cast as a threat to national advancement and symbols of weakness and backwardness, unable to discharge their moral duties of social participation and national improvement.[33]

China's cultural preoccupation with *suzhi* has been reproduced and reinforced in modern post-Mao China by strict birth-control and eugenics policies. Although the "one-child policy" and its various iterations are commonly understood as quantity-control measures, reproduction restrictions since the 1980s have been equally directed at controlling and improving population quality (*renkou suzhi*), based on a goal of "fewer but better" children. The goal of *renkou suzhi* was not explicitly used to justify China's twentieth-century eugenics policies, but Andrew Kipnis has noted numerous "conceptual continuities" between *suzhi* discourse and eugenics.[34] The idea of race improvement or *youshengxue* (literally "science of superior birth") gained traction in early twentieth-century China, as Western eugenics theory was imported and intersected with local fears of cultural, racial, or biological inferiority and degeneration.[35] Chinese eugenics discourse was initially premised on class bias; under the Communist Party, the focus shifted to reducing the burden on state and society of "inferior births". A national eugenics law, the Maternal and Infant Health Care Law ([*Mu Ying Baojian Fa*]), was passed in 1994, requiring prenatal testing and termination in cases of "serious disorder" and promoting abortion and sterilisation for those deemed unsuitable for reproduction. These policies, accompanied by extensive state propaganda idealising the enticing "norm of the healthy, educated single child",[36] helped popularise concern with low national *suzhi* as holding the nation back from "achieving its rightful place in the world".[37] In all, population quality control in China has consistently prioritised national interests over individual rights, with "individual bodies [controlled] for the sake of the nation's destiny".[38]

Of course, ableism is not a uniquely Chinese phenomenon, but China's *suzhi*-focused cultural and political context has arguably contributed to discrimination against persons with disability in Chinese society.[39] To the extent that *suzhi* implies a person's relative quality or worth as human capital can be quantified, the concept justifies a dehumanising, hierarchical vision of society in which "some bodies are recognised as having more value than others and therefore more deserving of the rights of citizenship".[40] In the early twentieth century, persons with disability were expressly placed at the bottom of the social hierarchy. Modern reform-era China has engaged extensively with disability and equality rights, both internationally and domestically, but there is also still a strong political and cultural emphasis on the notion of *suzhi* and the lesser value/higher burden of certain "imperfect" populations.[41] As Yee-Fui Ng has argued, "the preoccupation with 'quality' haunts the disability rights law, as there is simultaneous pressure to prevent disabled (or 'low quality') births and stress on disabled people to enhance their 'quality' in order to contribute to the socialist construction".[42]

Social prejudice against bodies of difference is signalled and reinforced by the low public visibility of disability in contemporary China, "as if those defined as abnormal, or disabled, are denied a place in society".[43] This discursive silence is due in part to an exclusionary medical model of disability, which views disability as an inherent, personal pathology, as opposed to a societal construct that results from barriers to public participation. Taken to its extreme, the medical model defines persons with disability as dysgenic pathologies to be eliminated, rather than as equal persons with differences to be accommodated.[44] Ng has argued that China's *suzhi* emphasis has accentuated a medical approach to disability in China, resulting in ineffective implementation of policies aimed at facilitating the independence and participation of people with disabilities in society.[45] For children with disabilities, this can mean exclusion from school, lack of access to special services, and isolation from the outside world. For their parents, stigma and exclusion can contribute to feelings of hopelessness when confronted with a child with a strange and unfamiliar medical condition, both about their ability as parents to cope and their child's chance of living a meaningful life. This was painfully described by Fisher and Shang in their detailed account of a Chinese father who had made the irreversible decision to withhold medical treatment from his disabled infant girl, a decision he later regretted:

> At that time [when we decided to give up Niuniu's life], I did not really realise that a life with disability could be so beautiful and with such rich content. It was Niuniu's blindness that opened my eyes to see how superficial and conceited I was before and to see such a world of people with disabilities that is defective but still nice and dynamic. She would have grown up to be an outstanding girl in this world, but I pushed her out of this world.[46]

Although many of my research participants spoke of the stigma and misunderstanding surrounding disability in modern China, most *gu'er* caregivers I spoke to felt that the main cause of relinquishment in rural China was the lack of social services and safety nets for families facing the heavy economic and emotional pressures of having a child with special needs. Like Sister Chen, they generally spoke sympathetically about the difficult choices facing parents in rural areas whose children are born with grave special medical needs. Despite enormous economic progress in recent decades, there is still widespread poverty in rural China and among migrant workers in urban areas. Families living in poverty often do not have access to prenatal health care or a healthy living environment, which can lead to higher incidences of maternal complications and infant disability and disease. These same families are less able to afford proper treatment and therapy for children with special needs.

China has expressed a strong commitment to the human rights of children with disabilities, both through domestic laws, such as the Law on the Protection of Minors ([*Weichengnianren Baohu Fa*] 1991) and the Law on the Protection of Disabled Persons ([*Canjiren Baozhang Fa*] 1990), and ratification of the UN Convention on the Rights of Persons with Disability. However, despite holding itself out as a progressive world leader in disability rights, there are many problems with China's practical implementation of disability protections.[47] China takes a largely residual approach to the care of children with disabilities. Families are presumed able to care for children with disabilities, so state spending on child disability support has mostly been focused on children who are in the care of the state.[48] Further, China does not yet have an effective national system of free public health care, and the availability and quality of special services or subsidies for families caring for children with disabilities varies widely from place to place. For example, eligible families can apply for disability certification on behalf of their special needs child, which in theory entitles the holder to special financial benefits and medical care. However, Shang and Fisher have noted that restrictive categorisations and unequal implementation due to local funding constraints have weakened access to support in many areas.[49] Although the trend is towards increasing welfare support in urban areas, in practice children with disabilities in less developed areas still face many barriers to accessing health care, special education, and other services,[50] resulting in heavy financial and emotional pressures on their parents. Shang and Fisher also report that some parents are unwilling to go through the registration process due to the negligible benefits available and concern that certification may lead to discrimination, even to the point of forced sterilisation.[51] Overall, in many parts of China, medical and rehabilitative support for disabled children in families is rudimentary at best, including as compared to the care provided to those who are relinquished to the state.[52]

For *gu'er* in the care of state-run institutions, a number of funding programmes and policies were developed in the wake of orphanage abuse scandals to address the medical needs of this population, including the Tomorrow Plan (discussed below). Although implementation is unequal and depends largely on local politics and resources, children relinquished into state institutional care are entitled to receive state-funded surgical and medical intervention. They are also entitled to free housing, health care, therapy, and special education.[53] As Shang has noted, for parents who cannot afford to pay for medical care or surgery out of pocket, and who face general economic insecurity even without the added pressure of a high-needs child, abandonment to the care of a state welfare home may seem like the only way to give their child a chance of survival, a situation which further challenges the narrative that "imperfect" or "low *suzhi*" abandoned children were simply unwanted by their birth families.[54]

Patterns of family building and the children left behind

Whatever the reasons or circumstances behind their abandonment, China's relinquished children do not all end up in institutional settings. Some children do not survive the circumstances of their abandonment; others become vagrant or street children. Further, research indicates that a large but unknown number of relinquished children have been taken in by informal adoptive families without any state involvement, families that have spontaneously emerged in rural areas in response to the abandonment crisis.[55] Here, too, sex and disability are significant factors that influence both patterns of family building and which children remain behind in institutional settings.

Adoption is a long-standing customary practice in China that has endured to modern times despite periods of active suppression by the state. Adoption across surname lines was at times formally prohibited in imperial China, and some normative texts argued against adoption outside of bloodlines, in line with the Confucian emphasis on family and continuing the ancestral line.[56] Despite this, various forms of adoption have long been used in China, not only to bring sons into sonless families but also for the sake of adding daughters to daughterless households (albeit sometimes with the intention of raising a "future daughter-in-law"). In the nineteenth century, in line with the growing importance of the child in society, the practice became more formalised, as state authorities began to exercise tighter supervision over the movement of children among families, and safeguards against child trafficking and slavery were put in place.[57] Johnson has argued that certain strains of both Confucianism and popular Chinese culture "support adoptive ties outside as well as inside bloodlines and support the use of adoption of both boys and girls to build family and kinship".[58] This competing ideology is evident in the long-standing use of the term *mingling zi*, or "mulberry insect children", to refer to adopted children. This usage

> derived from the belief that the wasp took the young of the mulberry insect and transformed them into young wasps, making them its "own children". According to folk belief, the wasp raps and taps outside its nest, in which it has put the mulberry insect's young, and prays, "Be like me, be like me." After a period of time, young wasps emerge. Thus, one who becomes the child of someone other than his or her birthparents is known as a *mingling zi*.... Confucian emphasis on upbringing and cultivation as the key to character provides further support for ties built on nurture and social relationships rather than biology and heredity [*footnotes excluded*].[59]

Despite this long history, it is often assumed that adoption is not a culturally accepted practice in modern China or happens only in a coldly calculated way, in order to add sons to sonless families. This has been challenged by ethnographic studies, which show that it is not only childless couples adopting and that many couples are adopting girls.[60] In their research in rural China in the 1990s and early 2000s, Johnson and her colleagues documented changing attitudes towards abandonment and adoption by interviewing over 350 parents who had relinquished children through abandonment, around one thousand families who had adopted children in this era, and over eight hundred families who "hid children through nonregistration, avoiding a record of the child's birth and existence".[61] In this sample, adoption of a stranger's child was not treated with misgiving, provided the child was generally in good health. The adoptive parents viewed their new parental rights and duties as permanent and complete, rather than fluid or tentative. They showed feelings of love and obligation towards their adopted children that were at least as strong as those for birth-children, with the "low status and fragility of adoptive ties that seemed to have characterised adoption practices in the past" only reflected in a small number of cases.[62]

This body of research suggests that, unlike in other cultures such as Korea where negative attitudes towards extra-familial adoption historically meant there were insufficient adoptive homes for homeless children, modern Chinese culture is broadly supportive of the adoption of unrelated children. Rather, the biggest obstacle to placing (healthy) abandoned children in Chinese homes has been government policy.[63] Until 1998, domestic adoption was actively suppressed by the state in line with higher-priority family-planning objectives, with adoption limited to childless couples over the age of thirty-five (other than for disabled and "truly orphaned" children).[64] Despite these restrictions, Johnson found a pattern of informal or de facto adoption (*shishi shouyang*) occurring outside of government procedures and oversight. Importantly, most of the adopted children in Johnson's sample were girls, with an estimated hundreds of thousands of unregistered adoptions of daughters taking place annually, even as international adoption was skyrocketing premised in part on the "unwanted baby Chinese girl" myth.[65] Due to the inability to legally formalise these adoptions, families usually faced a difficult choice: falsely report the adopted child as an over-quota birth and be exposed to heavy fines or in some cases sterilisation, or keep the child hidden and unregistered, living as a *hei haizi*, or "black child", without legal status as a citizen (the word "black" implies "illegal" in Chinese).[66] The extreme lengths so many parents have gone to in order to protect their newly forged family ties with adopted daughters cast further doubt on the constructed "unwanted baby girl" narrative that pervades international adoption discourse, as discussed above. These adoption patterns and practices also illustrate a cultural emphasis on *ernü shuang quan* (one boy–one girl family ideal)—despite China's long-standing son preference, daughters are also highly valued. Weiguo Zhang's research similarly suggests that the family institution is being reshaped in modern China, with girls increasingly valued for the "potential emotional and instrumental care that daughters provide to their parents".[67]

In all, Johnson has suggested that were it not for the active state suppression of local and customary adoption, "nearly all relinquished healthy daughters in the 1990s could have found families who wanted them in China, leaving few healthy children available for international adoption".[68] Health is key—while many healthy abandoned children are found and quickly adopted informally without ever coming to the attention of authorities, studies suggest that relinquished children with disabilities or illness are less likely to find new homes through de facto adoption, particularly if they are female, and so are more likely to end up in state care.[69] Similarly, disabled children are less likely to be taken in by extended family members in the event of their parents' death or incapacitation.[70] Sister Chen, like others of my research participants working with relinquished children with disabilities, had found that informal adoption was rarely an avenue for children such as Lina, presumably due to the same economic and cultural factors that contributed to their relinquishment in the first place. This is reflected in the very high rates of disability/special medical needs among *gu'er* in state welfare institutions, by some estimates as high as 90 per cent.[71]

The state response to "lonely children": child welfare institutions

In a Confucian, family-centred system of social ethics, the state should be benevolent towards its people, just as a father should be to his son, but the primary unit of care and welfare is the family; the state plays only a residual role, providing welfare for people without a clan.[72] So, in imperial China, children without parents were presumed to be the responsibility of extended kinship networks, not the state. However, infant abandonment, particularly of girls, was also common. In response, foundling hospitals for abandoned infants were established in some urban centres by local interest groups, beginning in the mid-seventeenth and eighteenth centuries (these hospitals were often plagued by mismanagement and scandal).[73] Other *gu'er* were taken in by foreign missionary orphanages.

The Confucian idea of a benevolent state took on new meaning with the founding of the People's Republic of China in 1949. As Carolyn Hsu has noted, under Chairman Mao, private charity was seen as "an affront to the ruling regime, an accusation that the Party-State was failing in its paternalistic duties.... the new regime cast itself as the paternalistic state *par excellence*, one which would be so sufficient that people would no longer need their clan networks".[74] In other words, the moral authority of China's Communist Party has always been linked with its ability to provide for the people. In the new Communist political-economic framework, welfare was seen as the prerogative of the state, to be provided through the economic units of society—urban state-owned enterprises and rural communes. In line with the move to this new "total society", the government set about monopolising care for *gu'er*. Private orphanages were either shuttered or taken over by the state, which took full financial and administrative responsibility for orphanages (*fuliyuan*) in urban centres across China; in rural areas, it was assumed that agricultural communes (*renmin gongshe*) could provide for the physical needs of children without families.[75] Shang has argued that the development of this system of state orphan relief was contingent on financial and political considerations, not the rights and interests of *gu'er*, with the situation of *gu'er* becoming "a kind of political symbol: either it was regarded as a manifestation of so-called socialist advantages or as something that brought shame to the socialist society when things were going wrong".[76] Similarly, Keyser has noted that the focus of child welfare in the early Maoist period was on ideological collectivism; in this framework, the argument was that *gu'er* were better off in state-run institutions.[77]

As China entered the post-Mao reform era in the 1980s, the system of agricultural communes was dismantled, resulting in a greater need for alternative care for *gu'er* in rural areas. Around the same time, as birth-planning policies were put in place, abandonment began to surge, leading to increased financial investment in the state orphanage system. However, the state continued to take a residual approach to *gu'er* care, with state orphanages only set up in urban areas. In rural areas, rather than take direct responsibility for housing *gu'er*, the state presumed that informal kinship networks would be the primary source of *gu'er* protection. The underlying assumption—that children will be cared for by extended family, friends, and neighbours—mirrors China's "utilitarian familism" approach to welfare generally, in which the family is promoted as the foundation of social welfare (this aligns with the long-standing Chinese view of the family as the basic unit of society).[78] Caring for extended family is an expected responsibility in Chinese culture.[79] It is also a legal requirement, with the Marriage Law specifying that grandparents and adult siblings are expected to care for children who lose their parents.[80] However, the same socioeconomic and cultural factors that contribute to parental relinquishment of children—gender, disability, weak social security for the elderly—could leave relatives unwilling or unable to care for children with special medical needs. As a result, demand for institutions to care for *gu'er* steadily rose in rural China in the 1980s and 1990s, leading to the emergence of social efforts to protect *gu'er* in need of care but without access to state orphanages. This "rural-urban duality" continues to characterise *gu'er* welfare in China today, with state orphanages mainly restricted to urban areas and only caring for a minority of the total *gu'er* population.[81] State-run orphanages include *ertong fuliyuan* (child welfare institutions), caring solely for children, and the more general *shehui fuliyuan* (social welfare institutions) that care for *gu'er* alongside adults with mental or physical disabilities and the elderly.[82]

The "dying rooms" scandal

Institutional care was historically a common way of caring for orphaned children in most parts of the world, but over the last century, developed countries have tended to move towards alternative care models, such as foster care and adoption, in line with emerging appreciation of the potential harms of institutionalisation. Child welfare experts now recognise that institutional care can be significantly damaging for infants and children; even assuming that a child's physical needs can be provided for in an institutional setting (not always a given due to funding constraints—orphanages are frequently linked with high mortality rates), institutional care does not provide an optimal environment for children to form relationships of attachment. But even accounting for the universal inherent disadvantages of institutional care, China's state orphanages gained an international reputation in the 1990s as particularly unsafe and potentially lethal places when news broke in Western media of shockingly high mortality rates and pervasive abuse practices in a number of state facilities.

In 1995, a British broadcaster aired *The Dying Rooms: China's Deepest Secret*, showing graphic and harrowing footage of abuse and fatal neglect in a number of state orphanages, footage that had been secretly captured by the filmmakers acting under the guise of international charity workers. The film was shortly followed in 1996 by a detailed exposé from Human Rights Watch/Asia called *Death by Default: A Policy of Fatal Neglect in China's State Orphanages*.[83] The Human Rights Watch/Asia report was based largely on eyewitness accounts and documentary evidence provided by whistle-blower Dr Zhang Shuyun, a former staff member of the Shanghai Child Welfare Institution (CWI). After trying for four years to expose abusive practices and high death rates at the Shanghai CWI to local and national authorities, Dr Zhang eventually resorted to going global, taking her findings to the international community. *Death by Default* documented evidence of systematic, extreme physical abuse at the Shanghai CWI and calculated a survival rate for children admitted in the late 1980s and early 1990s of just 10 per cent. The report contained pages of distressing photos of the bodies of children who had allegedly starved to death at the CWI, each child-sized bone showing clearly through paper-thin skin. Dr Zhang also reported a pervasive practice of "summary resolution", the selection of "unwanted infants and children for death by intentional deprivation of food and water" in what have come to be known as "dying rooms".[84] Human Rights

Watch/Asia calculated that for a newly admitted orphan in China's state institutions nationwide, the likelihood of survival beyond one year was less than 50 per cent in 1989. The report concluded that China's orphanages were only symbolically committed to the humane treatment of abandoned children, in practice "making almost no effort to keep them alive".[85]

Johnson has pointed out that the *Death by Default* report was arguably sensationalised, making a sweeping assumption of intentional fatal neglect in state orphanages across China based mainly on evidence from just one institution. While the very high mortality rates experienced in state orphanages across China in the early 1990s were well documented by local officials and Chinese government statistics, other factors behind these alarming rates included preexisting disabilities or illnesses, escalating numbers of admissions as abandonment rates rose, and underfunding.[86] In her research visits in the same period to several other major Chinese state orphanages, Johnson did not encounter "summary resolution".[87] Others did—despite Party denials of their existence, "dying rooms" have been documented by journalists, researchers, and by many of my contacts in the *gu'er* NGO sector, in multiple orphanages across China. For example, Anne Thurston, a China-based correspondent for the *Atlantic*, provided in 1996 a firsthand journalistic account of a dying room in a southern Chinese orphanage.[88] Importantly, Thurston also drew attention to how factors such as poverty and ignorance of the psychiatric harm of institutional care were contributing to the deplorable conditions in state institutions across China at the time (factors that were, of course, once equally at play in Western institutional settings, with similar harms inflicted on similarly vulnerable infants and children). Other researchers have described how low staff morale, chronic under-funding, and lack of professional staff have contributed to the emotional and social deprivation of institutionalised children in China, even when basic physical needs were being met.[89]

In discussing the well-documented problems that have plagued Chinese orphanages at various times, I do not mean to portray institutionalised children as the "abnormal unfortunate" and "exotic" other,[90] but simply to explore the human cost of those scandals and the resulting social response. In February 2011, hoping to put a human face to the *Death by Default* story, I travelled to London, England to meet with Dr Zhang in person. She served me home-cooked dumplings, and asked about my studies and family, before our conversation turned to her years at the Shanghai CWI. Dr Zhang was frank and measured as she related in person the account set out in *Death by Default*, determined to impress on me the horrors of what she had witnessed while working as a doctor at the institution. She showed me photograph after photograph of *gu'er* corpses. She told me of the extreme physical abuse she had seen meted out by apathetic employees responsible for the upbringing of hundreds of wards—children violently beaten, dunked in water, or forced to squat, arms outstretched, for long periods of time over bowls of boiling water so that they would be scalded when their legs inevitably gave out. She spoke of her dramatic escape from China via Hong Kong in 1995 and the pain of being unable to freely return to her homeland thereafter. She also introduced me to her friend and former ward, Aiming, one of the few survivors of his generation of Shanghai CWI intakes. When Dr Zhang was documenting the abuse and deaths in preparation for going public, Aiming had assisted her by secretly taking photographs of the bodies of his deceased friends. Throughout our meeting, Aiming sat silently and expressionlessly, with his eyes downcast. It is difficult to imagine the impact on Aiming of surviving twenty years at the Shanghai CWI while watching the vast majority of his *xiongdi jiemei* (brothers and sisters) die and impossible to know how the few other survivors of his generation have fared since leaving the orphanage. What is clear is that the "dying rooms" scandal had a lasting impact on orphan welfare in China, as well as adoption trends globally.

In one of the most provocative scenes in *The Dying Rooms*, the narrator comments that Chinese orphanages contain "proof that Chinese do indeed dump [baby girls] on the streets like kittens in a bag". While the documentary drew warranted critical attention to the issue of coercive family planning measures and the problems facing underfunded and overcrowded Chinese orphanages, it also helped popularise an unfairly simplistic image of China as full of "abject discarded girls ... waiting to be rescued from a country that did not want them and brought into a loving American family".[91] Johnson, herself one of the first American adoptive mothers of a Chinese daughter, was one of many to criticise this Orientalist portrayal of her child's motherland, pointing out that even before the scandal, China had put in place significant policy measures designed to improve *gu'er* lives.[92] These included opening up adoption—only a few years earlier, China's adoption laws had been extended to accommodate transnational adoption. The "dying rooms" exposés coincided, therefore, with the late-1990s boom in the movement of *gu'er* from China to the West, serving not only to motivate many potential adopters to choose China as a place to seek an adopted daughter or son but also to strengthen the "child rescue" overtones that have typically and controversially permeated the practice of East-to-West adoption.[93] As Johnson described it, "adoption agencies and editorial writers alike marvelled at how readily unwanted Chinese girls found loving homes in America, juxtaposing this to the alternative of languishing in the 'dying rooms' of Chinese orphanages, unwanted and unloved in their country of birth".[94] This narrative has had a lasting impact—in a recent detailed ethnographic account of the politics of China-West adoption, Leslie Wang has argued that even thirty years on, the shocking "dying room" images continue to shape the global imagination of Chinese orphanages and the geopolitics of international adoption.[95]

Blue skies tomorrow? State orphanages in the new century

The more immediate aftermath of the exposés was a swell of international outrage directed at China, resulting in a posture of angry defensiveness from the People's Republic of China (PRC). The dying room allegations cut to the core of China's national self-presentation as a child-loving culture. They also implicated the Communist Party's moral legitimacy and political prestige, already under fire due to harsh population control policies. The State Council, China's chief administrative authority, issued a rebuttal statement declaring the *Death by Default* report to be "totally without foundation", and subsequent press statements alleged that Dr Zhang had forged documentation of archives, death registers, and medical records, as well as fabricating the photographic evidence of malnourished corpses (it should be noted that Dr Zhang's evidence was corroborated by many other sources).[96] The *People's Daily*, official newspaper of the Chinese Communist Party, declared that Western reports of abuse in state institutions were wantonly fabricated, comprising stories made up to "cheat and fool the public".[97] In a separate report, the same newspaper went on a "whataboutism" offensive against America by publishing statistics on American school shootings, violent crimes against children, and child poverty to argue that "Americans who seem to care about the conditions of Chinese children are totally indifferent to the plight of children in their own country".[98] Many foreigners in China who had been volunteering in state orphanages reported that they were no longer allowed access after the exposés, which also resulted in "mutual denunciations between PRC spokespeople and international charities" and increased monitoring of foreign NGOs and charities.[99] But apart from this temporarily chilling of international efforts to access and assist state orphanages, the controversies were ultimately also a catalyst for increased political and social investment in *gu'er* welfare domestically.

Shang, like Johnson, has pointed to policies put in place even before the Human Rights Watch/Asia report, aimed at improving state orphanage conditions, including increased recourse to transnational adoption and cooperation with international charities.[100] This reform process began to accelerate in the wake of the exposés. In 2004, the Ministry of Civil Affairs (MCA, the central government agency responsible for social and administrative affairs, including welfare) launched the "Tomorrow Plan—Operations and Rehabilitations for Disabled Orphans". Under this three-year collaboration between the MCA, state orphanages, and almost three hundred Chinese hospitals, free medical treatment (including, where needed, surgical rehabilitation) was provided to thirty-five thousand *gu'er*.[101] Following this initial success, the Tomorrow Plan was made permanent and expanded in scope to cover some *gu'er* outside of state orphanages.[102] The initiative was an example of the new "welfare pluralism" model in action, in that it was initially financed jointly by central MCA funding, local state lottery income, and donations from society and NGOs.[103] According to the MCA, one important outcome of the Tomorrow Plan has been the adoption of tens of thousands of children who would otherwise not have found placements due to their costly medical needs,[104] although there is also concern that the attendant publicity about improved health care for *gu'er* may have been a factor for some parents in choosing to relinquish children with disabilities or grave medical needs into the state orphanage system.[105]

Soon after the Tomorrow Plan came the Blue Sky Plan.[106] This initiative was announced by President Hu Jintao during a 2006 Children's Day visit to a state orphanage, during which he called for all children to be able to develop equally under the same blue sky, with *gu'er* benefiting from the same opportunities as other children.[107] In line with this objective, the Blue Sky Plan was launched in 2007 as part of the government's eleventh national five-year plan (*Zhongguo wu nian jihua*) and subsequently extended into the twelfth planning period (2011–2015). The main thrust of the programme was the investment of billions of *yuan* of central and local government funding in the construction of new state orphanages in prefecture-level cities previously lacking state *gu'er* facilities and in the expansion and improvement of existing facilities.[108] The programme also emphasised that state orphanages should be used as hubs of medical, educational, and rehabilitative services for vulnerable children in the broader communities. Keyser reported that at a 2007 meeting of orphanage directors, the Blue Sky Plan was greeted with some scepticism, due to its focus on investment into hardware over software (buildings and infrastructure over staff training and policies) and concerns that the focus on state orphanages would lead to continued prioritisation of child institutionalisation over foster care placements.[109] These concerns may have been well founded in some locations: four of the foster homes included in this study, homes that had been working with state institutions during the first Blue Sky investment period, reported to me instances of *gu'er* being removed from family foster care placements in favour of reinstitutionalisation in newly constructed or renovated state orphanages.[110]

Another important policy document issued in conjunction with the Blue Sky Plan was the 2006 *Joint Ministerial Opinion on Strengthening Orphan Relief Work*.[111] This policy instrument was aspirational in tone, declaring that the Party and government have always cared for *gu'er* and setting out a number of views (*yijian*) on how existing relief measures could be improved. The Opinion exhorted all relevant departments at all levels of government to earnestly protect the rights and interests of *gu'er*, acknowledged the need for professionalisation of the orphan relief sector, and called for the mobilisation of social forces to assist in the task (although without setting out operational guidelines, service standards, or supervisory mechanisms). This openness to community involvement with state orphanages was a relatively new aspect of orphan relief in China—until the 1990s, orphanages had been banned from appealing to donations from the public for political reasons, and many had closed their doors to outside collaborators in the wake of the dying rooms scandal. But in the Blue Sky reform period, the MCA began to encourage greater community involvement.[112] Importantly, even international NGOs were permitted to be part of the new pluralist approach to state *gu'er* relief work, albeit closely monitored and at times with ambiguity about their proper place and role in the sector.[113] Community and NGO involvement with state orphanages in China now takes many forms, including fundraising/donations, volunteerism, and foster care.

The emerging foster family trend

One of the most important shifts in the work of China's state orphanages since the late 1990s has been towards placing children in local foster families or family group care settings, in lieu of large-group congregate care in institutions. The deleterious physical and psychological effects of orphanage life have been well documented—most obviously, institutional care negatively impacts on the ability of children to form attachments to family and social networks, which can lead to short- and long-term harm.[114] It is also less cost effective than family placements. Accordingly, the international trend in child welfare since the 1950s, and especially in developed countries, has been towards deinstitutionalisation, with family-based care now the preferred arrangement for children separated from their parents or guardians.[115]

Foster care is less common in developing countries, where social services infrastructure is often not sufficiently developed and professionalised to implement and regulate programmes outside of the traditional orphanage setting. Indeed, Shang and Fisher have noted that the Chinese government for a long time viewed institutional care as better for *gu'er*. In line with the official preference for institutions, foster families were only used to care for *gu'er* as a method of last resort.[116] For example, in the 1980s, innovative local foster care programmes were shut down by the central MCA, due to concerns about supervision and standards.[117] But in the late 1990s, as welfare generally began to socialise and international NGOs once more gained traction in collaborating with state orphanages, pilot foster care initiatives began to emerge in a number of provinces. These took the form of either in-house foster care (paid staff members tasked with providing a family environment to a small number of children on the orphanage grounds) or more traditional community-based programmes (locals recruited to provide daily care for a child or children in their home setting).[118]

One of the first pilot programmes was at the Shanghai CWI, which placed 220 children with local families between 1997 and 1999, with the advice and support of the British NGO Care for Children.[119] One study of the pilot programme found that recruitment of foster carers had been successful, with a substantial waiting list of applicants built up in a very short time, despite the fact that there was no tradition of state-sanctioned fostering in Chinese society at the time.[120] This can no doubt be linked in part to increased publicity surrounding the issue of *gu'er* following *Death by Default*—Keyser has noted that around 2000,

> public space for discussing and debating the "problem" of orphans also grew. Newspapers started carrying stories about society's responsibility to care for orphans, stories about the idea of fostering non-biological children, exposés on the joys of this kind of social action, as well as discussion about the legal and policy contradictions where it concerns the birth planning policies and domestic adoption policies.... The controversy surrounding orphan care led to alternative ways of thinking about how to care for orphans, and to the effort to engage society in caring for these children by providing a monetary benefit to citizen foster families.[121]

Foster care in China has some distinguishing features as opposed to in Western contexts. Where developed countries tend to place children in unrelated families mainly on a temporary basis, without extinguishing the parental rights or responsibilities of birth parents, the children who are fostered from orphanages in China have been orphaned or abandoned. They are also mostly disabled and therefore unlikely to be adopted. Accordingly, foster care in China, although technically temporary, usually has the "clear intention to create a permanent family environment for these children or, if this cannot be achieved, to maintain a family for as long as possible".[122] There is also a strong need for caregiving training for foster parents of *gu'er* with disabilities, something that state orphanages have not always been able to adequately provide.

Shang has described the shift to foster care as a "quiet revolution" in *gu'er* relief in China, one that has mainly been driven from the bottom-up, on the initiative of local officials in partnership with domestic and international NGOs.[123] In 2003, the MCA formally acknowledged the growing importance of foster care in *gu'er* relief, with the issue of temporary regulations to standardise the practice.[124] These were updated in 2014, with tighter controls put in place to improve care quality.[125] A number of domestic and international studies have concluded that foster care programmes are a promising aspect of China's renewed commitment to *gu'er* welfare in the new century,[126] and an estimated 50 per cent of state orphanages in China now provide some form of foster care for at least some of their residents.[127]

Ongoing challenges

Reports from the field suggest that conditions in many of China's state orphanages, particularly those in large wealthy urban centres such as Shanghai, Tianjin, and Beijing, have improved dramatically since the dying room images were broadcast to the world in the 1990s. Even by the end of that decade, facilities in many areas were benefiting from increased local and central government spending, more diverse sources of funding including international adoption and domestic donations, and greater openness to collaboration with NGOs.[128] There are, however, many ongoing problems with the state *gu'er* welfare system. First, and as discussed above, institutional care as compared to other forms of alternative care (foster care, family group care) is the least optimal form of care for vulnerable children. Although it should not be assumed that children in institutional settings do not also experience meaningful kinship experiences, research shows that institutions are generally detrimental for childhood social and emotional development.[129] Chinese academics have found that even post–Blue Sky, these issues have persisted in state orphanages despite improved facilities and staff ratios.[130] In light of these problems, the long-term trend both internationally and in China is towards deinstitutionalisation, although for the time being institutional care is still central to China's state programme of *gu'er* relief.

Apart from the overarching question of deinstitutionalisation, there are other more immediate challenges to providing high-quality care within the orphanage setting. These challenges vary from region to region because conditions largely depend on local factors such as leadership, provincial funding, and access to

NGO support. In a review of Chinese literature on state orphanage conditions, Meng and Kai have noted that the challenges facing facilities across China "range from poor quality of service and poorly trained staff to the institutionalised working model that emphasises administration rather than service, which fails to meet the diverse needs of children".[131] Many orphanages still struggle to provide anything other than the basic physical necessities of life, with *gu'er* unable to access compulsory education or corrective/rehabilitative surgical care, with lifelong negative consequences.[132] Despite improvements in infrastructure, NGOs and researchers report that the typical state orphanage is a socially deprived environment.[133] Orphanage care traditionally differs from family-like care, in that children are segregated by age and not assigned to permanent caregivers, which deprives them of the chance to form long-term emotional attachment to a family-like figure. Staff-child ratios and staff turnover can be very high, making it difficult for staff to interact with their charges warmly or attend to their emotional needs. In fact, staff are often not trained or supported in how to address emotional, psychological, and behavioural needs—in her 2009 large-scale survey of state orphanages, Shang gave the example of an orphanage that had only recently introduced the practice of holding babies.[134] This points to possibly the most urgent problem in the sector: professionalisation. In particular, more qualified counsellors, psychiatrists, and social workers are needed to provide staff training and improve overall service delivery.[135]

It is important to note that there are many state-run orphanages in China that provide high-quality nurturing services for *gu'er*. In the course of this research, I have spoken with scores of volunteers and NGO representatives who had worked closely with various state orphanages for many years and who emphasised that many directors and staff were making genuine efforts to help their wards to the best of their abilities and that the system had come a long way since the years of the dying room scandals. Others had witnessed ongoing problems with untrained staff, impersonal care, and inadequate medical treatment, even many years after the scandals first broke. Like other researchers, I have visited state orphanages with rooms full of infants who lay in bed for most of the day, and I have been beset by toddlers and children calling out "hold me" (*bao wo*) on seeing a different face enter the room, seemingly desperate for human touch. In her important sociological research on orphanage care and adoption in China, Leslie Wang verified that there were still dying rooms in some Chinese state orphanages—"spaces where very sick and disabled children are housed together and given few resources or individualized care"—as recently as 2011, decades after *The Dying Rooms* was first broadcast.[136] But she also pointed out that these rooms were no longer representative of orphanage care in China generally, despite their enduring impact on the sector's reputation internationally.

Conclusion: the need for private *gu'er* relief

Since the dismantling of many socialist safety nets in the modern reform era, economic hardship has intersected with birth-planning restrictions and ongoing stigma towards girls and children with disabilities. This intersection has had a coercive effect on tens of thousands of Chinese parents, in a way that has disproportionately impacted on girls with special medical needs. Further steps are needed to address these underlying causes of child abandonment, ensuring that the rights of children—to life, to health care, to a family—are more fully protected. The Chinese government has shown that it is aware of the importance of supporting families to stay together and has made positive progress towards that end. But for tens of thousands of families, such measures will come too late; accordingly, for the time being, state orphanages remain an important piece of the child welfare puzzle in China.

China's state orphanages have faced many hurdles in providing appropriate care for *gu'er*. Fortunately, as a country and culture that prides itself on caring for the vulnerable, the plight of China's *gu'er* has been increasingly in the public spotlight and consciousness in recent decades, including gaps and shortcomings in state *gu'er* relief. As awareness of these issues has grown, humanitarian workers and NGOs from China and abroad have stepped into the fray, with various projects aimed at addressing deficiencies within state orphanages. But China's state orphanages are only one part of the patchwork of state and society efforts that have evolved over the years to provide care for lonely children. In many parts of China, especially outside of urban centres, the more pressing issue than state orphanage standards has been the complete lack of any state-provided care options for *gu'er*. This gap in services resulted in hundreds of private orphanages, ranging widely in quality and professionalism, emerging in rural areas across China, as described in more detail in Chapter 3. In urban centres, meanwhile, in response to concerns about state orphanage standards, the foster home model developed, as described in Chapter 4.

To return to the children whose stories opened this chapter, Rose was brought out of her Henan orphanage and into a family of sorts at one such foster home, Compassion Family Life House, where she had access to the best care available in China for brittle bone disease. Josiah was given a chance of finding an adoptive family when he was selected for treatment at New Grace, and his congenital heart disease was diagnosed and surgically addressed. Although he had to wait for much longer than his "brothers and sisters" at New Grace to be matched, he eventually saw a photo of his waiting "forever family" and left soon after to join them in America. The remainder of this book introduces more such stories and studies—of individuals, organisations, and faith groups that have played various important and changing roles in orphan relief.

Notes

1 The term is commonly used in the international adoption community to refer to the day on which a child enters into the care of his or her adoptive parent(s).

2 In her anthropological study of a Chinese child welfare institution, Qian argues that scholarship on Chinese philanthropy overwhelmingly casts actors and organisations as positive civil society forces but often overlooks the discrimination and stigma reproduced when children are cast as the "unfortunate" objects of philanthropy:

Linliang Qian, "Consuming 'The Unfortunate': The Violence of Philanthropy in a Contemporary Chinese State-run Orphanage," *Dialectical Anthropology* 38, no. 3 (September 2014).

3 Adoption Law [*Shouyang Fa*] 1991, amended 1998 (People's Republic of China), article 4.

4 Ministry of Civil Affairs *et al.*, *Joint Ministerial Opinion on Strengthening Orphan Relief Work* [*Guanyu jiaqiang gu'er jiuzhu gongzuo de yijian*], 14 April 2006. Available at www.china.com.cn/chinese/PI-c/1183979.htm (retrieved 10 July 2018).

5 Children with one or both parents in jail are a "new kind of orphan" in China. In 2005, there were an estimated 600,000 dependent children of prisoners in China. This has not traditionally been a population targeted for *gu'er* service by the Ministry of Civil Affairs, but in recent years the population has received increased attention, albeit from a juvenile delinquency perspective: Liu Meng and Zhu Kai, "Orphan Care in China," *Social Work and Society International Online Journal* 7, no. 1 (2009), 3.3.

6 Ministry of Civil Affairs, *2016 Statistical Report on Social Service Development* [*2016 nian shehui fuwu fazhan tongji gongbao*], 3 August 2017, 2.2. Available at www.mca.gov.cn/article/sj/tjgb/201708/20170815005382.shtml (retrieved 4 July 2018). See, further, Chapter 3 at 62.

7 Meng and Kai, "Orphan Care in China," 3.1.

8 Xiaoyuan Shang, "Looking for a Better Way to Care for Children: Cooperation between the State and Civil Society in China," *Social Service Review* 76, no. 2 (June 2002), 207 (estimating 20,000 *gu'er* found nationwide annually); Xiaoyuan Shang, Karen R. Fisher, and Jiawen Xie, "Discrimination Against Children with Disability in China," in "Social Policy and Poverty," ed. Katja Hujo and Elena Gaia, special issue, *International Journal of Social Welfare* 20, no. 3 (2011), 298 (estimating ten thousand). The Chinese Disabled Persons' Federation in 2007 claimed that "tens of thousands" of children with disabilities are abandoned by their parents annually: Karen R. Fisher and Xiaoyuan Shang, "Protecting the Right to Life of Children with Disabilities in China," *Journal of Social Service Research* 4, no. 4 (2014), 561.

9 Meng and Kai, "Orphan Care in China," 3.1.

10 *People's Daily*, "Lankao Orphans' Death Rattles Society, Civil Organisations Face Restrictions," *people.cn*, 5 January, 2013. Available at http://politics.people.com.cn/GB/n/2013/0105/c70731–20099092.html (retrieved 13 August 2018).

11 Haiyan Li, Xiaoyuan Shang, and Jianpeng Cheng, "An Analysis of Reasons Behind the Abandonment of Orphans and Disabled Children in Beijing" [Beijingshi Gucan Ertong Bei Yiqide Yuanyin Fenxi], *Beijing Social Sciences* 4 (2004), 164–68; Kay Ann Johnson, Huang Banhan, and Wang Liyao, "Infant Abandonment and Adoption in China," *Population and Development Review* 24, no. 3 (September 1998), 479. For a rare example of anti-abandonment laws being enforced through the judicial system, see Hui Lü, "Children Without Parents," *China Today* (September 1994), reporting on a Zhejiang couple who abandoned their twin daughters at a hospital and were subsequently sued for outstanding hospital bills and ordered to give proper parental care to the children.

12 In using terms such as "Western" and "Chinese", I am in agreement with Hoffman and Zhao, who argue that such usage can result in "unwarranted generalization, leading to monolithic comparisons that erase internal differences" but that they might nevertheless be carefully used as "heuristic devices to illustrate broad cultural contrasts": Diane M. Hoffman and Guoping Zhao, "Global Convergence and Divergence in Childhood Ideologies and the Marginalization of Children," in *Education and Social Inequality in the Global Culture*, eds. Joseph Zajda, Karen Biraimah, and William Gaudelli (Dordrecht: Springer, 2008), 3.

13 Kay Ann Johnson, *Wanting a Daughter, Needing a Son: Abandonment, Adoption, and Orphanage Care in China*, ed. Amy Klatzkin (St Paul, MN: Yeong & Yeong,

2004); Kay Ann Johnson, *China's Hidden Children: Abandonment, Adoption, and the Human Costs of the One-Child Policy* (Chicago: University of Chicago Press, 2016).

14 Johnson, *Wanting a Daughter*, 50.

15 Johnson, Huang, and Wang, "Infant Abandonment and Adoption in China," 480.

16 Linda Wong, *Marginalization and Social Welfare in China* (London: LSE/Routledge, 1998), 173–74; Ronald C. Keith, "Legislating Women's and Children's 'Rights and Interests' in the PRC," *The China Quarterly* 149 (March 1997), 43; Michael Palmer, "Rethinking Children's Rights and Interests?: Economic Reform, Social Protection and Legal Culture in Post-Mao China," *Journal of Comparative Law* 5, 2 (2010), 261.

17 Julie Jimmerson, "Female Infanticide in China: An Examination of Cultural and Legal Norms," *UCLA Pacific Basin Law Journal* 8, no. 1 (Spring 1990), 52.

18 See, generally, Ann Waltner, "Infanticide and Dowry in Ming and Early Qing China," in *Chinese Views of Childhood*, ed. Anne Behnke Kinney (Honolulu: University of Hawai'i Press, 1995).

19 Shang, "Looking for a Better Way," 207.

20 Law on Protection of the Rights and Interests of the Elderly [*Laonianren Quanyi Baozhang Fa*] 1996 (People's Republic of China), article 11.

21 At the time of writing, analysts are expecting China to end birth-limits in the near future: Bloomberg News, "China Signals End to Child Birth Limits by 2020 at Latest," *Bloomberg.com*, 28 August, 2018, www.bloomberg.com/news/articles/2018–08–28/china-signals-end-to-limits-on-child-births-by-2020-at-latest (retrieved 30 January 2019).

22 See Yee-Fui Ng, "Disability Rights v Quality Birth Rhetoric: The Construction of Disability in China," *Lawasia Journal* (2012), 3 (noting strong resistance from pro-natal cultural tradition, and also noting periods of coercion and relative leniency); Wong, *Marginalization and Social Welfare in China*, 172 (noting charges of arbitrariness, cruelty and violation of human rights, and domestic resistance).

23 Johnson, *China's Hidden Children*, 2016. The United Nations Committee on the Rights of the Child has also expressed concern on this point: Comm. on the Rights of the Child, *Concluding Observations on the Combined Third and Fourth Periodic Reports of China (including Hong Kong and Macau Special Administrative Regions), adopted by the Committee at its sixty-fourth session (16 September–4 October 2013)*, U.N. Doc. CRC/C/CHN/CO/3–4, III.E.56 (29 October 2013).

24 Before relaxation of the one-child policy, a notable exception to the rule was that families with a child with disabilities were permitted to have a second child, a policy that the United Nations Committee on the Rights of the Child has noted promoted the stigmatisation of children with disabilities (Comm. on the Rights of the Child, *Concluding Observations*, 2013, III.F.58(a)).

25 Palmer, "Rethinking Children's Rights and Interests," 271.

26 Weiguo Zhang, "Who Adopts Girls and Why? Domestic Adoption of Female Children in Contemporary Rural China," *The China Journal* 56 (July, 2006), 66n18.

27 Shang, "Looking for a Better Way," 207; Li, Shang, and Cheng, "An Analysis of Reasons Behind the Abandonment of Orphans and Disabled Children," 2004.

28 Qian, "Consuming 'The Unfortunate,'" 254; Bi Ying Hu and Judit Szente, "The Care and Education of Orphan Children with Disabilities in China: Progress and Remaining Challenges," *Childhood Education*, 86, no. 2 (Winter 2009), 79; Catherine H. Keyser, "The Role of the State and NGOs in Caring for At-Risk Children: The Case of Orphan Care," in *State and Society Responses to Social Welfare Needs in China: Serving the People*, eds. Jonathan Schwartz and Shawn Shieh (Abingdon: Routledge, 2009), 46.

29 Hu and Szente, "The Care and Education of Orphan Children," 79.

30 Frank Dikötter, *Imperfect Conceptions: Medical Knowledge, Birth Defects and Eugenics in China* (New York: Columbia University Press, 1998), 152. See also

Charlotte Furth, "From Birth to Birth: The Growing Body in Chinese Medicine," in *Chinese Views of Childhood*, ed. Anne Behnke Kinney (Honolulu: University of Hawai'i Press, 1995), 164; Eleanor E. Holroyd, "Chinese Cultural Influences on Parental Caregiving Obligations toward Children with Disabilities," *Qualitative Health Research* 13, no. 1 (January 2003), 12–15 (discussing the "shame and blame" dimensions of parenting a child with disabilities).

31 Holroyd, "Chinese Cultural Influences on Parental Caregiving Obligations," 18.

32 Matthew Kohrman, *Bodies of Difference: Experiences of Disability and Institutional Advocacy in the Making of Modern China* (Berkeley: University of California Press, 2005), 62.

33 Dikötter, *Imperfect Conceptions*, 68–69; Zhou Xun, "The Discourse of Disability in Modern China," *Patterns of Prejudice* 36, no. 1 (2002), 107.

34 Andrew Kipnis, "*Suzhi*: A Keyword Approach," *The China Quarterly* 186 (June 2006), 305.

35 Dikötter, *Imperfect Conceptions*, 1998.

36 Ng, "Disability Rights v Quality Birth Rhetoric," 7.

37 Ann Anagnost, "The Corporeal Politics of Quality (*Suzhi*)," *Public Culture* 16, no. 2 (Spring 2004), 190.

38 Xun, "The Discourse of Disability in Modern China," 110. See also Dikötter, *Imperfect Conceptions*, 137 (discussing the "national consequences of dysgenic trends").

39 See, generally, Qian, "Consuming 'The Unfortunate,'" 259; Kipnis, "*Suzhi*: A Keyword Approach," 2006.

40 Anagnost, "The Corporeal Politics of Quality (*Suzhi*)," 194.

41 See, for example, Dikötter, *Imperfect Conceptions*, 162–64, 171–72; Xun, "The Discourse of Disability in Modern China," 111; Ng, "Disability Rights v Quality Birth Rhetoric," 22.

42 Ng, "Disability Rights v Quality Birth Rhetoric," 12.

43 Xun, "The Discourse of Disability in Modern China," 105.

44 Dikötter, *Imperfect Conceptions*, 81–82.

45 Ng, "Disability Rights v Quality Birth Rhetoric," 17–20.

46 Fisher and Shang, "Protecting the Right to Life of Children with Disabilities in China," 568.

47 Michael Ashley Stein, "China and Disability Rights," *Loyola of Los Angeles International and Comparative Law Review* 33, no. 1 (Fall 2010).

48 Karen R. Fisher, Xiaoyuan Shang, and Megan Blaxland, "Disability and Welfare Services," in *Handbook of Welfare in China*, eds. Beatriz Carrillo, Johanna Hood, and Paul Kadetz (Cheltenham: Edward Elgar, 2017), 252.

49 Xiaoyuan Shang and Karen R. Fisher, *Caring for Orphaned Children in China* (Lanham: Lexington, 2014).

50 Fisher, Shang, and Blaxland, "Disability and Welfare Services," 256–57.

51 Xiaoyuan Shang and Karen R. Fisher, *Disability Policy in China: Child and Family Experiences* (London: Routledge, 2016).

52 Fisher, Shang, and Blaxland, "Disability and Welfare Services," 255. But see Chapter 6 at 142 for more recent promising developments in this area.

53 Fisher, Shang, and Blaxland, "Disability and Welfare Services," 254–55.

54 Shang, "Looking for a Better Way," 207.

55 Johnson, *Wanting a Daughter*, 2004.

56 Weiguo Zhang, "Who Adopts Girls and Why?" 64; Johnson, Huang, and Wang, "Infant Abandonment and Adoption in China," 483.

57 Angela Ki Che Leung, "Relief Institutions for Children in Nineteenth-Century China," in *Chinese Views of Childhood*, ed. Anne Behnke Kinney (Honolulu: University of Hawai'i Press, 1995), 265.

58 Johnson, Huang, and Wang, "Infant Abandonment and Adoption in China," 483.

59 Johnson, Huang, and Wang, "Infant Abandonment and Adoption in China," 484.

60 Zhang, "Who Adopts Girls and Why?" 2006.
61 Johnson, *China's Hidden Children*, 4.
62 Johnson, Huang, and Wang, "Infant Abandonment and Adoption in China," 495.
63 Johnson, Huang, and Wang, "Infant Abandonment and Adoption in China," 503.
64 Adoption Law [*Shouyang Fa*] 1991 (People's Republic of China), articles 6 and 8; in 1998, the exception for adoptions involving disabled children and "true orphans" was extended to abandoned children whose parents cannot be found or ascertained, and the minimum age for other types of adoption was lowered to thirty.
65 See also Susan Greenhalgh and Edwin A. Winckler, *Governing China's Population: From Leninist to Neoliberal Biopolitics* (Stanford: Stanford University Press, 2005), 270 (estimating 80 per cent of adoptions were forced underground due to restrictions on domestic adoption).
66 Johnson, *China's Hidden Children*, 71. The problem of "black status" is not restricted to adopted children. The official (probably conservative) estimate is that thirteen million Chinese lack a *hukou* [personal record in the national compulsory household registration system]. This can be for a variety of reasons, including being born outside of family-planning quotas. For a recent account of a "black child" fighting for *hukou* registration in Beijing, see "Fighting for Identity; Bureaucracy" *The Economist*, London 411, no. 8887 (17 May, 2014), 43. The issue of "black status" children residing in unregistered private orphanages is discussed in Chapter 3 at 69–70.
67 Zhang, "Who Adopts Girls and Why?" 77.
68 Johnson, *China's Hidden Children*, 14.
69 Johnson, Huang, and Wang, "Infant Abandonment and Adoption in China," 500–501.
70 Xiaoyuan Shang, Morris Saldov, and Karen R. Fisher, "Informal Kinship Care of Orphans in Rural China," *Social Policy and Society* 10, no. 1 (January 2011): 110.
71 Shang and Fisher, *Caring for Orphaned Children in China*, 2014; Shang, Fisher, and Xie, "Discrimination Against Children with Disability in China," 299. A 2005 study of state orphanages reported that 80.5 per cent of children in state orphanages have some kind of disability (Xiaoyuan Shang, Xiaoming Wu, and Haiyan Li, "Social Policy, Social Gender and the Problem of Infant Abandonment in China" [*Shehui Zhengce, Shehui Xingbie Yu Zhongguo De Ertong Yiqi Wenti*], *Youth Studies* 4, [2005]). It should be noted, however, that orphanage directors reportedly tend to define "disability" very broadly so as to include relatively minor and easily treatable conditions such as cleft lips or birthmarks, possibly to counter the perception that even healthy children are abandoned due to repressive birth-control policies and backwards male-preferring cultural traditions. Interestingly, other researchers have similarly noted that disability is defined differently for different political purposes in other contexts—for example, broadly when it comes to implementation of the Maternal and Infant Health Care Law [*Muying Baojian Fa*] 1994 but narrowly in relation to disability rights (thereby reducing the financial responsibility of the state for persons with disabilities): Ng, "Disability Rights v Quality Birth Rhetoric," 16; Stein, "China and Disability Rights," 15–16.
72 Fang Zhao, Juha Erkki Antero Hämäläinen, and Honglin L. Chen, "Child Protection in China: Changing Policies and Reactions from the Field of Social Work," *International Journal of Social Welfare* 26, no. 4 (October 2017), 331.
73 Leung, "Relief Institutions for Children in Nineteenth-Century China," 251–54.
74 Carolyn L. Hsu, " 'Rehabilitating Charity' in China: The Case of Project Hope and the Rise of Non-Profit Organizations," *Journal of Civil Society* 4, no. 2 (September 2008), 87.
75 Shang, "Looking for a Better Way," 206.
76 Shang, "Looking for a Better Way," 206.
77 Keyser, "The Role of the State and NGOs," 50.

78 Wong, *Marginalization and Social Welfare in China*, 167.
79 For a discussion of cultural assumptions about the "public duty" of relatives to care for orphans in the extended family, as compared to the "private love" of parents for children, see Wu Hung, "Private Love and Public Duty: Images of Children in Early Chinese Art," in *Chinese Views of Childhood*, ed. Anne Behnke Kinney (Honolulu: University of Hawai'i Press, 1995), 91, 96, 105.
80 Marriage Law [*Hunyin Fa*] 2001 (People's Republic of China), articles 28 and 29. See also General Principles of the Civil Law [*Minfa Tongze*] 1986 (People's Republic of China), article 16.
81 The most recent government statistics showed a total of 465 state orphanages caring for 88,000 of a total *registered gu'er* population of 373,000: Ministry of Civil Affairs, *2016 Statistical Report on Social Service Development*, 2.2. This *gu'er* figure is likely underreported. There are also hundreds of hostels and protection centres caring for vagrant/street children, although these are beyond the scope of this book: see Xiaoyuan Shang and Xiaoming Wu, "The Care Regime in China: Elder and Child Care," in "Changing Care Regime for Children and Elderly – The East Asia Experiences," special issue, *Journal of Comparative Social Welfare* 27, no. 2 (June 2011), 129.
82 Segregated care is more desirable but has not been achieved throughout China, due in part to local funding constraints: Shang and Fisher, *Caring for Orphaned Children in China*, 47.
83 Human Rights Watch/Asia, *Death by Default: A Policy of Fatal Neglect in China's State Orphanages* (New York: Human Rights Watch, 1996).
84 Human Rights Watch/Asia, *Death by Default*, 5, 147–48.
85 Human Rights Watch/Asia, *Death by Default*, 77.
86 Johnson, *Wanting a Daughter*, 41–48.
87 Johnson, *Wanting a Daughter*, 43. See also Therese Hesketh, letter to the editor, "Orphanages in China Require More Funding," *British Medical Journal* 312, no. 7044 (8 June 1996), 1482.
88 Anne F. Thurston, "In a Chinese Orphanage," *The Atlantic* 277, no. 4 (April 1996), 28–41. See also Leslie K. Wang, *Outsourced Children: Orphanage Care and Adoption in Globalizing China* (Stanford: Stanford University Press, 2016), 9–12 (describing the author's observations of a dying room in a state orphanage in 2007).
89 Wong, *Marginalization and Social Welfare in China*, 1998; Wang, *Outsourced Children*, 2016.
90 Qian, "Consuming 'The Unfortunate,'" 2014.
91 Johnson, *China's Hidden Children*, 8.
92 Johnson, Huang, and Wang, "Infant Abandonment and Adoption in China," 1998.
93 While the rhetoric of "child rescue" remains prevalent in modern intercountry adoption, a number of parent-driven or family-driven objectives and arguments in favour of the practice have also emerged over time, with adoption increasingly seen as a mutually beneficial means of providing persons who are childless with children: Anna Jane High, "Pondering the Politicization of Intercountry Adoption: Russia's Ban on American 'Forever Families,'" *Cardozo Journal of International and Comparative Law* 22, no. 3 (2014), 506–9.
94 Johnson, *China's Hidden Children*, 8.
95 Wang, *Outsourced Children*, 12.
96 Human Rights Watch/Asia, *China: Chinese Orphanages; A Follow Up*, March 1996. Available at www.hrw.org/sites/default/files/reports/china96.pdf (retrieved 4 July 2018).
97 *People's Daily*, "The Description and Accusations about China's Children's Welfare Institutions by Britain's Channel Four and the Human Rights Watch/Asia Do Not Hold Water," *people.cn*, 2016, http://en.people.cn/whitepaper/13appendix.html (retrieved 4 July 2018).
98 Human Rights Watch/Asia, *China: Chinese Orphanages; A Follow Up*, 1996.

99 Renee Yuen-Jan Hsia and Lynn T. White III, "Working amid Corporatism and Confusion: Foreign NGOs in China," *Nonprofit and Voluntary Sector Quarterly* 31, no. 3 (September 2002), 336.
100 Johnson, *Wanting a Daughter*, 188; Shang, "Looking for a Better Way," 211.
101 Hu and Szente, "The Care and Education of Orphan Children with Disabilities in China," 83.
102 *People's Daily*, "Ministry of Civil Affairs Invests 1.3 Billion Yuan in 'Tomorrow Plan,'" *people.cn*, 30 May 2018, http://sn.people.com.cn/n2/2018/0530/c378287-31647255.html (retrieved 13 September 2018).
103 Xinhua News, "Huge Fund Spent on Operations for Disabled Orphans," *Xinhua News Agency*, 5 November 2005, www.china.org.cn/english/China/147656.htm (retrieved 9 July 2018).
104 *People's Daily*, "Ministry of Civil Affairs Invests 1.3 Billion Yuan in 'Tomorrow Plan,'" 2018.
105 Hu and Szente, "The Care and Education of Orphan Children with Disabilities in China," 80.
106 Ministry of Civil Affairs, *Child Welfare Institutions Blue Sky Construction Plan Implementation Programme* [*Ertong fuli jigou jianshe lantian jihua shishi fang'an*], 22 January 2007. Accessed from www.mca.gov.cn/article/xw/ywdt/200711/20071115003905.shtml (page no longer online) (retrieved 14 September 2018, on file with author).
107 Xiaofeng Guan, "Nationwide Plan for Better Care of Orphans," *China Daily*, 29 December 2006, www.chinadaily.com.cn/china/2006–12/29/content_770291.htm (retrieved 9 July 2018).
108 Hu and Szente, "The Care and Education of Orphan Children with Disabilities in China," 83.
109 Keyser, "The Role of the State and NGOs," 63n8.
110 See Chapter 4 at 101. Dr Shang likewise reported examples of re-institutionalisation to state orphanages in the 2000s: Shang and Fisher, *Caring for Orphaned Children in China*, 66.
111 Ministry of Civil Affairs *et al.*, *Joint Ministerial Opinion on Strengthening Orphan Relief Work* [*Guanyu jiaqiang gu'er jiuzhu gongzuo de yijian*], 14 April 2006. Available at www.china.com.cn/chinese/PI-c/1183979.htm (retrieved 10 July 2018).
112 Shang and Fisher, *Caring for Orphaned Children in China*, 60–63.
113 Keyser, "The Role of the State and NGOs," 2009.
114 Shang and Fisher, *Caring for Orphaned Children in China*, 63; David Howe, *Attachment Theory for Social Work Practice* (Basingstoke: Macmillan, 1995), 106.
115 Shang and Fisher, *Caring for Orphaned Children in China*, 17–19. There are, of course, potential downsides to foster care, including the risk of placement breakdown.
116 Shang and Fisher, *Caring for Orphaned Children in China*, 15–16, 65.
117 Shang, "Looking for a Better Way," 211–12.
118 Meng and Kai, "Orphan Care in China," 4.1.
119 Chris Beckett and June Thoburn, "Family Placements from a Chinese Institution," *Adoption and Fostering* 26, no. 3 (October 2002).
120 Beckett and Thoburn, "Family Placements from a Chinese Institution," 23.
121 Keyser, "The Role of the State and NGOs," 58–59.
122 Shang, "Looking for a Better Way," 204
123 Shang, "Looking for a Better Way," 223.
124 Ministry of Civil Affairs, *Interim Foster Care Management Measures* [*Jiating jiyang guanli zhanxiang banfa*], 27 October 2003. Available at www.gov.cn/gongbao/content/2004/content_62869.htm (retrieved 13 September 2018).
125 *People's Daily*, "New Family Foster Care Regulations Implemented on December 1," *people.cn*, 23 October 2014, http://pic.people.com.cn/n/2014/1023/c1016-25891201.html (retrieved 10 July 2018). The announcement of the new

measures included the slogan "*bushi qinren, shengsi qinren*" (not relatives, better than relatives).

126 Meng and Kai, "Orphan Care in China," 4.1; Xiaoyuan Shang, "Looking for Best Practice in Caring for Disabled Children: A Case of Socialized Foster Care in China," *Asia Pacific Journal of Social Work and Development* 22, no. 1–2 (March/June 2012), 127–38; Beckett and Thoburn, "Family Placements from a Chinese Institution," 2002; Shang and Fisher, *Caring for Orphaned Children in China*, chapters 8 and 13.

127 Fisher, Shang, and Blaxland, "Disability and Welfare Services," 255.

128 Johnson, *Wanting a Daughter*, 222.

129 Shang and Fisher, *Caring for Orphaned Children in China*, 18.

130 Meng and Kai, "Orphan Care in China," 3.1, 4.4.

131 Meng and Kai, "Orphan Care in China," 4.1.

132 Hu and Szente, "The Care and Education of Orphan Children with Disabilities in China," 83.

133 Hu and Szente, "The Care and Education of Orphan Children with Disabilities in China," 2009; University of Pittsburgh Office of Child Development, "Shift in Orphanage Demographics Brings New Challenges for China," October 2009. Accessed from www.ocd.pitt.edu/Shift-in-Orphanage-Demographics-Brings-New-Challenges-for-China/260/default.aspx (page no longer online, on file with author) (retrieved 9 February 2018); Meng and Kai, "Orphan Care in China," 2009; Shang and Fisher, *Caring for Orphaned Children in China*, chapter 7; Keyser, "The Role of the State and NGOs," 2009; Wang, *Outsourced Children*, 2016.

134 Shang and Fisher, *Caring for Orphaned Children in China*, 91.

135 Meng and Kai, "Orphan Care in China," 5.

136 Wang, *Outsourced Children*, 12.

Bibliography

Anagnost, Ann. "The Corporeal Politics of Quality (*Suzhi*)." *Public Culture* 16, no. 2 (Spring 2004): 189–208.

Beckett, Chris, and June Thoburn. "Family Placements from a Chinese Institution." *Adoption and Fostering* 26, no. 3 (October 2002): 19–27.

Dikötter, Frank. *Imperfect Conceptions: Medical Knowledge, Birth Defects and Eugenics in China*. New York: Columbia University Press, 1998.

"Fighting for Identity; Bureaucracy." *The Economist*, 17 May 2014.

Fisher, Karen R., and Xiaoyuan Shang. "Protecting the Right to Life of Children with Disabilities in China." *Journal of Social Service Research* 40, no. 4 (2014): 560–72.

Fisher, Karen R., Xiaoyuan Shang, and Megan Blaxland. "Disability and Welfare Services." In *Handbook of Welfare in China*, edited by Beatriz Carrillo, Johanna Hood, and Paul Kadetz, 252–65. Cheltenham: Edward Elgar, 2017.

Furth, Charlotte. "From Birth to Birth: The Growing Body in Chinese Medicine." In *Chinese Views of Childhood*, edited by Anne Behnke Kinney, 157–91. Honolulu: University of Hawai'i Press, 1995.

Greenhalgh, Susan, and Edwin A. Winckler. *Governing China's Population: From Leninist to Neoliberal Biopolitics*. Stanford: Stanford University Press, 2005.

Hesketh, Therese. Letter to the editor. "Orphanages in China Require More Funding." *British Medical Journal* 312, no. 7044 (8 June 1996): 1482.

High, Anna Jane. "China's Orphan Welfare System: Laws, Policies and Filled Gaps." *University of Pennsylvania East Asia Law Review* 8, no. 2 (2013): 127–76.

High, Anna Jane. "Grassroots NGO Regulation and China's Local Legal Culture." *Socio-Legal Review* 9, no. 2 (2013): 1–50.

High, Anna Jane. "'It's Grace and Favor, It's Not Law': Extra-Legal Regulation of Foreign Foster Homes in China." *University of Pennsylvania Asian Law Review* 12, no. 3 (Spring 2017): 357–405.

High, Anna Jane. "Pondering the Politicization of Intercountry Adoption: Russia's Ban on American 'Forever Families.'" *Cardozo Journal of International and Comparative Law* 22, no. 3 (Spring 2014): 497–560.

Hoffman, Diane M., and Guoping Zhao. "Global Convergence and Divergence in Childhood Ideologies and the Marginalization of Children." In *Education and Social Inequality in the Global Culture*, edited by Joseph Zajda, Karen Biraimah, and William Gaudelli, 1–16. Dordrecht: Springer, 2008.

Holroyd, Eleanor E. "Chinese Cultural Influences on Parental Caregiving Obligations toward Children with Disabilities." *Qualitative Health Research* 13, no. 1 (January 2003): 4–19.

Howe, David. *Attachment Theory for Social Work Practice*. Basingstoke: Macmillan, 1995.

Hsia, Renee Yuen-Jan, and Lynn T. White III. "Working amid Corporatism and Confusion: Foreign NGOs in China." *Nonprofit and Voluntary Sector Quarterly* 31, no. 3 (September 2002): 329–51.

Hsu, Carolyn L. "'Rehabilitating Charity' in China: The Case of Project Hope and the Rise of Non-Profit Organizations." *Journal of Civil Society* 4, no. 2 (September 2008): 81–96.

Hu, Bi Ying, and Judit Szente. "The Care and Education of Orphan Children with Disabilities in China: Progress and Remaining Challenges." *Childhood Education* 86, no. 2 (Winter 2009): 78–86.

Human Rights Watch/Asia. *China: Chinese Orphanages; A Follow Up*. March 1996. Available at www.hrw.org/sites/default/files/reports/china96.pdf (retrieved 4 July 2018).

Human Rights Watch/Asia. *Death by Default: A Policy of Fatal Neglect in China's State Orphanages*. New York: Human Rights Watch, 1996.

Hung, Wu. "Private Love and Public Duty: Images of Children in Early Chinese Art." In *Chinese Views of Childhood*, edited by Anne Behnke Kinney, 79–110. Honolulu: University of Hawai'i Press, 1995.

Jimmerson, Julie. "Female Infanticide in China: An Examination of Cultural and Legal Norms." *UCLA Pacific Basin Law Journal* 8, no. 1 (Spring 1990): 47–79.

Johnson, Kay Ann. *China's Hidden Children: Abandonment, Adoption, and the Human Costs of the One-Child Policy*. Chicago: University of Chicago Press, 2016.

Johnson, Kay Ann. *Wanting a Daughter, Needing a Son: Abandonment, Adoption, and Orphanage Care in China*. Edited by Amy Klatzkin. St Paul, MN: Yeong & Yeong, 2004.

Johnson, Kay Ann, Huang Banhan, and Wang Liyao. "Infant Abandonment and Adoption in China." *Population and Development Review* 24, no. 3 (September 1998): 469–510.

Keith, Ronald C. "Legislating Women's and Children's 'Rights and Interests' in the PRC." *The China Quarterly* 149 (March 1997): 29–55.

Keyser, Catherine H. "The Role of the State and NGOs in Caring for At-Risk Children: The Case of Orphan Care." In *State and Society Responses to Social Welfare Needs in China; Serving the People*, edited by Jonathan Schwartz and Shawn Shieh, 45–65. Abingdon: Routledge, 2009.

Kipnis, Andrew. "*Suzhi*: A Keyword Approach." *The China Quarterly* 186 (June 2006): 295–313.

Kohrman, Matthew. *Bodies of Difference: Experiences of Disability and Institutional Advocacy in the Making of Modern China.* Berkeley: University of California Press, 2005.

Leung, Angela Ki Che. "Relief Institutions for Children in Nineteenth-Century China." In *Chinese Views of Childhood*, edited by Anne Behnke Kinney, 251–78. Honolulu: University of Hawai'i Press, 1995.

Li, Haiyan, Xiaoyuan Shang, and Jianpeng Cheng. "An Analysis of Reasons Behind the Abandonment of Orphans and Disabled Children in Beijing." [*Beijingshi Gucan Ertong Bei Yiqide Yuanyin Fenxi*]. *Beijing Social Sciences* 4 (2004): 164–68.

Lü, Hui. "Children Without Parents." *China Today* (September 1994): 42–45.

Meng, Liu, and Zhu Kai. "Orphan Care in China." *Social Work and Society International Online Journal* 7, no. 1 (2009): 43–57.

Ministry of Civil Affairs. *Interim Foster Care Management Measures* [*Jiating jiyang guanli zhanxiang banfa*]. 27 October 2003. Available at www.gov.cn/gongbao/content/2004/content_62869.htm (retrieved 13 September 2018).

Ministry of Civil Affairs. *Child Welfare Institution Blue Sky Construction Plan Implementation Programme* [*Ertong fuli jigou jianshe lantian jihua shishi fang'an*]. 22 January 2007. Accessed from www.mca.gov.cn/article/xw/ywdt/200711/20071115003905.shtml (page no longer online) (retrieved 14 September 2018).

Ministry of Civil Affairs. *2016 Statistical Report on Social Service Development* [*2016 nian shehui fuwu fazhan tongji gongbao*]. 3 August 2017. Available at www.mca.gov.cn/article/sj/tjgb/201708/20170815005382.shtml (retrieved 4 July 2018).

Ministry of Civil Affairs *et al. Joint Ministerial Opinion on Strengthening Orphan Relief Work* [*Guanyu jiaqiang gu'er jiuzhu gongzuo de yijian*]. 14 April 2006. Available at www.china.com.cn/chinese/PI-c/1183979.htm (retrieved 10 July 2018).

Ng, Yee-Fui. "Disability Rights v Quality Birth Rhetoric: The Construction of Disability in China." *Lawasia Journal* (2012): 1–25.

Palmer, Michael. "Rethinking Children's Rights and Interests?: Economic Reform, Social Protection and Legal Culture in Post-Mao China." *Journal of Comparative Law* 5, no. 2 (2010): 260–80.

Qian, Linliang. "Consuming 'The Unfortunate': The Violence of Philanthropy in a Contemporary Chinese State-run Orphanage." *Dialectical Anthropology* 38, no. 3 (September 2014): 247–79.

Shang, Xiaoyuan. "Looking for a Better Way to Care for Children: Cooperation between the State and Civil Society in China." *Social Service Review* 76, no. 2 (June 2002): 203–28.

Shang, Xiaoyuan. "Looking for Best Practice in Caring for Disabled Children: A Case of Socialized Foster Care in China." *Asia Pacific Journal of Social Work and Development* 22, no. 1–2 (March/June 2012): 127–38.

Shang, Xiaoyuan, and Karen R. Fisher. *Caring for Orphaned Children in China*. Lanham: Lexington, 2014.

Shang, Xiaoyuan, and Karen R. Fisher. *Disability Policy in China: Child and Family Experiences*. London: Routledge, 2016.

Shang, Xiaoyuan, Karen R. Fisher, and Jiawen Xie. "Discrimination Against Children with Disability in China." In "Social Policy and Poverty," edited by Katja Hujo and Elena Gaia. Special issue, *International Journal of Social Welfare* 20, no. 3 (July 2011): 298–398.

Shang, Xiaoyuan, Morris Saldov, and Karen R. Fisher. "Informal Kinship Care of Orphans in Rural China." *Social Policy and Society* 10, no. 1 (January 2011): 103–16.

Shang, Xiaoyuan, and Xiaoming Wu. "The Care Regime in China: Elder and Child Care." In "Changing Care Regime for Children and Elderly – The East Asia Experiences." Special issue, *Journal of Comparative Social Welfare* 27, no. 2 (June 2011): 123–31.

Shang, Xiaoyuan, Xiaoming Wu, and Haiyan Li. "Social Policy, Social Gender and the Problem of Infant Abandonment in China" [*Shehui Zhengce, Shehui Xingbie Yu Zhongguo De Ertong Yiqi Wenti*]. *Youth Studies* 4 (2005).

Stein, Michael Ashley. "China and Disability Rights." *Loyola of Los Angeles International and Comparative Law Review* 33, no. 1 (Fall 2010): 7–26.

Thurston, Anne F. "In a Chinese Orphanage." *The Atlantic*, April 1996.

Waltner, Ann. "Infanticide and Dowry in Ming and Early Qing China." In *Chinese Views of Childhood*, edited by Anne Behnke Kinney, 193–217. Honolulu: University of Hawai'i Press, 1995.

Wang, Leslie K. *Outsourced Children: Orphanage Care and Adoption in Globalizing China*. Stanford: Stanford University Press, 2016.

Wong, Linda. *Marginalization and Social Welfare in China*. London: LSE/Routledge, 1998.

Xun, Zhou. "The Discourse of Disability in Modern China." *Patterns of Prejudice* 36, no. 1 (2002): 104–12.

Zhang, Weiguo. "Who Adopts Girls and Why? Domestic Adoption of Female Children in Contemporary Rural China." *The China Journal* 56 (July 2006): 63–82.

Zhao, Fang, Juha Erkki Antero Hämäläinen, and Honglin L. Chen. "Child Protection in China: Changing Policies and Reactions from the Field of Social Work." *International Journal of Social Welfare* 26, no. 4 (October 2017): 329–39.

3 *The sisters will take her*

China's grassroots private orphanages

I met Tian Jinna in 2010 at Guanghui Children's Home, a Catholic orphanage in rural Hebei province. Jinna, who was blind and intellectually impaired, had called Guanghui home for as long as she could remember, over twenty years. She lived there with around forty other children and young adults, all with special medical needs of varying severity, cared for by eight nuns (*xiunü*, sisters) and a rotating cast of volunteer nannies and teachers from nearby Catholic villages. When I introduced myself to Jinna on my first morning at Guanghui, she excitedly waved me into the small whitewashed concrete room that she shared with two other girls. Foreign visitors were a rare event in Jinna's world. She was pleased to have an opportunity to practice the few phrases of rote-learned English that she knew and eagerly invited me to "sit down, I will play for you". Her rendition of *Für Elise* on an old electric keyboard was clunky but earnest, and she beamed with joy throughout. Afterwards, she showed me around her bedroom and introduced me to some of her *xiongdi jiemei* (brothers and sisters), chatting freely about her life at Guanghui. She told me that she did not have a father or mother but that the Catholic sisters were her family and that she felt very blessed.

Caring for unrelated *gu'er* is not an exclusively Christian undertaking, but it is a moral obligation that is firmly entrenched in the Judeo-Christian ethic. The Bible portrays God as "father to the fatherless"[1] and admonishes believers to copy God's supreme example of concern for the "least" in society as a reflection of the redemption narrative. For the nuns of Guanghui, this meant their work was a God-given task. They trusted in divine providence to meet their physical needs, and they were bringing their *gu'er* up in the traditions of their faith, like believers in hundreds of Christian orphanages across China.[2] Early every morning, Jinna would gather the other children to her in a circle of rusty wheelchairs and wobbly wooden walking frames in the central courtyard of the Children's Home to lead them in their morning *wanfu Maliya* (Hail Mary) prayers while the sisters attended mass at the neighbouring abbey. She would then help her *xiongdi jiemei* with their breakfast before heading to an adjoining arts and crafts building to "work" for the day with the other capable teenagers and young adults of Guanghui. This consisted of making figurines and trinkets from plastic beads, to be sold to visitors to raise funds to support the Guanghui community.

I was first told about Guanghui Children's Home by a Beijing-based Hong Kong physician, Eleanor Anders. At the time, Eleanor was running a foster home for *gu'er* and working on a number of related health care initiatives with various state orphanages across China. She was also in regular contact with three grassroots Catholic orphanages in Hebei province, including Guanghui and St Martin's (introduced in Chapter 1). On Eleanor's introduction, I rang Sister Yang, Guanghui's director, and arranged to visit. Eleanor warned me that I might find the conditions at Guanghui confronting but assured me that I would be warmly welcomed by the sisters. I arrived at Guanghui late at night after a long, hot, and dusty day of travel. I was shown to a dormitory room that I would be sharing with three volunteers from nearby villages (the sisters lived in an adjoining convent). In this room were six Chinese-style beds with firm boards instead of mattresses, a small fan to provide some relief from the summer heat, and a lone framed picture of the Sacred Heart of Jesus on the concrete wall. Our room was off a central concrete courtyard, next door to a basic reception and meeting room, and across from a row of dormitory rooms where the children and young women like Jinna slept (boys were moved to a separate dormitory building when they reached adolescence). In the morning, I awoke to the sounds of the sisters singing hymns, unaccompanied, coming through the window behind my bed and a persistent, quiet moaning coming from the courtyard through the window on the opposite wall. Venturing outside, I was taken on a tour of the orphanage by one of the kind sisters. She was holding a giggling baby girl of around six months. The baby had a golf ball–sized hole in her face between her eyes, a flattened, misshapen skull, and a large protuberance on her head with scarred skin stretched over it. Looking around the courtyard, I saw a small pond, green with algae, a few pieces of broken plastic play equipment, and around a dozen young children. Some were simply sitting, and a few were tied to their chairs, which the sister explained was to prevent them from injuring themselves during spasms or fits. We crossed into the dormitory wing, and my guide pointed out a small figure sitting in a low chair at the end of the corridor, facing the wall. She looked to be around three years old at a glance, but she had an expressionless, old-woman face. I was told she had been living at Guanghui for over twenty years. Her limbs were like twigs, and I rarely saw her leave her post in the corridor during my stay. Nearby was the boy who I had heard moaning all morning, Pangpang. He sat in a wooden chair with small wheels, rocking his body back and forth, his arms and torso loosely bound to the chair, a soiled bandage wrapped around his head, and his face stained with tears. Pangpang was also rake thin—his legs looked far too fragile to support his weight—and he was almost always in this chair, although I did later see him standing unaided on one occasion. His cries soon became a familiar background noise at Guanghui. He was almost always crying, sometimes silently, sometimes loud wails, but his cries never sounded beseeching; he sounded to me like he knew nobody was going to respond, which added to the sadness. A moment later, I met Jinna, and her piano performance momentarily drowned out the other sounds of Guanghui.

Sister Yang had welcomed me to Guanghui both as a researcher and as a volunteer, but I felt frustrated and ineffectual in the latter role. The children's basic physical needs were being provided for, something that had not always been the case in the past due to financial constraints; but emotionally, many of the children seemed desperate for stimulation and affection, and I worried constantly about my limitations and boundaries as a short-term visitor. I spent a great deal of time with a five-year-old called Shanshan, a beautiful, bright, wheelchair-bound girl. Shanshan had fat rosy cheeks and was paralysed from the waist down. On my first morning, she called out to me as I crossed the courtyard—*jiejie, guolai, guolai* ("older sister, come here, come here")—full of smiles, and when I went to her, she immediately reached up to be held, saying *bao wo, bao wo* ("hold me"). There were no toys in sight other than the broken swings, so I fetched my notepad and pen and drew some animals for her. This was a source of delight, and she quickly began scribbling away. Whenever I had to leave Shanshan, she would start silently weeping, but she never protested. She seemed accustomed to short bursts of attention from passersby. I would often notice her sitting quietly in the courtyard, wiping her own tears, and if I was able to go to her in those moments, she would always cling tightly to my neck and rest her cheek against mine, desperate not to be let go.

The history of Guanghui is tied up with the history of the local Catholic church that supports the home financially. The sisters I spoke to at Guanghui characterised their church as "unofficial"—meaning not strictly associated with the approved China Catholic Patriotic Association—but enjoying in recent years a measure of stability in terms of its relationship with state authorities. The church's buildings had been seized by the state in the 1950s, then returned to local control in 1988. In the interim period, Catholic believers from the area had met in various house groups for prayer and worship. In 1982, a baby was found abandoned at the door of one such house-church. In the following years, several more foundlings were left at house churches across the county. The local bishop urged his parishioners to treat these children as members of God's family and take them in, and by 1988 there were over a dozen *gu'er* in various Catholic homes in the area. At that time, the church leadership decided it would be better to bring the children together in a central facility, to be cared for under one roof by the sisters of the Guanghui convent. They rented additional buildings for this purpose, and Guanghui Children's Home was born. Following its establishment, word of this unofficial orphanage spread throughout the county, and more and more *gu'er* were relinquished into the sisters' care. Eventually the nuns had to paste signs in the surrounding villages requesting parents to stop abandoning their children at Guanghui's door, and the intake rate gradually slowed down. In Sister Yang's estimate, she and the other nuns of Guanghui have cared for nearly five hundred special-needs *gu'er* since 1988. Of these, around forty were eventually reunited with their birth parents, and close to one hundred were informally adopted by local villagers. In addition to the forty-odd children living on the orphanage grounds, fifty more children with lesser disabilities were staying with nearby village families as short- or long-term foster children. Guanghui paid these families a small monthly stipend to cover the associated costs.

The organic development of grassroots orphanages

This chapter introduces the changing story of grassroots private orphanages in China, with reference to two in-depth Catholic case studies—Guanghui Children's Home, home to Jinna, and St Martin's Home for the Handicapped, home to Lina.[3] It is based primarily on data gathered in 2009 and 2010. Interviews were carried out with directors, staff, and volunteers from a total of seven private orphanages, as well as six expatriates with decades of experience supporting mostly Catholic orphanages across China. The stories of the sisters and children of Guanghui and St Martin's provide a snapshot of an alternative, parallel, and often unacknowledged system of care for *gu'er* in China.

I use the term "private orphanage" to describe non-governmental group homes for *gu'er* (it is also a term sometimes used by the sisters themselves—*gu'er yuan* or *gu'er suo*). "Orphanage", like "orphan", is a term loaded with meaning, and I do not use it so as to evoke assumptions about substandard care or emotional deprivation of the children who have grown up in these contexts. Rather, I use "orphanage" to distinguish congregate *gu'er* care from family-based care models (informal kinship care, foster care, and adoption).[4] Private orphanages care for a larger number of children than would normally live in one household and often rely on a team of support workers or volunteers, like the sisters. Generally speaking, the consensus of child development experts is that congregate care offers fewer opportunities for attachment and individualised attention than family-based care, and is therefore a less desirable option. In pointing this out, I do not mean to devalue the bonds of love and kinship that can develop in communities such as Guanghui, or to underemphasise the abuse and neglect that children can suffer in traditional family contexts.[5]

China's private orphanages emerged organically and reactively, in response to demands in rural parts of China where the state had not historically taken direct responsibility for supporting *gu'er*, and state facilities were consequently not available for families and children in need. Following the taking in of one or more *gu'er* in a particular region, a home or church group could quickly gain a reputation as a safe place for local parents to leave a child or for community members to bring foundlings, leading to more and more intakes over time. This pattern aligns with Johnson's finding that relinquishing birth parents in China often prefer to target specific doorsteps of people they believe to be good-hearted and so more likely to take in a foundling, rather than anonymously abandoning their child in a public space.[6] Even if a state orphanage is within travelling distance, children relinquished into the state system effectively disappear as far as birth parents are concerned, whereas by leaving one's child with a local family or private orphanage, it would often be possible to keep watch from afar. At both St Martin's and Guanghui, parents had on occasion come back for their child after a change of heart; more commonly, relinquishing parents kept their distance while occasionally leaving furtive donations and notes at the gates. Whether the emergence and availability of local grassroots orphanages like Guanghui impacts the decision of local birth parents to relinquish is unclear. Sister Yang's posters requesting people to stop leaving *gu'er* at Guanghui's gates were effective, but there is no way of knowing if this was due to birth parents choosing to keep their children after all or simply making alternative abandonment plans.[7]

The Ministry of Civil Affairs carried out the first national survey of private orphanages in China in 2014, in the aftermath of the deadly fire at Yuan Lihai's de facto orphanage in Lankao, when informal *gu'er* relief was receiving widespread attention. The survey found that there were almost ten thousand children being cared for in 878 "locally-run adopting groups" (*minban shouyang jigou*), of which 583 were run by religious organisations.[8] My research suggests both that this is an extremely conservative estimate[9] and that most religious orphanages were run by Catholic and Protestant groups working in a rapidly shifting political climate. The story of these grassroots Christian orphanages is one thread in the broader narrative of China's gradual and unsteady shift from welfare statism to welfare pluralism, a thread complicated by the broader context of historically strained and mutually suspicious relations between religious groups and the state. As social groups like the sisters of Guanghui and St Martin's claimed space left behind by the retreating welfare state and forged for themselves a role in *gu'er* relief, state regulation and oversight were typically reactive, informal, and unpredictable. Until the Lankao fire of 2013, private orphanages were technically illegal, widely tolerated, and generally unsupported by the state. As this chapter explores, this was a source of frustration for the sisters and impacted on the quality of life they could offer to their charges.[10]

"Give us this day our daily bread"

It was not always easy for Guanghui and St Martin's to provide even the basic necessities of life for their many charges, particularly given their serious medical needs. The orphanages experienced severe financial hardship throughout most of the 1990s and into the 2000s, struggling to find sufficient resources to feed, clothe, and medically treat the hundreds of children in their care. Each orphanage had received only a symbolic "condolence fund" (*weiwen kuan*)[11] from local county authorities when they were first established, of five thousand *yuan* and two thousand *yuan* respectively.[12] Local state officials also occasionally gifted donations-in-kind (clothing, diapers, formula) and Spring Festival *hongbao* (red envelopes) containing token amounts—a few hundred *yuan* here, a few hundred there. But other than these small gestures, the orphanages received no regular government funding (until 2010, in the case of Guanghui). Instead, they had always been almost entirely dependent on donations of funds, goods, and services from ordinary people, primarily obtained through local church networks. These donations were referred to and understood by the sisters as God's provision in response to prayer. Sister Yang described it to me as

> a mighty thing. Whenever we were without food and meals, the bishop would go to the village churches to reason with them, saying "If you want to love Jesus, you must love these little children and donate some of your produce". And because we had just a few nuns here caring for the children, he would also invite the faithful to come and help. And in this way the custom was established, so since then the children have had food to eat. The nuns were here, and we had meals from the faithful. Sometime in the 1990s, we began growing our own vegetables and raising chickens. But in general, we are dependent for our living on the support of the local church—food as well as labour, like building our houses.... So, in this church district, under the exhortations of our bishop, we've formed this convention. Every year the faithful leave a portion of their goods for the good of the orphans.
>
> *(Sister Yang, Guanghui, 2010)*

Financial hardship was a major factor impacting the quality of care that Guanghui and St Martin's could provide. Keyser has noted that children are often brought to grassroots orphanages by relinquishing parents who believe that altruistically motivated Christians will provide higher-quality care than state orphanages but that this may not be the case due to serious financial limitations and the inability to access state support.[13] Like St Martin's, Guanghui had the air of a place where the sisters were doing their best with very few resources. The children wore the same clothes for days at a time—Shanshan's favourite was a secondhand velvet party dress adorned with grubby ruffles and dull sequins. There were very few luxuries such as toys or books. The sisters and volunteers seemed to spend most of their time watching the higher-needs infants, with children over the age of three or four often left to fend for themselves for long stretches of time. St Martin's was in a slightly less isolated location than Guanghui, being near a large university, and so benefitted during the summer months from a steady stream of students who came to cheerfully help the sisters in their work. Sister Chen spoke poignantly of the relief she and her sisters felt when they were able to share their workload with those hardworking students: "That's when we can relax. All year long, I long for the holidays." By 2010, St Martin's was also receiving enough donated funds to hire young local *ayis* to assist the nuns with caregiving. But the work was physically and emotionally taxing, and the staff turnover rate was very high (*lailai, zouzou*, or "they come and go", as Sister Chen put it). All of the children cared for on-site at St Martin's and Guanghui had some sort of disability or special medical need (healthy *gu'er* could usually be fostered out to nearby village families), but few of the sisters or *ayis* had medical training. Deaths were common in the 1980s and 1990s, due in part to the sisters being unable to afford hospital admittance fees. Sometimes the cook at Guanghui would serve us chopped leaves from a tree in the courtyard for lunch, and the sisters would reminisce about those harder years, when there was no money for vegetables and leaves were the only greens available. Eleanor Anders spoke of winter visits to a nearby Catholic orphanage in those years and finding that there was not enough money to buy coal to heat the children's rooms. Some children were tied to chairs all day in freezing conditions, and a slipped glove here or there could easily go unnoticed by the overworked sisters, leading to advanced, irreversible frostbite.

Conditions at the Catholic orphanages had generally improved by the time of my initial fieldwork. After years of building up their homes with insufficient funds and donations, years in which children and sisters alike were often underfed, cold, and sick, the sisters often expressed gratitude for the increased stability they had experienced in more recent years. But they also appeared generally very tired after years of caring for the children in basic facilities with limited staff numbers. Despite improved funding, money was still tight, and their work was still very taxing. I would often find myself taken aback at the quality of care they were providing. This was partly because as an Australian researcher, I brought certain expectations of first-world care practices and living standards with me to the field. Stepping outside Guanghui's gates and strolling around the village was an important reminder of context. Guanghui was located in a small village in a county that was at that time officially designated as "poverty stricken". Right outside the gates were two large rubbish pits, picked through by wild dogs as a local goatherd watched on. Around the corner were an eye clinic and pharmacy, also run by the church, where people were only asked to pay what they could afford. There was also a large seminary and Sunday school. In a town of dirt lanes, strewn garbage, and crumbling buildings, the well-tended church structures were an oasis from the otherwise prevailing sense of poverty.

As a visible outsider, the people of the village were very generous to me, despite their poverty. On my evening walks through the village, I would constantly have small gifts pushed upon me—ice-creams from the shopkeeper, fried fish from a street vendor, tofu from a group of grandmothers playing cards on the street. Over the course of Guanghui's thirty-year history, hundreds of children had been fed and clothed as a result of this local spirit of generosity. As Richard Madsen has noted, Catholic villages in China tend to be very good at marshalling collective resources and have "above average community solidarity, which is based on a spirit of 'generalised reciprocity' ".[14] Generally, China does not have a strong tradition of donation-dependent charitable organisations.[15] This can be attributed in part to a Confucian "utilitarian familist" approach to welfare: because the basic "cell" of Chinese society (*shehui xibao*) was the family, altruism centred on extended kinship networks, which were expected to provide for their vulnerable members (children without parents, persons with disabilities, the elderly).[16] Persons without families were seen as the responsibility of the paternalistic, benevolent state, which would step in to look out for its subjects as a father cares for his children. But for the Catholic and Protestant communities donating to charitable orphanages like Guanghui, the concept of family extended beyond blood relatives to the family of God, and utilitarian familism had thereby taken on new dimensions. Both the sisters and the congregations who supported their work were following the example of Jesus when he urged his followers to care for the hungry, sick, and homeless as if caring for his sisters and brothers.[17] They saw the *gu'er* in their midst as members of an extended spiritual "family of

God". For most of their history, Guanghui and St Martin's relied solely on this extended family to provide for their needs, under the spiritual leadership of their bishops. They prayed for money when it was needed and expressed trust that God would provide for their needs through his people.

The nonlegal status of private orphanages

Private orphanages have a long history in China, but their legal status was called into question when the Communist Party came to power. Angela Ki Che Leung has described the network of non-governmental institutions that spread across China, beginning in the seventeenth and eighteenth centuries, to care for abandoned infants.[18] These "foundling hospitals" were frequently accused of mismanagement, corruption, and negligence, due in part to high mortality rates (for example. one Yangzhou hospice was nicknamed *shaying tang*, or "the killing infants hospice"). Imperial-era foundling hospitals, like the modern network of state orphanages, were also not geographically accessible to poorer rural families, being based mainly in urban centres. Accordingly, in the eighteenth century, philanthropists began to organise "relay stations" (*jieying tang* or *liuyang tang*) to collect *gu'er* from remote districts and relay them to urban orphanages. Following the turbulent and socially destructive Taiping Rebellion (1850–1864), this indigenous system of *gu'er* relief was, in some areas, also supplemented by a system of "outdoor relief"—providing money, food, and clothing to at-risk families as a way of discouraging abandonment or infanticide. Also in the nineteenth century, Western missionaries entered the scene and began to set up competing Christian orphanages. These were widely seen by Chinese people as a humiliating act of imperialism and regarded with suspicion, leading to renewed political interest in bolstering Chinese-led efforts at orphan welfare.[19] When the Communist Party came to power in 1949, "imperialist" foreign orphanages were specifically denounced, and private orphanages generally were either shut down or appropriated by the state—for example, two orphanages run by Catholic churches in Nanjing were taken over and merged to establish the government-run Social Children's Welfare Home of Nanjing City.[20] In this way, institutional care for vulnerable children became the prerogative of the state, to be provided through state-run and state-funded *fuliyuan* (welfare institutions).

As discussed in Chapter 2, this ostensible state monopoly on *gu'er* welfare was politically and ideologically significant, in that it aligned with the Party-State's self-presentation as the ultimate and sufficient provider for its people.[21] Owing to this context, state orphanages were initially required to rely solely on government appropriation for funding, with fundraising and NGO collaborations "implicitly or explicitly banned for political reasons".[22] In other words, the state monopoly was not only administrative, but also financial. Shang has argued that this monopoly resulted in the "interests of the orphans themselves ... [being] hidden from view by political considerations".[23]

The "welfare statism" model of sanctioned *gu'er* relief continued until well into the 1990s. Around that time, as China began to experience both economic progress and increasing welfare pressure, the nonprofit sector gradually experienced a resurgence. The political climate changed as the state pivoted to a "small government, big society" approach to welfare, implementing various central programmes aimed at encouraging a shift to welfare pluralism. For example, in 1999 the Ministry of Civil Affairs formally introduced a new policy of "social welfare privatisation"; Shang has reported that in related conference proceedings, the Ministry instructed local Civil Affairs bureaus to promote the development of NGOs as service providers and to shift their focus from delivery to supervision of the "new mixed welfare economy".[24] In the field of *gu'er* welfare specifically, state orphanages were facing particular pressures in the 1990s due to rising abandonment rates, and there was increasing national and international attention on the plight of *gu'er*. Adoption was also on the rise as a result, but orphanage resources were generally stretched thin caring for large numbers of unadopted *gu'er*, most with significant and costly disabilities or medical needs. In response, the Ministry recognised the need to "mobilise resources from all walks of life" and gave permission to state orphanages to move towards pluralism and begin looking for new sources of funding and support, including donations from society and partnerships with NGOs.[25]

At the same time, a new generation of private care providers had already begun spontaneously emerging across China in response to demand for more services for *gu'er*. These varied greatly in size—from individual "love mothers" (*aixin mama*) like Lankao's Yuan Lihai, independently caring for dozens of children at a time, to much larger church-based orphanages such as Guanghui with hundreds of charges.[26] These private orphanages were typically informal and unofficial, without legal status or personality, and it is unclear whether such arrangements were legally or politically permissible. China's first authoritative law on child welfare, the 1991 Law on the Protection of Minors, was written in aspirational, vague terms (this is a feature of statutes in China generally). It urged all levels of society, from state organs to grassroots organisations, to protect minors; but it also provided that *gu'er* were to be taken in and cared for by child welfare organisations (*ertong fuli jigou*) established by Civil Affairs bureaus, which could be read as a duty exclusively bestowed on government.[27] Even as the state welfare system was transitioning to a pluralist funding model, orphan-targeted policy instruments in 1999 and 2000 continued to presume that orphanages would generally be state-run (NGO-funded orphanages were permissible but only if pre-approved by and jointly established with Civil Affairs).[28] This presumption was further clarified in 2008 when the Ministry of Civil Affairs issued a notice specifying that foundlings should be reported to the police and sent to state-approved facilities, rather than being taken in by informal caregivers.[29] In short, there was no clear legal or political authorisation for independent, grassroots parties to deliver services that had always been monopolised by the state.

On the ground, the experience of the sisters of Guanghui in the 1990s and 2000s was that local authorities refused to register their orphanage as an official *gu'er* care provider and denounced their work as "illegal" (*feifa de shiqing*).[30]

Repeated requests for some form of formal recognition as an orphanage were denied. Speaking in 2010, Sister Yang described her frustration at the situation:

> The government does not acknowledge (*chengren*) us as a formal (*zhengshi de*) orphanage. We are not a state welfare institution, and so we do not have legal status (*faren de zige*).... We've asked for this many times, but from the city level up to the provincial level, the government does not want to manage us (*buxiang guan*).... We find it very hard to get government support (*zhichi*). It's as though we are an illegal organisation, and there's no way around that (*mei banfa*). We have appealed to them so many times for help, but they just think it's too troublesome (*mafan*) and are unwilling to take us on. And given that we are caring for so many children, and are so busy every day looking after them, we also don't have the energy to deal with this. It's like we were knocking on government doors every day—I used to appeal to them frequently. But now I'm exhausted. I don't want to go anymore. I don't have the energy to try to establish a relationship with the government. If we have food to eat each day, then that's enough. I don't want to think too much about the rest.

Although by the 1990s, the Ministry of Civil Affairs had signalled openness to a multieffort, pluralist approach to welfare delivery generally, the experience of Guanghui, St Martin's, and the other private orphanages I interviewed was that when it came to *gu'er* welfare, officers at local Civil Affairs bureaus were hesitant to officially recognise, endorse, or support their role as *gu'er* caregivers. Some of my research participants believed this hesitance was due to apathy towards *gu'er*, while others felt that the officials they encountered were supportive in theory but wary of becoming politically or possibly financially accountable for the work of grassroots charities, especially those associated with church groups. An independent consultant for Catholic orphanages in Hebei argued that

> the government should somehow recognise the sector, but I can also see the fear of government in managing structures that are very poorly run. How can they present themselves to the outside world and say "this [orphanage] is recognised" but leave the children in these conditions? ... If they register these private homes, they have to guarantee [the homes] are doing the right thing.
>
> *(Charles Kramer, adviser to Guanghui, 2010)*

Guanghui and St Martin's were also unable to simply register as authorised NGOs with a *gu'er* relief focus, not least because this required finding a supportive government agency to act as sponsor/supervisor (*yewu zhuguan danwei*, known colloquially as a *popo* or mother-in-law). As Yuwen Li has noted, most NGOs in China are unable to satisfy the many arduous registration requirements, and most government departments are unwilling to act as NGO sponsors. This is because doing so brings the potential of political liability if the organisation's actions are later assessed negatively.[31] Other registration barriers for grassroots groups like Guanghui include minimum capital requirements and the lack of administrative capacity to pursue an application. As a result, the vast majority of NGOs in China—between one million and three million, depending on how the term is defined—are unregistered, which is technically illegal but generally tolerated.[32] Also at play for Catholic orphanages was the religion factor. Sister Yang reported being constantly bounced between the local Religious Affairs bureau, Civil Affairs bureau, and county leaders, all telling her that church-affiliated orphan relief was properly the responsibility of a different department and all apparently unwilling to get involved in the politically fraught question of a faith-based *gu'er* welfare organisation.

Stuck in a political and legal grey zone, legal status was not an attainable goal for Guanghui. The orphanage was caring for hundreds of children without registration, which Keyser has described as an "openly acknowledged non-legal arrangement".[33] However, being outside of the legal framework for *gu'er* welfare did not mean that Guanghui was treated as an illicit organisation that should be shut down. Sister Yang spent years intentionally drawing attention to the home's nonlegal status, but Guanghui was never threatened with this. She even went so far as to ask the state to take over the orphanage and run it as a state orphanage, a suggestion that was ignored—taking over Guanghui would have resulted in the local Civil Affairs bureau becoming guardians overnight to scores of children with varying complex medical needs, potentially a very costly responsibility. Instead, the bureau, like all the departments Sister Yang approached, continued to turn a blind eye to Guanghui's frustrations and appeals. The sisters were permitted to continue caring for *gu'er* but without any formal recognition of their role, needs, or shortcomings.

One eye closed—the impact of nonregulation

The approach of the state to informal private orphanages was regularly described to me as *zheng yizhi yan, bi yizhi yan*—"one eye open, one eye closed". The "closed eye" was happening at different levels of government (I return to the "one eye open" below). First, the central Ministry of Civil Affairs, prior to the turning point of the 2013 Lankao fire, had not clarified the legal position of unregistered orphanages, meaning they continued to exist in a political and legal grey zone. Shang and Fisher have described national policy debates in the 1990s and early 2000s as to whether non-governmental *gu'er* relief homes should be permitted and the proper role of the state in providing oversight and support,[34] but these questions were not seriously addressed at the national level until the 2013 Lankao fire highlighted the extent of the problem. Second, at the local level, authorities commonly turned a blind eye to private orphanages, even homes like Guanghui that were actively seeking collaboration, support, and legal status from the state. Hundreds of private orphanages were permitted to quietly address local needs, but did so without any formal support or oversight. This "non-legal arrangement" had significant ramifications for the *gu'er* in their care.

Hukou *and* gu'er *status*

The main impetus for Guanghui's persistent lobbying for recognition in the 1990s was the legal status of its children. China operates a household registration system, in which the government assigns each citizen a *hukou*. Without a *hukou*, a person is essentially unregistered, an "illegal" in her own country (*bu hefa de gongmin*) who does not officially exist—a popular term for children without hukou is *hei haizi*, literally "black child". The problem of *hei haizi* is long-standing and widespread in China, where strict birth-planning policies have resulted in millions of over-quota children being hidden from local authorities and going without *hukou* as a result.[35] As residents of an informal orphanage, Guanghui's children were themselves unregistered for many years. It was only in 2003, after almost a decade of constant doorknocking, that the local Civil Affairs bureau finally agreed to organise *hukou* for the Guanghui children. But Guanghui was an exception rather than the rule in this respect. Of the dozens of other Catholic orphanages in Guanghui's province, Sister Yang reported that only Guanghui had succeeded in negotiating a solution to the *hukou* problem (St Martin's children were given *hukou* in 2010). Sister Yang attributed this to the sheer size of Guanghui as compared to other orphanages, which she thought made it harder for officials to simply ignore the *hukou* issue.

In 2010, I interviewed a retired senior Ministry of Civil Affairs official and asked him about the problem of *hei haizi* in informal orphanages. He dismissed this as a concern, saying that being without a *hukou* is not such a big deal in rural areas.[36] But in fact the consequences of being a *hei haizi* can be far-reaching, particularly for already-marginalised *gu'er*. For example, children without *hukou* can encounter major difficulties in accessing education and welfare entitlements—Guanghui and St Martin's were reliant on goodwill and *guanxi* (networks of contacts) to enrol their *hei haizi* in local primary schools. Other private orphanages I interviewed expressed huge frustration at the *hukou* problem, giving examples such as being unable to arrange for a child to travel for medical treatment or to be admitted to high school because she or he did not legally exist. Those who age out of private orphanages without a *hukou* resolution could also encounter problems with finding employment or getting married, in addition to the potential psychological harm of being treated as a noncitizen in one's own country.[37]

Living in an unregistered orphanage also significantly impacted a child's adoption prospects. For children who are relinquished into the care of China's state orphanages, there is a formal process for proving *gu'er* status, which includes a mandatory "looking for the parents" waiting period and certification of abandonment.[38] At that point, the child becomes a ward of the state and is typically waitlisted for domestic and possibly international adoption.[39] For *gu'er* in unregistered orphanages, there were no such safeguards or procedures. Adoptions were only possible on a local and informal basis, which would not necessarily resolve any underlying *hukou* problems; this was one of the most pressing concerns expressed to me in interviews with private orphanages in 2009 and

2010.[40] Even at Guanghui, where the *hukou* issue was resolved in 2003, the orphanage itself remained unregistered, so its children were not on the official adoption waitlist. Instead, Guanghui had to seek out potential adoptive parents themselves in the local community. And international adoption was never an option for unregistered *gu'er* in informal orphanages (it is worth noting here that anecdotally, children with disabilities tend to have better chances of adoption if they are on an international waiting list). Sister Yang expressed great frustration at the limited adoption prospects of her children, describing this as her biggest quandary—not only because of the pressures faced by the sisters in caring for a large, ageing population of high-needs children but because these children were missing out on the chance to reintegrate into society by becoming part of a traditional family unit.

Financial support

As unregistered orphanages, none of my research subjects were receiving anything more than token financial assistance from the state. Unlike state orphanages, informal orphanages did not have access to the targeted government *gu'er* relief funds introduced in Chapter 2, such as the Tomorrow Plan. Because their children were *hukou* holders, and after years of lobbying, Guanghui had recently begun receiving the national minimum living standard guarantee, set at around fifty *yuan* per child per month.[41] For other private orphanages, access to this guarantee or to the other welfare allowances was hampered by their nonlegal status. For example, Sister Chen of St Martin's, far less tenacious than Sister Yang in her dealings with state officials, had applied to Civil Affairs and county leaders for financial support once or twice but stopped bothering when the answer was always "no". As Keyser has also noted, it seems that most *gu'er* in China who were not registered as such through the state-run welfare system were effectively not counted when it came to *gu'er* welfare benefits.[42]

Shang has written extensively on the missing role of the state as fund provider to private orphanages and other community-based *gu'er* caregivers. Her landmark 2005 investigation of *gu'er* living conditions pointed to a worrying lack of welfare support for private *gu'er* caregivers in rural areas, particularly those caring for children with disabilities.[43] In response to Shang's findings, the State Council issued a 2010 Opinion on *gu'er* protection, directing local and central government to establish a national flat-rate "orphan allowance".[44] The allowance, which came into effect in 2011, was set at a minimum of one thousand *yuan* per month for children in state orphanages and no less than six hundred *yuan*[45] per month for *gu'er* living with extended family.[46] But its implementation was also, in practice, "hampered by constrained local resources and priorities" and effectively restricted to "formally registered children, households, and alternative care providers", by and large failing to reach the unregistered *gu'er* living with informal caregivers or in unregistered orphanages.[47] For example, Guanghui's Sister Yang heard news of the allowance, but did not succeed in convincing the relevant departments that it should be extended to the scores of *gu'er* in her care. Furthermore, because Guanghui and St Martin's were not registered as legal NGOs or charities, they were also not permitted to organise public fundraising campaigns.[48] Like other Catholic orphanages across China, the homes survived because their primary caregivers were nonsalaried nuns who worked without pay, training, or holidays.

Standards and transparency

The kindness and concern of the sisters and other caregivers I met during the course of my fieldwork was touching. Even after years of caring for severely ill children in basic facilities with limited staff numbers, each child who pulled through a tough start to life was a cause for celebration. At Guanghui, one of the sisters recounted with quiet amazement how a three-year-old boy in her care had taken his first steps just that week—when he arrived as a premature baby, he weighed only one kilogram, his head was the size of a grapefruit, and his arms thin as an adult's finger. She never thought he would survive, let alone one day learn to walk. Like the other caregivers of Guanghui, this sister worked tirelessly and without complaining, in line with her spiritual beliefs. The Guanghui sisters also did their best to reach out to NGOs and medical professionals for support in their task of bringing up children with special needs, determined to do their best by each child. But experience from the West clearly shows that the goodwill of Christians does not guarantee chid safety.[49] At both Guanghui and St Martin's, the lack of medical training, disability support, or organisational management was obvious. The homes were understaffed and underfinanced. I often encountered troubling caregiving practices, such as tying children to chairs or beds (although it must also be said that in general, the quality of care seemed on par with what I had observed in some state orphanages and certainly more personal and individualised, with better child-to-caregiver ratios). Further, Guanghui and St Martin's likely represented a relatively higher-quality group of private orphanages, given how open they were to receiving a foreign researcher to scrutinise their operations. In the course of my research, I also interviewed six expatriates with decades of experience working with informal orphanages across China. Each of them related worrying examples of neglect in the field, even after taking contextual poverty and lack of training into account—two had gone so far as to lobby church leaders in the Vatican to shut down particularly problematic Catholic orphanages but to no avail. One offered a particularly bleak assessment of the poorest of these homes: "The sisters are killing themselves running the Catholic orphanages badly because they're underfunded. They need more money or to shut down" (*Matthew Thomas, adviser to grassroots NGOs, 2010*).

As discussed in Chapter 2, research suggests that many of China's state orphanages were also unsafe places for *gu'er*, at least until well into the 1990s. But in the wake of the dying room scandals, the Chinese government attempted to reform and standardise the quality of care provided in state facilities. For example, in 2001 the Ministry of Civil Affairs published detailed guidance on the minimum living and care standards to be provided in state orphanages, covering everything from how often bedding should be changed, to emotional/mental development and staff qualifications.[50] This was followed by a 2003 measure which guided state orphanages on how to find suitable foster families for *gu'er*, in an effort to reduce harmful institutionalisation and promote family-based care.[51] But these important measures, designed to safeguard the rights and interests of *gu'er* and caregivers alike, were not reaching informal orphanages like Guanghui, due to their lack of legal status. There were no inspections or audits of Guanghui care practices. As Shang and her colleagues have also pointed out, the state was failing to adequately supervise, regulate, and facilitate this sector of *gu'er* welfare.[52] Instead, private orphanages were subject only to self-regulation and internal standards, and any attempts to professionalise were completely self-driven. This is not to suggest that formalising and funding the sector would have necessarily led to immediate improvements in care quality but simply to note that in a system in which tens of thousands of children were outside the formal gaze of the state, a large number of these were missing out on the potential benefits of important state-led protections, entitlements, and developments.

Closely related to care standards is the issue of NGO accountability and governance. The lack of state supervision here was not a concern raised by my research participants—generally the attitude was that apart from issues of funding and *hukou*, nonregistration gave private orphanages the freedom to spend income on their *gu'er* as they saw best. Guanghui and St Martin's were almost wholly dependent on civil donations to fund their work but as unregistered organisations were not subject to any of the financial transparency requirements imposed by NGO laws. As the orphanages had no legal personality, donations were handled on a cash-in-hand basis or through personal bank accounts, and donors trusted that the sisters would apply the funds appropriately. This generally did not pose any problems for their local Catholic supporters but did likely impact on the homes' ability to professionalise and expand their donor base. This in turn confirmed them in their low-level engagement and inability to participate in civil society on a larger scale:

> ... so the rural unregistered orphanages are of course not involved in advocacy or lobbying for enforcement of better standards. They just do their own thing, on their own, without reference to the rapidity of change in this country.
>
> *(Matthew Thomas, adviser to grassroots NGOs, 2010)*

I saw nothing at any of my research sites (including Star Village, introduced below) to suggest that funds were being intentionally misapplied (although I did hear many stories of suspected cases of corruption). But there was also clearly a supervision gap in this regard, one with the potential to undermine both government and public trust.[53] The case of Star Village, a non-state orphanage that has frequently been accused of profit-making off the backs of *gu'er*, is instructive here.

Star Village was founded in 2000 by Madam Leng, a former prison guard who had become concerned for the fate of the children of her prison's inmates. During conversations with imprisoned mothers, Madam Leng repeatedly heard of children who had been shunned by extended family and were living on the streets. In response, she began tracking down the homeless children of long-term prisoners, and set up Star Village as a non-government group home—essentially a specialised type of *gu'er yuan* (literally "lonely child institution" or orphanage), which grew to the point where it was caring for over one hundred children, aged zero to eighteen. The infants and toddlers lived in a group building staffed by two full-time *ayis*. The school-aged children lived in groups of around twelve in small, sparsely furnished cabins, with the older children helping the group's *ayi* to care for their younger "siblings". Like Guanghui and St Martin's, Star Village was not able to register as an NGO or orphanage. As a result, it received no state funding and had also had difficulty arranging schooling and health care for those of its children without local *hukou*. To support such a large number of children, therefore, Star Village engaged in intensive, and apparently very successful, fundraising efforts. Over time, the organisation had built up and capitalised on a strong reputation as a "philanthropic tourism" destination. One of the first buildings I encountered on the Star Village campus was a small arts and craft factory, selling artwork made by the older children. In the reception building, the walls were plastered with full-height posters depicting the history and mission of Star Village, including many photographs of tearful reunions between prison inmates and their children and emotional "before and after" stories of children who had found respite at Star Village from trauma and hardship—a prominent testimony displayed on the wall read "*you yige kunle keyi shuijiao de difang*" ("I've finally a place where I can rest when I'm tired"). On summer weekends, Star Village was often crowded with large groups of visitors from nearby suburbs. A large auditorium was constructed to screen lengthy documentaries on Madam Leng's humanitarianism, which would be followed by passionate appeals for donations from charismatic staff members. Star Village had also invested in a 1,700-acre farm, replete with fruit trees and small livestock and a canteen that could feed hundreds of workers and volunteers at a time during harvest season. Supporters could "sponsor a tree" or pay to pick strawberries from the gardens. Unwanted donated goods were sold in a makeshift market near the auditorium.

These activities eventually raised questions about whether Star Village was, in fact, a profitable business, rather than a nonprofit welfare group, an accusation that Madam Leng has always vigorously denied. Admittedly, Star Village was registered as a commercial enterprise (an "educational consultancy") with the State Administration of Industry and Commerce—this is a very common strategy for nonprofit groups to obtain the convenience and legitimacy of having a legal personality. In 2005, China Development Brief estimated there were two hundred thousand Chinese NGOs registered as businesses, due to being unwilling or unable to register under the restrictive NGO framework.[54] However, it may also be viewed as an evasion of the financial transparency obligations imposed on NGOs. In Star Village's case, this arrangement periodically aroused suspicion in the media, with one report describing it as a "financial black hole". This was a cause of frustration for Madam Leng, who had repeatedly appealed to various government bureaus for registration as an NGO, but to no effect: "We do not have any option other than registering commercially. It is really not our wish. We try to do it transparently, to standards. We are self-disciplined. The loving people who support us all put their faith in us" (*Madam Leng, founder of Star Village, 2010*).

One eye open—informal oversight and support

Being outside the legal framework for *gu'er* welfare did not mean the orphanages were simply left to their own devices. Despite their unofficial status, the private orphanages in my sample had never tried to hide the nature of their work from local authorities. Rather, they accepted that village chiefs, birth-planning officials, and Civil Affairs would supervise their work, albeit informally—the "one eye open" approach to an unregulated sector. Consistent with this, my research participants generally put much more emphasis and importance, in our conversations, on recognition (*chengren/renke*), legitimacy, and permission than on questions of registration and formal legality. They wanted government officials to acknowledge the legitimacy of their work and contributions to society, to permit them to continue in their mission, and to provide practical assistance—funding, *hukou*, and training. Only Sister Yang of Guanghui and Madam Leng, founder of Star Village, expressed frustration regarding their inability to formally register. My other research participants were equivocal as to whether registration would be in their best interests, implicitly or expressly arguing that "it's easier to do things if nobody knows you are doing it". For example, one longtime supporter of a Christian orphanage in Shanxi expressed concern that registration would bring interference in the form of increased state regulations and demands: "So we are caught in a dilemma: how much control do we want to lose in order to become legal?" (*Hannah Wang, volunteer coordinator for Home of Joy orphanage, 2009*).

For Guanghui and St Martin's, unofficial support for their work was signalled in various forms, but trust had to be earned over time. Both homes occasionally received small token gifts from local village leaders at Chinese New Year. School administrators would admit their children without the proper documents. Sometimes local police would bring foundlings directly to them to be taken in, in the absence of any state-provided alternatives nearby. Based on such gestures, Sister Chen of St Martin's spoke of St Martin's as having effectively been given a "green light" (*kai lüdeng*) from the city's leaders, albeit on the understanding that the orphanage would not seek financial support from the government. In the orphanage's first few years, officials would occasionally drop by unannounced to check that nothing "illegal" (child trafficking, for-profit adoptions) was going on. But as the years passed, and as St Martin's continued to quietly care for *gu'er* without rumours or scandals, these informal inspections dropped off, officials came to "feel at ease" (*fangxin*), and the sisters were basically left alone. Another private orphanage I visited, one province over, described local officials as being very hostile in their early years—they experienced a number of police "raids", that is unannounced inspections and threats to remove the children from their care. Years later, the same police department was bringing children to their doors, having determined that the orphanage was a legitimate and above-board caregiver. Guanghui's relationship with the state had similarly evolved over time, as described by Sister Yang:

> The government in its speech and in its tone does not want to be as provocative as previously—*your work is illegal!* At the very least, they recognise that the work we do is charitable work and do not use the same inhumane words of before. Now they recognise that we are doing charitable work, at least that's what they say.
>
> *(Sister Yang, Guanghui, 2010)*

In all, informal orphanages were generally able to cultivate at least some level of legitimacy in the eyes of both donors and state actors by working hard and being transparent and open to informal oversight. Madam Leng of Star Village described this process as a transition from "red" to "amber" to "green" status, in terms of the perceived attitude of state actors to nonlegal orphanages. But they were also vulnerable to being shut down or forced out at any point, given their nonlegal status.[55] For that reason, many orphanages intentionally kept a low profile, following certain unspoken rules (not engaging in political advocacy, not allowing foreigners to visit) so as not to draw attention to their unofficial role plugging gaps in state welfare. This is a point that scholars have made about China's millions of unregistered NGOs generally: that their ambiguous legal position has had a chilling effect on civil society.[56] On the other hand, some of my research participants felt it was highly unlikely that large, well-established organisations would ever be shut down, as this would require the state to take financial responsibility for large numbers of high-needs *gu'er* (not to mention the potential negative publicity involved in removing children from their lifelong homes). Given that social policy in China is mostly funded at the local level, this would probably not be feasible in poorer, more rural areas, such as the county where Guanghui was located.[57] Instead, by allowing nonlegal orphanages to act, local governments could essentially outsource their obligations towards *gu'er* but without taking on the responsibility of funding or formally regulating the sector. For the sisters of Guanghui, this was a source of great frustration:

> We hope the government will one day see the needs of these children and see how, with sincere intentions, we are taking on the government's responsibility to care for them. We are willingly giving our hearts, in the spirit of China, to help better this nation. And we are willing to collaborate. We hope that one day we will be recognised for this. We have been doing this work for twenty-two years, the first child we took in is now thirty years

> old.... Their law says this: *gu'er* are the responsibility of the government. But maybe that's not possible. There are too many people. So, we are the ones doing the work.
>
> *(Sister Yang, Guanghui, 2010)*

Of course, given the decentralised nature of Chinese bureaucracy, state-society relationships vary greatly from province to province, from county to county, and from township to township—as Hsu and Jiang have pointed out, Chinese social groups build ties with particular state actors, not "the state", which is "polymorphous, with fissures between the central and local governments, and competing agendas between different localities, departments and individual officials".[58] While Guanghui had been unsuccessfully lobbying for recognition and support for many years, another Christian orphanage in a nearby township had come to a mutually beneficial understanding of sorts with the county-level Civil Affairs bureau. Rainbow House had a similar origin story to Guanghui. In the 1990s, an elderly church member in the area had begun taking homeless *gu'er* into his home. His fellow parishioners supported him with donated clothing and pocket money. Eventually the church let him use some rooms to set up a group home, and so Rainbow House opened its doors in 2000, caring for six *gu'er*. By the time of my visit in 2010, the orphanage was caring for over seventy, from newborns to high schoolers. Rainbow House was relatively well resourced—its facilities were impressive, there were many volunteers on site, and the orphanage could even afford to hire a full-time tutor to assist the older children with their schoolwork (one of their *gu'er* had recently been admitted to university, which was a point of great pride for the directors). As the directors told it, the orphanage had initially faced strong opposition from county officials who did not approve of their work:

> At first, the government did not understand our work because it was a Christian orphanage. So they had opinions about this and were always calling on us, and when we started up it was very difficult. There was a lot of misunderstanding. It was very difficult to do our work in the face of this opposition. As a new orphanage, you couldn't yet see our achievements. We only had a few children. But slowly they came to feel that our work was of high quality, that we were helping to transform children's lives. And so, over time, the relationship improved.
>
> *(Mrs Moses, co-director of Rainbow House, 2010)*

Eventually, local county officials came to respect the role Rainbow House was playing in the community and agreed to treat it as the county orphanage. This seemed to amount mainly to a plaque on the gate that read "[X] county orphanage" (*gu'er yuan*, not *fuliyuan*, the term used for state welfare institutions) as a signal of the government's approval, as well as occasional face-giving visits from important local officials (photos of these visitors were prominently displayed in the orphanage meeting room). In addition, Rainbow House's *gu'er* were issued with *hukou* for the first time. The arrangement also improved the organisation's standing in the community, which facilitated more effective fund-raising. Even so, all of Rainbow House's funds continued to come from the church and private local donors—including the county Party Secretary himself, in his personal capacity. Rainbow House had not been fully appropriated or taken over by the state as an official state orphanage (*fuliyuan*),[59] but it had been given a valuable stamp of political approval, of sorts. This improved Rainbow House's legitimacy in the eyes of society—due in part to traditional suspicion of both charities and non-governmental groups, it is common for NGOs in China to "borrow" legitimacy from the state (the ultimate provider for its people) by fostering and publicising these types of informal state endorsements.[60] The directors of Rainbow House described this as a win-win arrangement, in that local needs were met at no cost to the county, and Rainbow House retained its autonomy. This autonomy allowed Rainbow House to continue raising *gu'er* in the Christian faith. The transmission of faith to Rainbow House children was done carefully and quietly—not through formal religious instruction, which is frowned upon in China, but through the influence of Rainbow House Christian leaders, *ayis*, and volunteers.[61]

For church-affiliated orphanages, religion was an important factor in navigating relationships with state actors, given China's long-standing scepticism and severity towards religion. McCarthy has noted that many officials in China are wary of the mixing of religion with state-endorsed charitable services, which has led faith-based registered organisations to tread carefully when it comes to asserting their religious motivations in the public sphere.[62] That same scepticism seemed to have impacted negotiations between informal, faith-based orphanages and state authorities. For example, Guanghui was associated with a Catholic community that had historically had antagonistic relationships with the state. Catholicism in China came under threat when the People's Republic was founded, because its leaders were unwilling to accept subordination to the quasi-religious Maoist regime, and the Maoist regime saw allegiance to a higher power as a threat to Communist rule.[63] In an attempt to contain and closely monitor the religion, the new Party-State established the Chinese Catholic Patriotic Association (CCPA) as the only state-approved assembly of Catholics. Defiant believers set up illegal "underground" church groups in response, risking severe punishment in doing so. This public/underground distinction continues today, although in a somewhat blurrier manner.[64] Yang has characterised the religious market in China as tripartite, consisting of red (officially permitted, such as the CCPA church), black (officially banned, such as Falun Gong and non-CCPA "underground" Catholic communities) and grey sectors (religions of ambiguous legal status).[65] The Guanghui church was technically "black"—underground and unregistered—but by the time of my visit, the diocese was being treated more as a grey-zone group. It was not at all clandestine or subject to ongoing sanctions (one sister described it as *bu shang, bu xia*, neither above or below-ground). The church was still under the watchful eye of the local Religious Affairs bureau but was a fairly powerful and autonomous social force. The sisters did remember harder times, and this history of persecution seemed to weigh on them, contributing to their sense of disempowerment when it came to lobbying the state for support (this may also have been reinforced by the male-officials/female-caregivers dichotomy involved). But overall the relationship between Guanghui church leaders and local authorities had evolved into something relatively non-confrontational and non-contentious—one volunteer at Guanghui described it as "more openness, less fear" (an important point to make, given that many studies of China's religious sector tend to assume dichotomous, antagonistic state-religion interactions).[66] Accordingly, the community was given a large degree of freedom in its various mission projects, including the orphanage, even though this had not translated into meaningful financial support or registration. As one sister described it, "You can't do this [type of work] in other places—but here, the government has considerable confidence in [our church] and does not interfere too much" (*sister of Guanghui, 2010*). In other dioceses, the dynamics were different. During my 2010 visit to Guanghui, Sister Yang heard from contacts at a Catholic orphanage across the province that their home was under tight police surveillance, making it difficult for NGOs and volunteer doctors to visit. This was apparently related to problems with the associated "underground" church community, whose bishop had only recently been released from prison.

Conclusion: the missing state

The question of who should look after vulnerable children is inherently emotive and complex. In modern China, the Party-State claims responsibility for *gu'er* welfare but has not always been able to respond adequately to increasing vulnerability, especially in rural areas. At the grassroots level, private orphanages emerged as a common, organic, and unregulated response to urgent local welfare needs.[67] At the time of my 2009/10 fieldwork, central law and policy had not kept pace with these grassroot practices, so unregistered orphanages were in a legal grey zone—not expressly permitted, not given formal guardianship of their charges, but not prohibited in practice. Faced with stretched resources, local authorities in parts of China allowed Sister Yang, Sister Chen, Yuan Lihai, and hundreds of others to take in children as needed. This was done on a discretionary basis, with authorities keeping an eye open for problems and sometimes providing informal support but frequently turning a blind eye to important questions of legal status, guardianship, financing, and care standards. Professor Shang has described this as "the missing role of the state".[68] Although the highest child protection law, the Law on the Protection of Minors, called on society to aid vulnerable children, there was no framework in place to facilitate the work of independent, grassroots orphanages like Guanghui. This was not a concern for the sisters, at least not when they took in their first foundlings—they saw children like Jinna in need and chose to respond. As Sister Chen of St Martin's said to her bishop when the home was set up, "what society isn't doing, we the church must do". They regarded their holy work as legitimate (*heli*), regardless of whether it was lawful (*hefa*). As local authorities came to see the importance of their work, in time they were left in peace to carry this work out.

The story of private grassroots orphanages mirrors research findings on NGOs in China more generally. Most Chinese NGOs are unregistered, technically illegal, and widely tolerated provided they do not pose a political threat. Being unregistered arguably contributes to low levels of ability, professionalism, and civic engagement.[69] In 2010, Tsinghua University Professor Guosheng Deng described this blind eye approach to unregistered NGOs as a "three 'no' policy"—no recognition, no banning, no intervention.[70] Under this approach, although these NGOs are not recognised as having any legal status, neither are they banned by the government or subjected to interference in terms of their internal affairs, provided they do not pose a threat to state security or social stability.[71] The "three 'no' " approach, whether intentional or not, shields Civil Affairs bureaus from the political liabilities associated with actively recognising, banning, or intervening in the activities of grassroots NGOs. At the same time, local governments can benefit from the contributions of local groups to the social good where the state's resources are stretched thin. As Shang has noted, it would be beyond the capability of locally funded welfare departments in indigent provinces to take over the responsibility of caring for the large numbers of children in informal orphanages.[72] At the same time, a "three 'no' ", blind eye approach has resulted in organisations developing slowly and cautiously, hampered by their lack of legal status, unsupported in terms of finances and professionalisation and constrained by hidden political rules.

Some private orphanages, like Rainbow House, did in time receive some measure of recognition, endorsed by local authorities to lesser or greater degrees; others, like St Martin's, were unconcerned at their lack of state support or oversight. For others, like Guanghui, their pleas for registration and support were repeatedly ignored. Local officials were apparently hesitant to formally acknowledge this work, possibly for fear of incurring political or financial liability were anything to go wrong. In China, the issue of *gu'er* relief has always been political, tied up with criticisms of birth-planning policies, welfare gaps, and charges of state-sanctioned neglect in government orphanages. But the state was not entirely missing from the field—informal oversight happened, especially in the orphanages' early days, to check for potential scandals or obvious criminal activity like child trafficking. Over time, the sisters were able to gain the trust and respect of local officials despite their nonlegal status, although this did not necessarily translate into meaningful support. The government benefitted from local caregivers addressing local needs, keeping an eye on goings-on but without taking on the responsibility of supervising or financing the relief efforts. As Sister Yang put it, speaking in 2010: "This is rightly the government's burden. But if people like us are doing this work, they prefer to leave us doing it, it saves them from having to do it". And so grassroots orphanages continued on as outsiders, often struggling with low standards and inadequate resourcing; their *gu'er* were ostensibly the responsibility of the state, but as unregistered *gu'er* in unrecognised *gu'er yuan*, they could not easily access their entitlements, like the orphan allowance or adoption opportunities.

In this way informal orphanages were able to develop open, symbiotic relationships with the state; in the cases presented in this chapter, the homes generally enjoyed a great deal of autonomy—as one of Guanghui's supporters put it, "They have courage. The nuns have built up their own way. They went against the current and now have some freedom" (*Charles Kramer, adviser to Guanghui, 2010*). But while it may be true that autonomy made it easier for the homes to get on with their work, that would be equally true for individuals motivated by corruption or failing to provide even the most basic standard of care. In 2005 Shang argued that the state's "missing role in law, regulation and policy-making" was dangerous for children and that a major policy breakthrough was urgently needed in the field of non-state *gu'er* relief. In 2009, Keyser noted that the problem of unregistered children in private orphanages was "bubbling to the surface of policy discussion". But it was only in 2013, when the Lankao tragedy struck, that a coordinated, central response to the unregulated private orphanage sector was devised.

Notes

1 Ps 68:5 (NIV).

2 Cathy Neimetz, in her fieldwork at a Protestant orphanage in China, similarly observed three themes linking orphan relief work with the Christian faith: dependence on God for provisions, in the face of intense financial hardship; providing a familial connection for children as God brings the lost and needy into His "family"; and the cautious but confident transmission of faith to *gu'er* ("Christian Distinctives in Orphan Care in China: Reflections on an Agency Visit," *Social Work and Christianity* 41, no. 1 [2014]). For an ethnographic description of how the state and religious sector intersect in the context of a Chinese state-run orphanage, see Linliang Qian, "Everyday Religiosity in the State Sphere: Folk Beliefs and Practices in a Chinese State-run Orphanage," *China Information* 30, no. 1 (2016).

3 My interest in this topic was sparked by Professor Shang's important 2005 *China Quarterly* article, also based on fieldwork investigating non-government orphanages: Xiaoyuan Shang, Xiaoming Wu, and Yue Wu, "Welfare Provision for Vulnerable Children: The Missing Role of the State," *The China Quarterly* 181 (March 2005).

4 For an overview of alternative care models, see Xiaoyuan Shang and Karen R. Fisher, *Caring for Orphaned Children in China* (Lanham: Lexington, 2014), 13–18.

5 For discussion of how a family-like environment can be cultivated within an institutional setting, see Catherine Neimetz, "Navigating Family Roles Within an Institutional Framework: An Exploratory Study in One Private Chinese Orphanage," *Journal of Child and Family Studies* 20 (2011).

6 Kay Ann Johnson, *China's Hidden Children: Abandonment, Adoption, and the Human Costs of the One-Child Policy* (Chicago: University of Chicago Press, 2016).

7 Johnson, Hu and Szente, and Shang have all similarly reported on state orphanages experiencing an increase in abandonments as a result of media coverage: Kay Ann Johnson, *Wanting a Daughter, Needing a Son: Abandonment, Adoption, and Orphanage Care in China*, ed. Amy Klatzkin (St Paul, NM: Yeong & Yeong, 2004), 13–14; Bi Ying Hu and Judit Szente, "The Care and Education of Orphan Children with Disabilities in China: Progress and Remaining Challenges," *Childhood Education* 86, no. 2 (Winter 2009), 80; Xiaoyuan Shang, "Looking for a Better Way to Care

for Children: Cooperation between the State and Civil Society in China," *Social Service Review* 76, no. 2 (June 2002), 208.

8 Xinde Review, *Chinese Non-Government Child Adoption Seminar* [*Zhongguo minjian ertong yangyu yantaohui*] (Shijiazhuang: *Xinde wenhua yanjiusuo* [Xinde Cultural Institute], 2014) (on file with author). See also Catherine H. Keyser, "The Role of the State and NGOs in Caring for At-Risk Children: The Case of Orphan Care," in *State and Society Responses to Social Welfare Needs in China: Serving the People*, eds. Jonathan Schwartz and Shawn Shieh (Abingdon: Routledge, 2009), 56–58.

9 See also Keyser, "The Case of Orphan Care," 56 (estimating that "most of the estimated 250,000 or more unregistered children" reside in private orphanages).

10 The Lankao fire and the resulting policy changes are discussed below in Chapter 5.

11 The term does not translate easily to English but indicates a monetary gift given as a token of appreciation or support.

12 Five thousand *yuan* is approximately seven hundred US dollars; two thousand *yuan*, approximately three hundred US dollars.

13 Keyser, "The Case of Orphan Care," 56–57.

14 Richard Madsen, *China's Catholics: Tragedy and Hope in an Emerging Civil Society* (Berkeley: University of California Press, 1998), 51–52.

15 Carolyn L. Hsu, "'Rehabilitating Charity' in China: The Case of Project Hope and the Rise of Non-Profit Organizations," *Journal of Civil Society* 4, no. 2 (September 2008).

16 Linda Wong, *Marginalization and Social Welfare in China* (London: LSE/Routledge, 1998), chapter 8. See also Lai Ching Leung, "Gender Mainstreaming Childcare Policy: Barriers in a Confucian Welfare Society," *Journal of International and Comparative Social Policy* 30, no. 1 (2014): 42 (noting that altruism as promoted by Confucian teachings rests on "principles of familial responsibility and obligation"); Hsu, "'Rehabilitating Charity,'" 84 (noting a long, rich tradition of voluntary giving to the needy in China but in a framework that valorises giving to kin).

17 Matt 25:40 (NIV) ("The King will reply, 'Truly I tell you. Whatever you did for one of the least of these brothers and sisters of mine, you did for me'").

18 Angela Ki Che Leung, "Relief Institutions for Children in Nineteenth-Century China," in *Chinese Views of Childhood*, ed. Anne Behnke Kinney (Honolulu: University of Hawai'i Press, 1995), 251–69. See also Peifeng Liu, "Development of Charities in China since the Reform and Opening Up," in *NGOs in China and Europe: Comparisons and Contrasts*, ed. Yuwen Li (Farnham: Ashgate, 2011), 72.

19 Leung, "Relief Institutions for Children," 256–57.

20 Xiaoyuan Shang, "Moving Towards a Multi-Level, Multi-Pillar System: Institutional Care in Two Chinese Cities," *Journal of Social Policy* 30, no. 2 (2001), 262, 264.

21 See Chapter 2 at 38.

22 Shang, "Moving Towards a Multi-Level, Multi-Pillar System," 262.

23 Shang, "Moving Towards a Multi-Level, Multi-Pillar System," 262.

24 Shang, "Moving Towards a Multi-Level, Multi-Pillar System," 279.

25 Shang, "Moving Towards a Multi-Level, Multi-Pillar System," 263–64.

26 See also Shang, Wu, and Wu, "The Missing Role of the State," 129 (noting that non-state institutions for *gu'er* range from five to two hundred beds and are provided by churches, individuals, NGOs, and private enterprises). Legally speaking, there is probably little difference between an unregistered "orphanage" providing group care and an informal "foster/adoptive parent" who takes in children without registration (for example, Yuan Lihai's Lankao home was variously described as an orphanage (*gu'er suo*) and an informal adoptive home (*shouyang ying'er de jia*) in different media reports). The investigation into private orphanages that followed the Lankao fire of 2013 encompassed the entire spectrum: see Chapter 5 at 118n14.

27 Law on Protection of Minors [*Weichengnianren Baohu Fa*] 1991 (People's Republic of China), articles 5, 29 (the 2006 revised Law on Protection of Minors contained the same provision in articles 6 and 43).

28 Ministry of Civil Affairs, *Social Welfare Institutions Interim Measures* [*Shehui fuli jigou guanli zhanxiang banfa*], 30 December 1999. Available at www.mca.gov.cn/article/fw/bmzn/shfl/flfg/201804/20180400008415.shtml (retrieved 3 September 2018); Shang, "Looking for a Better Way," 210 (noting a 1996 Joint Ministerial Notice on *gu'er* welfare development that required local governments to "take full responsibility for protecting orphaned or abandoned children" and a 2000 State Council notice on the socialisation of social welfare, stating that "children's welfare homes would still be mainly managed by the government").

29 Ministry of Civil Affairs, *Notice on Resolving Issues Concerning Private Adoption of Children by Domestic Citizens* [*Guanyu jiejue guonei gongmin sizi shouyang zinü youguan wenti de tongzhi*], 5 September 2008. Available at www.gov.cn/zwgk/2008–09/22/content_1102097.htm (retrieved 22 August 2018).

30 See also Shang, Wu, and Wu, "The Missing Role of the State," 132 (concluding that "it is illegal for NGOs to run children's welfare homes"); Liu Meng and Zhu Kai, "Orphan Care in China," *Social Work and Society International Online Journal* 7, no. 1 (2009), 6 (noting that NGOs are taking an increasing role in caring for *gu'er* but "lack the legislative support that authorizes these NGOs' duties and responsibilities and even rights in service delivery process").

31 Yuwen Li, "Introduction: Challenges and Opportunities for NGOs in Different Parts of the World," in *NGOs in China and Europe: Comparisons and Contrasts*, ed. Yuwen Li (Farnham: Ashgate, 2011), 2–3.

32 Guosheng Deng, "The Hidden Rules of Governing China's Unregistered NGOs: Management and Consequences," *The China Review* 10, no. 1 (2010), 188.

33 Keyser, "The Case of Orphan Care," 56.

34 Shang and Fisher, *Caring for Orphaned Children in China*, 67.

35 Johnson, *China's Hidden Children*, 2016.

36 Interview with retired senior-level Ministry of Affairs official, Beijing, 12 August 2010 (on file with author).

37 Johnson, *Wanting a Daughter*, 174–77.

38 Keyser, "The Case of Orphan Care," 57.

39 Not all state orphanages partner with international adoption agencies. For disabled children from orphanages that are closed to international adoption, the prospects of being placed with a "forever family" may be much lower. Robert Gilbertson, founder of Prince of Peace Village (introduced in Chapter 4), expressed disappointment on behalf of these children—including one Prince of Peace boy who had been at the foster home for nine years, awaiting adoption: "I think it's sad for him, when he sees all his friends getting adopted and he wonders why he can't get adopted. It's kind of hard to figure out how to deal with that" (*Robert Gilbertson, founder of Prince of Peace Village, 2017*).

40 See, further, *People's Daily*, "Shenzhen Yet to Put an End to Private Adoption of Orphans," *people.cn*, 9 January 2013, www.people.com.cn/GB/24hour/n/2013/0109/c25408–20145535.html (retrieved 29 August 2018), interviewing a state orphanage director on the issue of informal adoption and related *hukou* problems.

41 Fifty *yuan* is approximately seven US dollars.

42 Keyser, "The Case of Orphan Care," 49.

43 Xiaoyuan Shang, *Zhongguo gu'er zhuangtai yanjiu* [Study of the condition of orphans in China] (Beijing: China Social Sciences Academic Press, 2008). Shang, Wu, and Wu presented an English overview of the missing role of the state as fund provider for unregistered orphanages in "The Missing Role of the State" (2005).

44 Office of the State Council, *Opinion on Strengthening Orphan Protection Work* [*Guowuyuan bangong ting guanyu jiaqiang gu'er baozhang gongzuo de yijian*], 16 November 2010. Available at www.gov.cn/zwgk/2010–11/18/content_1748012.htm (retrieved 28 August 2018).

45 Approximately one hundred and fifty, and ninety, US dollars, respectively.

46 Ministry of Civil Affairs, *Expansion of Government Guarantees for Vulnerable Children* [*Jiang kunjing ertong naru zhengfu baozhang woguo ertong baohu dingceng sheji mai chu yidabu*], 2 June 2016. Available at www.gov.cn/zhengce/2016-06/02/content_5078937.htm (retrieved 29 August 2018).
47 Shang and Fisher, *Caring for Orphaned Children in China*, 232.
48 Law on Public Welfare Donations [*Gongyi Shiye Juangzeng Fa*] 1999 (People's Republic of China), article 10.
49 Shang, Wu, and Wu, "The Missing Role of the State," 135.
50 Ministry of Civil Affairs, *Basic Standards for Child Social Welfare Institutions* [*Ertong shehui fuli jigou jiben guifan*], 6 February 2001. Available at http://shfl.mca.gov.cn/article/bzgf/etfl/200807/20080700018266.shtml (retrieved 29 August 2018).
51 Ministry of Civil Affairs, *Interim Foster Care Management Measures* [*Jiating jiyang guanli zhanxiang banfa*], 27 October 2003. Available at www.gov.cn/gongbao/content/2004/content_62869.htm (retrieved 13 September 2018).
52 Shang, Wu, and Wu, "The Missing Role of the State," 134–35.
53 Jillian S. Ashley and Pengyu He, "Opening One Eye and Closing the Other: The Legal and Regulatory Environment for 'Grassroots' NGOs in China Today," *Boston University International Law Journal* 26, no. 1 (Fall 2008), 86.
54 Tina Qian and Nick Young, "Rule on Names Starts to Close Door to NGO 'Businesses,'" *China Development Brief* (15 April 2005) (on file with author).
55 See also Keyser, "The Case of Orphan Care," 61 (noting that domestic, non-governmental, nonregistered groups are at the mercy of local government).
56 Ashley and He, "Opening One Eye and Closing the Other," 80.
57 Shang, Wu, and Wu, "The Missing Role of the State," 132.
58 Carolyn L. Hsu and Yuzhou Jiang, "An Institutional Approach to Chinese NGOs: State Alliance versus State Avoidance Resource Strategies," *The China Quarterly* (March 2015), 104.
59 Although apparently rare, this has been known to happen on occasion. For example, the Suishang Child Welfare Institution (CWI) in Yinshang county, Anhui province, home to over two hundred children, began as a "folk orphanage" (*minjian gu'er yuan*). When the county received Blue Sky funding to build a state orphanage, the folk orphanage's children were brought into the state system and the founder was given the position of honorary director. This eased the financial pressure and resolved *hukou* and education problems: Beijing Times, "Media Report State Orphanages Lack Funds, Private Orphanages Lack Policies" *people.cn*, 11 January 2013, http://legal.people.com.cn/GB/n/2013/0111/c188502–20165512.html (retrieved 13 September 2018).
60 Hsu, "'Rehabilitating Charity,'" 2008.
61 Cathy Neimetz's ethnography of another Christian-run orphanage in China describes in more detail how faith can be transmitted from caregivers to children, even when religious instruction is expressly banned: "Christian Distinctives in Orphan Care in China," 2014.
62 Susan K. McCarthy, "Repurposing the State: Religious Charity and Resistance in China," *The China Journal* 70 (July 2013).
63 Madsen, *China's Catholics*, 34.
64 Madsen, *China's Catholics*, 483 (noting that "there is now no clear distinction between an open church which the government controls politically and an underground church which it does not").
65 Fenggang Yang, "The Red, Black and Grey Markets of Religion in China," *The Sociological Quarterly* 47 (2006).
66 Qian, "Everyday Religiosity in the State Sphere," 82.
67 The emergence of private orphanages parallels Kay Johnson's finding, based on extensive ethnographic research, that informal adoption was a common grassroots response to abandonment in one-child-policy China (*China's Hidden Children*, 2016).
68 Shang, Wu, and Wu, "The Missing Role of the State," 2005.

69 For example, a study by Charlotte Goodburn of "black" (unregistered) schools for children of migrants in Beijing found the schools were unable to register as licensed schools, due to substandard conditions, but were unable to access funding and improve standards due to their lack of registration: Charlotte Goodburn, "Learning from Migrant Education: A Case Study of the Schooling of Rural Migrant Children in Beijing," *International Journal of Educational Development* 29 (2009).
70 Deng, "The Hidden Rules of Governing China's Unregistered NGOs," 2010.
71 Deng, "The Hidden Rules of Governing China's Unregistered NGOs," 190.
72 Shang, Wu, and Wu, "The Missing Role of the State," 132.

Bibliography

Ashley, Jillian S., and Pengyu He. "Opening One Eye and Closing the Other: The Legal and Regulatory Environment for 'Grassroots' NGOs in China Today." *Boston University International Law Journal* 26, no. 1 (Fall 2008): 29–96.

Deng, Guosheng. "The Hidden Rules of Governing China's Unregistered NGOs: Management and Consequences." *The China Review* 10, no. 1 (2010): 183–206.

Goodburn, Charlotte. "Learning from Migrant Education: A Case Study of the Schooling of Rural Migrant Children in Beijing." *International Journal of Educational Development* 29 (2009): 495–504.

High, Anna Jane. "China's Orphan Welfare System: Laws, Policies and Filled Gaps." *University of Pennsylvania East Asia Law Review* 8, no. 2 (2003): 127–76.

High, Anna Jane. "Grassroots NGO Regulation and China's Local Legal Culture." *Socio-Legal Review* 9, no. 2 (2013): 1–50.

High, Anna Jane. " 'It's Grace and Favor, It's Not Law': Extra-Legal Regulation of Foreign Foster Homes in China." *University of Pennsylvania Asian Law Review* 12, no. 3 (Spring 2017): 357–405.

Hsu, Carolyn L. " 'Rehabilitating Charity' in China: The Case of Project Hope and the Rise of Non-Profit Organizations." *Journal of Civil Society* 4, no. 2 (September 2008): 81–96.

Hsu, Carolyn L., and Yuzhou Jiang. "An Institutional Approach to Chinese NGOs: State Alliance versus State Avoidance Resource Strategies." *The China Quarterly* (March 2015): 100–22.

Hu, Bi Ying, and Judit Szente. "The Care and Education of Orphan Children with Disabilities in China: Progress and Remaining Challenges." *Childhood Education* 86, no. 2 (Winter 2009): 78–86.

Johnson, Kay Ann. *China's Hidden Children: Abandonment, Adoption, and the Human Costs of the One-Child Policy*. Chicago: University of Chicago Press, 2016.

Johnson, Kay Ann. *Wanting a Daughter, Needing a Son: Abandonment, Adoption, and Orphanage Care in China*. Edited by Amy Klatzkin. St Paul, MN: Yeong & Yeong, 2004.

Keyser, Catherine H. "The Role of the State and NGOs in Caring for At-Risk Children: The Case of Orphan Care." In *State and Society Responses to Social Welfare Needs in China; Serving the People*, edited by Jonathan Schwartz and Shawn Shieh, 45–65. Abingdon: Routledge, 2009.

Leung, Angela Ki Che. "Relief Institutions for Children in Nineteenth-Century China." In *Chinese Views of Childhood*, edited by Anne Behnke Kinney, 251–78. Honolulu: University of Hawai'i Press, 1995.

Leung, Lai Ching. "Gender Mainstreaming Childcare Policy: Barriers in a Confucian

Welfare Society." *Journal of International and Comparative Social Policy* 30, no. 1 (2014): 41–52.

Li, Yuwen. "Introduction: Challenges and Opportunities for NGOs in Different Parts of the World." In *NGOs in China and Europe: Comparisons and Contrasts*, edited by Yuwen Li, 1–20. Farnham: Ashgate, 2011.

Liu, Peifeng. "Development of Charities in China since the Reform and Opening Up." In *NGOs in China and Europe: Comparisons and Contrasts*, edited by Yuwen Li, 71–94. Farnham: Ashgate, 2011.

Madsen, Richard. *China's Catholics: Tragedy and Hope in an Emerging Civil Society*. Berkeley: University of California Press, 1998.

McCarthy, Susan K. "Repurposing the State: Religious Charity and Resistance in China." *The China Journal* 70 (July 2013): 48–72.

Meng, Liu, and Zhu Kai. "Orphan Care in China." *Social Work and Society International Online Journal* 7, no. 1 (2009): 43–57.

Ministry of Civil Affairs. *Basic Standards for Child Social Welfare Institutions* [*Ertong shehui fuli jigou jiben guifan*], 6 February 2001. Available at http://shfl.mca.gov.cn/article/bzgf/etfl/200807/20080700018266.shtml (retrieved 29 August 2018).

Ministry of Civil Affairs. *Expansion of Government Guarantees for Vulnerable Children* [*Jiang kunjing ertong naru zhengfu baozhang woguo ertong baohu dingceng sheji mai chu yidabu*], 2 June 2016. Available at www.gov.cn/zhengce/2016-06/02/content_5078937.htm (retrieved 29 August 2018).

Ministry of Civil Affairs. *Interim Foster Care Management Measures* [*Jiating jiyang guanli zhanxiang banfa*], 27 October 2003. Available at www.gov.cn/gongbao/content/2004/content_62869.htm (retrieved 13 September 2018).

Ministry of Civil Affairs. *Notice on Resolving Issues Concerning Private Adoption of Children by Domestic Citizens* [*Guanyu jiejue guonei gongmin sizi shouyang zinü youguan wenti de tongzhi*], 5 September 2008. Available at www.gov.cn/zwgk/2008-09/22/content_1102097.htm (retrieved 22 August 2018).

Ministry of Civil Affairs. *Social Welfare Institutions Interim Measures* [*Shehui fuli jigou guanli zhanxiang banfa*], 30 December 1999. Available at www.mca.gov.cn/article/fw/bmzn/shfl/flfg/201804/20180400008415.shtml (retrieved 3 September 2018).

Neimetz, Cathy. "Christian Distinctives in Orphan Care in China: Reflections on an Agency Visit." *Social Work and Christianity* 41, no. 1 (2014): 60–78.

Neimetz, Cathy. "Navigating Family Roles Within an Institutional Framework: An Exploratory Study in One Private Chinese Orphanage." *Journal of Child and Family Studies* 20 (2011): 585–95.

Office of the State Council. *Opinion on Strengthening Orphan Protection Work* [*Guowuyuan bangong ting guanyu jiaqiang gu'er baozhang gongzuo de yijian*], 16 November 2010. Available at www.gov.cn/zwgk/2010-11/18/content_1748012.htm (retrieved 28 August 2018).

Qian, Linliang. "Everyday Religiosity in the State Sphere: Folk Beliefs and Practices in a Chinese State-run Orphanage." *China Information* 30, no. 1 (2016): 81–98.

Qian, Tina, and Nick Young. "Rule on Names Starts to Close Door to NGO 'Businesses.'" *China Development Brief* (15 April 2005) (on file with author).

Shang, Xiaoyuan. "Looking for a Better Way to Care for Children: Cooperation between the State and Civil Society in China." *Social Service Review* 76, no. 2 (June 2002): 203–28.

Shang, Xiaoyuan. "Moving Towards a Multi-Level, Multi-Pillar System: Institutional Care in Two Chinese Cities." *Journal of Social Policy* 30, no. 2 (2001): 259–81.

Shang, Xiaoyuan. *Study of the Conditions of Orphans in China* [*Zhongguo gu'er zhuangtai yanjiu*]. Beijing: China Social Sciences Academic Press, 2008.

Shang, Xiaoyuan, and Karen R. Fisher. *Caring for Orphaned Children in China*. Lanham: Lexington, 2014.

Shang, Xiaoyuan, Xiaoming Wu, and Yue Wu. "Welfare Provision for Vulnerable Children: The Missing Role of the State." *The China Quarterly* 181 (March 2005): 122–36.

Wong, Linda. *Marginalization and Social Welfare in China*. London: LSE/Routledge, 1998.

Xinde Review. *Chinese Non-Government Child Adoption Seminar* [*Zhongguo minjian ertong yangyu yantaohui*]. Shijiazhuang: *Xinde wenhua yanjiusuo* [Xinde Cultural Institute], 2014 (on file with the author).

Yang, Fenggang. "The Red, Black and Grey Markets of Religion in China." *The Sociological Quarterly* 47 (2006): 93–122.

4 *We just pray*

The faith-based foster home movement

New Grace Foster Home was founded by expatriates David and Martha Dale. The Dales moved their family to China in 1994 when David was offered a senior management position with a large international company. Soon after arriving in Beijing, the course of their lives changed dramatically. Their bible study group had been studying passages on caring for orphans and decided to visit a nearby state orphanage to deliver donated goods and play with the children. At the orphanage, rather than staying with the main group, Martha, a doctor, asked to be taken to see the sickest children. She and David were deeply distressed at what they saw next. They were taken to a room of around two dozen babies, lying two to three in a cot, who seemed to be listlessly waiting for death, with just one woman assigned to change nappies and distribute bottles. There were no spare hands to hold or soothe the babies, who spent all their time in the cots and had learned as a result not to cry. Many of the babies were brain-damaged, most were skeletal, and only one reached up to be held; the others seemed to have shut down emotionally. It was around this time that *The Dying Rooms* was broadcast into living rooms around the world, and many state orphanages across China began closing their doors to such volunteer groups in response.[1] It was another four years before David and Martha were able to return to the orphanage, but when they did, they came prepared. In the meantime, David had resigned from his high-paying executive position, and they had moved their family to a small village on the outskirts of Beijing. There, they used personal savings and donations from supporters abroad to begin constructing a multibed home to care for as many orphans as they could cope with at a time. They then invited the director of the same orphanage to visit the construction site and hear their vision—to bring some of the sickest of the orphanage *gu'er* to New Grace for privately funded medical treatment, followed by long-term individualised care. The director agreed to begin sending select infants from his institution to be "fostered" to New Grace. In February 2000 the Dales began their mission work, beginning with two baby girls in need of urgent surgery to correct severe neurological defects. One of these girls went on to become their daughter through adoption, and the other eventually joined a "forever family" in America.

In the years that followed, David and Martha continued to bring children with urgent, untreated conditions out of state orphanages, where their chances of survival and adoption were very low. The Dales would then provide family-style care, arrange for medical treatment, and prayerfully await a "forever family" for each child. With each child who was adopted, a bed would become free, and another *gu'er* could be brought into the New Grace fold. In time David and Martha came to rely on a global network of donors to support their work—some donated funds to cover *ayi* salaries and running costs; doctors provided *pro bono* surgery in China, Hong Kong, Singapore, or the United States; and volunteers helped ferry children around China and overseas to access treatment as needed. Once children had received surgery or treatment and were deemed stable, they could typically be placed on China's international adoption waiting list. Although New Grace was unable to arrange adoption, the organisation could work with adoption agencies to advocate for a particular child, and many were ultimately placed with Western Christian families familiar with the New Grace mission.

The main New Grace site was a clean and bright fifty-six-bed facility with a communal dining hall, dormitories and apartments for short- and long-term volunteers, a kindergarten classroom, and a physical therapy space. The home was located on a large rural plot surrounded by cornfields, on a road between a village and a hamlet. In summer, the children would walk with their *ayis* to the hamlet's main square, play on the big playset in New Grace's front yard, or go swimming in the home's large paddling pool. In winter, the home was well heated and cosy, and there were festive celebrations for both Christmas and Chinese New Year. A regular succession of volunteer teachers, physical therapists, doctors, nurses, and administrators came from around the world to be part of the mission. The New Grace *gu'er*, who were usually able to remain at New Grace until adoption could be arranged, came from state orphanages near and far. Beginning with their original partnership with a local state orphanage, the Dales went on to make foster care arrangements with orphanages in provinces across China, to the point where demand for their services eventually far exceeded their capacity. They also went on to open on-site "special care" units at a number of state orphanages across China. As of 2018, over two thousand children had passed through the doors of New Grace Foster Home and its sister facilities across China.

In a nearby city, two years after David and Martha brought their first foster children to New Grace, a Chinese Christian named Linda Zhou happened to start down a very similar path to the Dales. Linda had been praying for some time about God's concern for "widows and orphans" and began volunteering at a state orphanage in response. At the orphanage, she came to know a three-year-old boy called Xiao Ping, who had cerebral palsy. Xiao Ping spent his days alone in his bed, looking at the ceiling and at his hands, without any human interaction. His caregivers either did not realise, due to his severe physical limitations, that he was mentally capable or did not have the time, training, or concern to attempt to interact with him despite those limitations. Linda began to spend long periods of time with Xiao Ping, and in time he began to respond to her, in his own subtle ways. Concerned for his wellbeing if he were to stay at the orphanage, Linda convinced the orphanage's director to let her take Xiao Ping home with her as a foster child. Xiao Ping was the inspiration and impetus for setting up Still Waters Foster Home, a group home for *gu'er* with cerebral palsy.

When I visited in 2017, Still Waters was home to twenty-eight *gu'er* from nearby state orphanages, cared for by fourteen full-time workers. The home was funded almost entirely by donations from unofficial home churches in the area, as well as some international churches that had learned of Linda's work over the years. Xiao Ping was about to turn nineteen and had been in Linda's care for almost sixteen years. He and the other children and caregivers of Still Waters lived in a large two-storey rented house, near the centre of a gated housing estate in a relatively prosperous Hebei city. The estate centred around a small lake filled with lily pads and surrounded by leafy trees and flowerbeds. A small plaque on the gate to the Still Waters premises was all that distinguished the foster home from the other spacious family homes in the compound—that and the dozens of sheets drying in the summer sunshine in the front yard. As soon as I entered the reception room of Still Waters, I was warmly welcomed by a group of volunteers and invited to sit down and hold Wang Lei, a two-year-old boy with cerebral palsy. His body was limp, but he maintained steady eye contact. A group of older boys in wheelchairs were playing video games in the air-conditioned living room next door, while most of the younger children were upstairs sleeping through the summer midday heat while Christian praise music played quietly in the background. There were many Bibles and Christian picture books lying around, and homemade posters of Bible verses decorated the walls. The home was somewhat shabby but tidy and well equipped. The storage rooms were stocked full of hand-me-down clothes and medical supplies, and there was an air of cheerful productivity in each room, with various caregivers and volunteers busily attending to their work.

A new model of private orphan relief

A major catalyst for increased non-government involvement in Chinese *gu'er* relief was the "dying rooms" scandal of the mid-1990s, which brought national and international attention to the needs of China's orphan population. In the late 1990s, as the state became increasingly receptive to welfare pluralism generally, orphanages that had closed their doors to outsiders in the immediate aftermath of the scandal began once again to be receptive to private aid. The most visible of these efforts involved large-scale, registered international groups, such as Save the Children, Care for Children, and UNICEF, working at the national level with the Ministry of Civil Affairs or state research institutes, to provide child-targeted programmes across China.[2] A number of national and international NGOs became involved in advocating for the deinstitutionalisation of *gu'er*, assisting state orphanages in setting up family foster care programmes.[3] International adoption agencies and adoption advocacy groups also became increasingly active in China in the late 1990s and early 2000s as adoption of Chinese *gu'er* to Western families surged. These groups, such as Holt International and

Families with Children from China, often donated funds directly to state orphanages through collaborative projects to improve the quality of life of unadopted children.[4] But only a relatively small number of high-profile, politically connected NGOs have been successful in setting up national, formalised orphan relief initiatives in China. This chapter introduces the development of a less visible, more informal model of collaboration with China's troubled state orphanages: foreign-run and Chinese-run foster homes such as New Grace and Still Waters.

As discussed in Chapter 2, foster care first emerged as a key policy initiative for China's state orphanages towards the end of the 1990s. Typically, foster care is provided by a preexisting family unit to one or two children at a time.[5] In contrast, I use the term "foster home" to describe organisations such as New Grace and Still Waters providing off-site care for much larger numbers of children, fostered from state orphanages on an ostensibly temporary basis and tended by paid employees and volunteers. The foster homes in my sample varied greatly in size, from those caring for around a dozen babies in rented houses or high-rise apartments to homes with over one hundred children of all ages living on spacious, purpose-built campuses alongside scores of employees. But they all had in common that they were set up as a means of ministering, physically, emotionally, and spiritually, to China's lonely children and that the children in their care came almost exclusively from state orphanages. Children were typically brought from state orphanages on the basis of their individual surgical or medical needs. These children remained in the legal guardianship of their home state orphanages but were sent on a long-term basis to the foster home, which typically could provide higher-quality care, at least as compared with state orphanages in less developed parts of China—better child-staff ratios, trained caregivers, intentional attachment opportunities, and medical treatment in China's best hospitals or even abroad. Many foster homes had developed a reputation over time as specialists in certain medical conditions, such as congenital heart disease in the case of New Grace Foster Home and cerebral palsy in the case of Still Waters Foster Home. All of the homes provided free medical care on the understanding that the child would be permitted to stay on at the foster home for as long as possible, ideally until they could be placed for adoption, rather than being returned to state facilities where post-operative care might be inadequate or lacking.[6] In many cases, private treatment, combined with visibility via social media to foreign supporters of the foster home, would ultimately lead to better adoption outcomes. When an adoption match could not be made, children would often end up being cared for in the foster home on a permanent basis, even beyond the period of treatment.[7] These groups could be contrasted with the private orphanages introduced in Chapter 3, which took in children directly, without interacting with state authorities or state-run welfare institutions in the process.

It is difficult to know how many foster homes were operating in China at the time of my fieldwork, as many were intentionally keeping a low profile, at least domestically, due to the political sensitivity of their work. Based largely on word-of-mouth, my fieldwork uncovered at least a dozen in the greater Beijing area alone (foster homes tended to be located in large, prosperous cities, for easy access to leading hospitals). This review of China's foster home sector is based on in-depth, semi-structured interviews and participant observation at seventeen foster homes in the vicinity of Beijing, Shanghai, and Xi'an in 2009, 2010, and 2017. Fifteen of these foster homes were founded by Western expatriates and two by Chinese nationals. Many of the homes had intertwined histories—for example, it was common for staff from one home to eventually leave to set up a new home targeting a different medical specialism or working with a new state orphanage partner. All of the foster homes were faith-based, set up by Christians inspired by biblical exhortations to care for orphans and commonly in response to the shocking "dying room" pictures and stories coming out of state orphanages in the 1990s. As Leslie Wang has noted, faith-based *gu'er* relief groups, even those run by foreigners, have been permitted to operate in China provided they avoid overt evangelism or political activism, as did all of the homes in my sample.[8]

This chapter introduces the development of modern China's Christian foster homes, including the social and political constraints faced by Christians and foreigners in the field. It is based primarily on the data gathered in 2009 and 2010. In more recent years, the foster home sector has come under increasing pressure as the Chinese government has taken a harder line towards informal *gu'er* caregivers, faith-based organisations, and foreign-funded NGOs alike. By the time of my final fieldwork in 2017, a number of research participants who I had met in 2009 or 2010 were no longer willing to host a foreign researcher, speaking only via email or telephone. And between the time of my 2017 fieldwork and the time of finalising this manuscript in early 2019, many of the foster homes in my sample had been ordered to return their charges to their home provinces. These developments are discussed in more detail in Chapter 5 and Chapter 6. But even before these closures, the humanitarians running foster homes in China had always faced ambiguity regarding the legality, permissibility, and future of their work, which took place in a constantly shifting political context. All began as very local grassroot initiatives and as unregistered and technically illegal organisations, similar in this respect to the private orphanages introduced in Chapter 3. But unlike the private orphanages, foster homes were constantly in contact with state-employed orphanage directors, in addition to frequent, informal negotiations with local Public Security (police) and Civil Affairs officials. As unregistered organisations with foreign ties, these interactions with the state were often fraught. A minority of foster homes were eventually able to leverage their welfare contributions and good government connections to formally register as approved NGOs or welfare providers. But most simply existed in legal limbo, subject to informal, local oversight and unspoken rules, the "one eye open, one eye closed" approach. The response of Christian foster homes to these challenges and ambiguities was twofold—creative, strategic workarounds and prayerful submission to providence in the face of any insurmountable hurdles: "We have a delicate situation. We just pray" (*Bob, St Matthew's Foster Home, 2010*).

Improving care standards, importing resources

My first stay at New Grace was at the end of 2005. After a semester studying in Beijing, I spent the winter vacation volunteering at the foster home with a university friend. There were nearly sixty children living at New Grace at the time. Our days were spent teaching English nursery rhymes and ABCs to the older children; in the evenings, we put together memory scrapbooks for the babies who were soon to leave both New Grace and China to join their adoptive families abroad. I saw how David and Martha tried to treat every child they cared for as they would their own, including by celebrating each birthday and milestone. Martha spent many evenings stitching handmade quilts, which would be given to each child on adoption to serve as a reminder of their first family at New Grace. Spending that winter in the warm, comfortable foster home, surrounded by kind *ayis* and other volunteers, was an easy and feel-good way to be a small part of a mission that I did not, at that time, truly appreciate the need for.

A few weeks into our time at New Grace, we were asked by David to travel to a city in Henan province, an overnight train ride away. One year earlier, David and Martha had opened an on-site special care unit at a state orphanage in that city, after hearing from an American volunteer there that fatal neglect of seriously ill babies was still a common practice, even years after *The Dying Rooms* had first aired. The Dales felt compelled to offer the orphanage their assistance with its higher-needs population. They met with the orphanage's director and convinced him to let them provide hospice care, on their own dime but on his premises, for his sickest children, those who would be unlikely to survive even with the best of care. The on-campus unit was to be independently managed, staffed, and funded by the Dales. The director gave them the use of the fifth floor of his administration building for the project, which they quickly renovated, kitting it out with incubators, oxygen tanks, and medical supplies.

After a long train and taxi ride, we arrived at this state orphanage, where we were to stay for a few weeks filling in as supervisors of the New Grace special care unit. We greeted the nannies, local women who worked twelve-hour shifts caring for two babies each, and met their ten charges. The unit did not have the lively, hopeful air of the main foster home back in Beijing. The babies in the special care unit were not expected to live long lives and had very serious, often painful, medical conditions. Living in the unit, even for such a brief time, was sobering. On our first night, one of the *ayis* came to tell us that an infant called Yi Lin seemed to be in more pain than usual and needed morphine. This tiny baby girl had a severely enlarged head due to a build-up of spinal fluid in her brain. She was not expected to live for much longer. After checking our dosage calculations again and again, I held Yi Lin close and gave her an injection. Eventually her pain seemed to subside and she was able to sleep, but it was hard to put her back in her cot. I could not stop thinking about the rooms I had seen in the rest of the orphanage earlier that day and what this baby's life and death might have been like without access to the care provided by the Dales. Yi Lin was in a great deal of pain, but she was clean, fed, and on pain relief. There were many more, just floors away, who were not.

On our tour of the orphanage, the contrast between the privately funded special care unit and the remainder of the institution had been made starkly apparent. The main buildings were severe concrete constructions, freezing cold and bleak in the January frost. On one floor, we saw a room of around two-dozen toddlers being watched by two clearly very tired and disengaged women. There were a few old toys scattered around, but the room was depressingly dark and shabby overall and smelled pungently of urine. The children were all bundled up in many layers of quilted smocks and jackets to guard against the cold. Some had fallen over but were unable to get back up and were instead just laying quietly. In another cold room with grimy walls and sooted-over windows, we saw row upon row of cots, each holding two or three still and silent babies, some with bottles propped up next to them but out of reach, and just one worker in sight. It was a relief to return to the sanctuary of the warm and cosy fifth floor, with its cheerful hand-painted Disney wall murals, physiotherapy equipment, and well-stocked supply cupboards, and to see the attentive nannies filling out medical charts, rocking fussy babies, and keeping a close eye out for signs of distress or pain. Most of these infants would not recuperate from their medical conditions, but each child who passed away was named, held, and remembered. After opening this first special care unit, David and Martha went on to set up similar independent on-site care units at multiple other state orphanages in the same province, while continuing to bring *gu'er* from across the country to their main foster home for treatment at Beijing's top-rate hospitals and long-term care in the New Grace family.

Tens of thousands of children have received privately funded care in foster homes across China. In 2017, New Grace alone cared for a total of 397 children, with 104 new admissions across their various units and foster home. In her ethnography of the importation of first-world resources and practices into Chinese orphanages, Leslie Wang has noted that the care available to *gu'er* in state orphanages is frequently stratified, depending on whether an individual child is chosen to benefit from these streams of private humanitarian aid.[9] Many are not chosen, as demand for such supplementary services far outpaces supply. As one of the oldest foster homes in China, New Grace had developed a strong reputation among state orphanages over time, to the point of frequently having to turn down requests for help from orphanage directors; the other large foster homes in my sample similarly had very long waiting lists.

During my next stretch as a New Grace volunteer in 2007, I was sent, with another Australian, to a different Henan state orphanage. We were there to collect a baby boy, Paul, who had been chosen to receive treatment at New Grace, and to bring him back to the foster home by overnight train. This slight boy of around eight months had a severely cleft lip and palate, with related breathing and feeding difficulties, and was understandably unsettled at being taken from his *ayis* to go with strangers on a twelve-hour train ride. We shared our first-class compartment with two well-dressed businessmen who had paid for the luxury, peace, and quiet of a four-berth cabin, away from the crowded and raucous economy seat carriages. I felt sure they would not take kindly to having to share the space with an upset baby, one with confronting physical deformities at that. In fact, the businessmen, along with the train conductor and passengers from neighbouring cubicles, went out of their way to help us comfort Paul throughout the long night. They each took turns to bounce him on their knees, showing us the "correct Chinese way" to hold an infant and pacing the corridor to jiggle him to sleep.

This touching glimpse of China's child-loving culture was also a small glimpse of the scale and impact of the movement of *gu'er* from state to private facilities. As Wang has noted, this movement frequently resulted in children benefiting from an imported "first-world vision of care that relies on access to education, training, and economic resources outside the reach of most local people".[10] Foster homes like New Grace had spent decades importing not only foreign funds and resources, oftentimes literally packed in the suitcases of inbound volunteers, but also first-world medical and child-development practices. Wang has explored how this at times resulted in negotiations and tension between Western and local Chinese logics of care, with the latter often more focused on short-term physical health ("pragmatic logic of care") and the former on the individualised emotional and physical potential of each child ("intensive logic of care").[11] But it was not only foreign groups that were running private *gu'er* facilities guided by an intensive logic of care and a rights-based conception of children with special needs. Two of the foster homes in my sample, Still Waters and Mercy Home, were set up by Chinese Christians, independently of any foreign funding or collaboration (at least initially). Although the conditions at these homes were somewhat less comfortable and flashy than at New Grace (older, rented buildings rather than custom-built premises; more children to each room; more reliance on donated secondhand toys and clothes rather than new items brought to China from Western department stores), these foster homes had the same aim as the foreign foster homes: to provide potentially lifesaving care for children with special medical needs in the short-term and a family-style upbringing and a sense of belonging and permanence in the long term until adoption could be arranged.

"China looks after its own": foreign intervention in Chinese *gu'er* relief

All of the foreign foster homes I visited employed solely or predominantly Chinese staff, with any Western volunteers and staff playing mainly administrative, supervisory, or behind-the-scenes roles. This was not just for pragmatic reasons, such as language. One foster home manager explained how important it was to send a clear message to state officials and Chinese society alike that foreign foster homes were helping the state to save children from abandonment, not to save them "from being Chinese".[12] This concern speaks to a complicating contextual factor for foreigners trying to supplement state *gu'er* relief: China's historically rooted scepticism of the intervention of outsiders in matters of domestic welfare. Until at least the second half of the twentieth century, Western intervention in Chinese welfare generally had problematic colonial overtones. In the case of China's *gu'er*, foreign relief work has had a particularly controversial history. Large numbers of foreign missionaries entered China in the latter half of the nineteenth century, in the wake of the humiliating Opium Wars. Protestants and Catholics alike began to set up orphanages that were in competition with the native Qing-dynasty "foundling hospitals" discussed in Chapter 2. These foreign missionary homes were seen as an insulting, imperialist criticism of China's ability to care for its own and were widely regarded with suspicion (for example, accusations of infanticide, kidnapping, and baby-selling were common).[13] They also could not simply be closed down, given the large numbers of children in their care. But the presence of foreign orphanages did result in renewed interest in native *gu'er* relief efforts as a way to offset the unwanted intrusion—as Leung has described it, "the establishment of more native foundling homes was no longer simply a manifestation of compassion but now was seen by the authorities as an essential political measure to counter imperialism".[14] With the founding of the People's Republic in 1949, foreign orphanages were shut down, and their perceived "imperialist cultural aggression" came to an end.[15]

The extent to which this historical narrative has shaped contemporary attitudes in China about foreign involvement in *gu'er* relief is a matter of conjecture. However, most of my research participants felt that modern discourse was at least a parallel, if not a continuance, of these historical controversies. Many foreigners running foster homes had encountered state officials who seemed wary of acknowledging the extent of foreign involvement in the field of domestic *gu'er* welfare. Some had been explicitly rebuffed by orphanage directors on the basis that China "didn't need foreigners to look after its own children". Others had been consistently impressed by the willingness of state officials to partner with and support foreign-funded organisations in order to benefit as many *gu'er* as possible. In other words, individual state actors varied from time to time and place to place in terms of their openness to foreign-funded efforts. But all of the foreign foster homes were aware of the complicated historical context. Perhaps as a result, they were also generally aware of the importance of "giving face" to state authorities and not embarrassing China by focusing on deficiencies in state welfare. One research participant, the founder and director of a Xi'an foster home, described it as living in a "twilight zone between the reality of what it is and what I have to portray it to be" (*Alana, founder/director of Red Thread Foster Home, 2009*). When she referred in her blog to a healthy child who had died on returning to her home orphanage, she was immediately subjected to days of government visits and threats that her home would be shut down: "I can understand why—I embarrassed them".

More generally, a number of China NGO scholars have written extensively about the legal and political barriers faced by foreign NGOs seeking to establish a lawful presence in China.[16] This is frequently attributed to the state's ambivalence and scepticism towards foreign involvement in domestic Chinese affairs, particularly in the wake of the Eastern European "Colour Revolutions",[17] and an "entrenched ... traditional official idea that the main needs of individuals should not be met by foreign relationships".[18] The foreign-run foster homes I surveyed were not "foreign NGOs" in the sense of being already established abroad; rather, they had emerged locally in China, at a grassroots level, but happened to be run by foreigners.[19] In this respect they had more in common with other local, grassroots welfare movements, such as the private orphanages discussed in Chapter 3, and Chinese-run foster homes like Still Waters. But as foreign-affiliated groups, there was an added dimension to their interactions and negotiations with local state officials, and they frequently encountered the same scepticism and mixed messaging from state officials as have been documented in relation to international NGOs trying to make inroads in China.

Forgiveness, not permission: gradual growth of Christian foster homes

Both New Grace Foster Home and Still Waters began when Christians witnessed "orphans in distress" in state institutions and felt compelled to help, beginning with just one or two children at a time. This was a common origin story for China's foster homes. The oldest and largest of these foster homes was Prince of Peace Village, which was set up by the Gilbertsons, an American couple. In the 1990s, the Gilbertsons began fostering children from a large state orphanage in north-east China ("Wuhui orphanage") and bringing them to stay in their own home in a nearby housing estate ("the Dongjian estate").[20] They registered a charity in the USA to collect donations to support their work, which allowed them to bring home more and more *gu'er*. A wealthy Chinese neighbour, Mr Huang, saw the difference that foster care and privately funded medical treatment was making and decided to support the cause by loaning the Gilbertsons several of his other houses on the estate, free of charge, to facilitate their work.

Over the years, the Gilbertsons inspired other like-minded expatriate neighbours and church friends. For example, Bob and Diana, American friends of the Gilbertsons, moved to the estate in 1999 to help out and later began taking in older boys from the same orphanage, caring for them in a home that came to be known as St Matthew's Foster Home. This was a special group with lower prospects of adoption and often very serious behavioural issues: "They never had a birthday and they never had a gift. They don't know how to handle it, being here with 'parents'" (*Bob, St Matthew's Foster Home, 2010*). Another American foster home, Compassion Family Life House, opened down the street and developed expertise in treating children with brittle bone disease. A French couple set up Good News (introduced in Chapter 1 and home to Tessa) to specialise in caring for blind *gu'er*. By 2002, there were six foreign-run foster homes in the Dongjian housing estate. Around this time, the Gilbertsons were anxious to expand but were beginning to feel uneasy about their dependence on Mr Huang's goodwill. They began looking for an alternative location and struck up a deal with the authorities in nearby Wuhui, a politically progressive city. The government in Wuhui, aware of the potential employment opportunities a large, newly constructed foreign-funded home would bring to the area, sold the Gilbertsons the rights to a large block of rural land for one *yuan*, or about fifteen cents (the translator dryly remarked at the time, "I think you should take it, it's a good deal"). There, the Gilbertsons began constructing a purpose-built campus with enough beds to home scores of children at a time. The move to the new campus was completed in 2006.

Within just a few years, the organisation was one of the largest employers in its area, with over one hundred full-time staff members, and apparently a source of pride for local officials. Speaking in 2009, one of the Village's American managers explained how police officers would often visit with gifts and how the Wuhui Civil Affairs Bureau held the Village up as an example of a "model foster home". The home was caring for hundreds of *gu'er* with special medical needs. From the initial relationship with the Wuhui orphanage, the Gilbertsons' reputation for providing free, high-quality health care spread until the foster home was caring for children from dozens of state orphanages across the country, with a long waiting list. All the Village buildings were purpose-built, clean, and beautifully furnished. In the main reception and administrative building, a double-height entrance foyer with stone flooring and wood panelling was hung with framed black-and-white photos of the many hundreds of babies and children who had passed through the foster home, both before and after the move to the new location. This building also included many offices, staff rooms, and a library for visitors. Passing through the building and out the double French doors at its rear, all seven acres of the campus, with its many pristine buildings and play areas, could be admired. The campus included a clinic, a preschool and elementary school, an arts-and-craft workshop, a community outreach centre, and a hotel for visiting volunteers. The various buildings were connected by paved walkways that weaved through landscaped ornamental gardens. More than six hundred children had been and gone, the majority to new families formed through adoption.

Privately funded "welfare institutions" are permissible in theory in China under the *Social Welfare Institutions Interim Measures* of 1999, but only if pre-approved by and jointly established with Civil Affairs, something that is reportedly rarely, if ever, granted in practice.[21] None of the foster homes in my sample had permission to set up welfare institutions when they began taking in children from state orphanages. A number had tried to get some form of pre-approval from city or provincial authorities, but all had been rebuffed. Instead, the foster homes had generally adopted the same "forgiveness rather than permission" approach as Prince of Peace, beginning with informal home-based care of a small number of foster children as a way of building trust with receptive state orphanage directors. Over time, as trust developed, each home's capacity and scope expanded, sometimes to the point where several hundred children were being cared for at any one time, including *gu'er* sent from very distant provinces like Inner Mongolia and Xinjiang. Other homes intentionally remained smaller as a way of maintaining a "family feel" or avoiding unwanted attention from local officials.

For the foster homes that had remained behind in the Dongjian housing estate, such unwanted attention from state authorities had begun to increase around 2006 and 2007. As the number of *gu'er* living in the compound rose, the area began to experience increased notoriety and visibility, particularly in online adoption communities. Large numbers of foreign volunteers and prospective adoptive families were passing through, and all the homes were soliciting donations for their work through much-trafficked websites. This seems to have made Dongjian city officials uncomfortable, given the political sensitivity of *gu'er* issues and foreign involvement in Chinese domestic welfare; as my research participants described it, there was a "losing face" (*diu mian*) problem due to so many foreigners caring for Chinese children in one area.[22] Dongjian officials began to exert pressure on the homes, through frequent surprise inspections and phone calls, mostly in the form of suggesting or demanding the foreigners and their *gu'er* move on: "They were basically just saying: we don't want this to be our problem—go somewhere else" (*Alain, Good News Training Centre, 2009*); "They didn't tell us to close, they told us to move. At first it was friendly. Then it became more pressured, with constant knocks on the door. In April 2007, they said, 'That's it! Out! Now!'" (*Tony, Compassion Family Life House, 2009*). Some of the homes report being told to change their names to more neutral terms "because there are only state-run orphanages in China". It also appears that pressure was exerted upstream on the nearest state orphanage, which soon pulled its children from the various Dongjian foster homes. Some of these children had been living in the Dongjian homes for years: "We lost nineteen kids in one day.... That was heart-breaking—the older kids had been there all their lives. They were seven and eight and nine. This was all they knew, suddenly taken to the orphanage. It must have been like getting hit in the face with a two-by-four" (*Bob, St Matthew's Foster Home, 2010*). Eventually, the larger homes moved to new locations where they could take on more employees and *gu'er*; three smaller homes, each caring for around two dozen *gu'er*, were able to lie low and stay in Dongjian until the pressure eased: "The guards [at the housing estate] would tell us that the police were coming and you better hide the kids. The government vehicles were regularly patrolling the area.... We made sure we [foreigners] were never seen with the kids" (*Bob, St Matthew's Foster Home, 2010*). Bob of St Matthew's believes that once the larger homes moved on, the city decided the de facto *gu'er* village that had emerged in the housing estate was "shut enough". Speaking in 2010, another Dongjian foster home manager said simply, "*na shijian, kunnan shihou, wanle*" (that time, the hard time, is over now) (*Ivy, manager of Friendship Outreach*).

Unstable legal status

As was the case for private orphanages, NGO registration was not usually a feasible option for foster homes, whether Chinese or foreign-run, due mainly to the unwillingness of government agencies to take on the responsibility of acting as "mother-in-law".[23] For foster homes funded by foreign charities, a further obstacle was the lack of legal pathways for foreign NGOs to register in China.[24] Instead, at the time of my fieldwork in 2009 and 2010, the foster homes in my sample were all either registered as commercial enterprises or managing to function without legal personality in China. In interviews, this was referred to as being "half under the table" or being in a "legal grey area". Commercially or nonregistered NGOs are formally illegal, at least since the *Banning of Illegal NGOs Measures* were passed in 2000,[25] but have remained extremely common despite periodic crackdowns (these could often be evaded by measures as simple as a name change).[26] Registration as a business is a long-standing, creative means for nonprofits to address some of the practical disadvantages of operating without a legal identity. Good News' commercial registration, for example, which gave it license to carry on as "consultants for visual impairment equipment", facilitated the opening of bank accounts and the issuance of visas for foreign staff. Other foster homes got by without having any legal identity in China at all, instead using individual names for transactions (signing contracts, employing staff, opening bank accounts). As Keyser has also noted, this created uncertainty for founders and managers, who were essentially bearing the legal risks for the organisation in question.[27]

The foster homes were all facing similar practical challenges as a result of their lack of NGO status. For example, most homes were employing staff by way of verbal agreement, or a simple written contract signed by an individual as employer in their personal capacity, and were therefore unable to purchase social insurance for their employees. These arrangements also meant employees were not legally protected by the Labour Bureau in the event of workplace accidents or disputes with employers: "What made it all work was trust—they trusted me—that I would treat them well and do the right thing. This trust was built up over time" (*Will Peters, founder of Autumn Rain Orphan Care, 2009*). Homes without a legal identity were also unable to open organisational bank accounts, meaning donations, salaries, and operating expenses were typically handled using personal bank accounts. Because there are various daily and annual caps on personal bank account withdrawals in China, most foster homes were forced to adopt complex banking practices involving multiple accounts opened by volunteers or friends to channel multimillion-*yuan* operational budgets. These arrangements sometimes caused transparency concerns for donors, especially overseas charities funnelling foreign donations to China. As the founder of Good News put it, "We are operating way below the international financial ethics standards.... We don't like it, of course, but we don't have a choice" (*Alain, Good News Training Centre, 2010*). Foster homes that had registered commercially faced the added cost of paying taxes on expenditure, although some had successfully negotiated with their local tax offices for reduced rates or exemption, based on the charitable nature of their work. Ashley and He have pointed out that such negotiations are risky, in that they bring attention to the impropriety of the organisation being registered commercially in the first place and acting outside the mandate of their business licenses.[28] Finally, unregistered foster homes were not permitted to actively fundraise in China. Many did so anyway, by using a sympathetic government-organised NGO (GONGO)[29] to collect donations on their behalf, for which an administration fee of up to 12 per cent would typically be charged.

Alliances with state orphanages

The founders of foster homes in China had similar motives to the sisters of Guanghui and St Martin's. But unlike private orphanages, foster homes were working closely with the state welfare apparatus, taking in registered *gu'er* from willing state institutions. These alliances between foster homes and state orphanages depended largely on personal ties with orphanage directors. As Spires has noted, such successful alliances between unofficial NGOs and state actors are possible in China but tend to always be "contingent on each side's calculation of need, risk, and benefit".[30] My research participants acknowledged and described these calculations in our conversations. Given their lack of express authorisation or registration, either as NGOs or approved welfare institutions, most of the foster homes described their work as "not technically legal". They were aware that because of this, there was always a risk of the Chinese government putting a stop to their work—as a Prince of Peace manager put it: "The reality is that if anybody decided they didn't want us to care for kids, that million-dollar investment [in the new campus] would be irrelevant" (*Mark, director of Prince of Peace, 2009*). However, they had persevered despite this risk, due to the higher moral norm that sick children must be cared for, no matter the legal restrictions on doing so: "We know our cause is worthwhile, so we're willing to act illegally" (*Will Peters, founder of Autumn Rain Orphan Care, 2009*).

On the state orphanage side, only one director was willing to be interviewed for this study, and he denied knowledge of any foster homes, despite the fact that I had already met dozens of children from his orphanage in foster homes around Beijing.[31] However, he and scores of state-employed orphanage directors across China had made the decision to collaborate with foster homes, in spite of their unclear legal status. In doing so, some directors were no doubt motivated by the specialist care available in foster homes, with beneficial outcomes for individual children. Although the Chinese government had increased funding for state orphanages over the years, and put in place the Tomorrow Plan to address *gu'er* medical needs, these funds could be difficult to access in a timely manner, time being of the essence for infants with serious conditions such as heart disease. Moreover, there were clear financial incentives to state orphanages in maintaining foster care arrangements with relatively wealthy, privately funded homes. Fostered *gu'er* would officially remain under the guardianship of their sending orphanage, which would continue to receive the state per capita orphan allowance even as they outsourced their caregiving responsibilities (one of the foster homes in my sample actually paid its partner state orphanage an annual fee of around 3,000 US dollars in order to be allowed to care for a group of older teenage girls on a long-term basis). Surgical intervention provided by the foster homes also often resulted in children becoming "adoptable", where they were previously destined to live out their lives in state facilities at the state's expense.

On the other hand, the foster homes understood that partnering orphanage directors were potentially putting their own careers at risk by allowing children to travel across provincial borders to live at independent, unsupervised facilities—were anything to go wrong, questions would be asked about why orphanages were partnering with unapproved welfare providers, often Christian or foreign-run organisations at that, and without direct oversight:

> It's always a risk; the state orphanages are walking a fine line, a tightrope—because the MCA [Ministry of Civil Affairs] doesn't trust foreigners. So we sort of bow to the state orphanages and how they want to do it—if they want us to come to dinners with officials or if they want us to not be visible. It all depends on their relationship with the MCA.
>
> *(Gail, director of Mustard Seed Creations, 2010)*

As a result, partnerships between foster homes and state orphanages generally developed slowly, as foster homes needed to build up strong track records of care in order to earn the trust of orphanage directors: "Our standard of work gives them a bit of safety" (*David, founder of New Grace Foster Home, 2009*). The foster homes also expressed a keen awareness of the need to "give face" to state orphanages and to be mindful of the various pressures on orphanage directors: "We don't want to tell the orphanages what to do—we try to do what they feel comfortable with" (*Zelda, Mustard Seed Creations, 2009*).

At the same time, at least at the time of my earlier fieldwork, my research participants felt that the chances of the foster homes actually being shut down were slim, due to their established role as legitimate, respectable care providers and the negative publicity that could result: "That would get nasty—we have so many employees and babies here" (*Zelda, Mustard Seed Creations, 2009*).[32] Some spoke of how orphanages in some parts of China even seemed to receive political credit for innovative cross-country foster care arrangements: "Our work is a star in [the orphanage director's] crown" (*David, founder of New Grace Foster Home, 2009*). The larger foster homes, with million-dollar operating budgets, were bringing large influxes of capital and increased employment opportunities to local communities. But despite these advantages, foster care arrangements were still subject to change without notice, in line with changing top-down policies on *gu'er* relief generally. For example, as Blue Sky Plan[33] funding began to be distributed to state orphanages around 2007 and 2008, directors with new but empty beds reportedly came under political pressure to reinstitutionalise children who had been fostered out to private organisations.[34] Different directors responded differently, but most of the foster homes in my sample were required to return some of their children to state facilities around this time, regardless of how long they had been fostered or their medical status. Some fought against this—for example, Alain of Good News recounted how he visited an orphanage director who had recently recalled a number of Good News *gu'er* and successfully argued that the children should be allowed to return to his care. But overall the security of the children resident in foster homes was tenuous and subject to change without notice. Given the foster homes' dedication to creating opportunities for home-style care and kinship bonding—between caregivers and children, "older sisters", and "younger brothers"—the removal of children was always a huge blow for everyone involved.

Not permitted, not forbidden: hidden rules and informal oversight

The formal legislative framework for *gu'er* welfare and nonprofit organisations was, in a practical sense, largely irrelevant to the people setting up and running foster homes in China—registration was simply not a feasible option. Like the majority of small, local nonprofit groups in China, the foster homes existed in legal limbo, hampered by restrictions and ambiguities in the NGO legislative framework.[35] Like so many grassroots nonprofit groups in China, and as was the case for the private orphanages introduced in Chapter 3, the foster homes were not clearly permitted in law. But they were also not forbidden in practice. They had negotiated a place for themselves in the grey area between lawful and unlawful, tolerated and not tolerated. For example, when Alain and Brigitte set up their home for blind *gu'er*, where Tessa would later have her "gotcha day" party as described in Chapter 1, they named it Good News Foster Home. But over time, numerous officials encouraged them to change their name—but not, importantly, the nature of their work—from "foster home" to something more neutral such as "training centre" because "it's illegal for foreigners to foster Chinese children". Alain explained how he had frequently encountered this type of mixed messaging from state officials in his years working in China: "They don't want to tell us what to do—they wouldn't tell us to do something illegal—rather they keep it blurry. It's not clear. They don't tell you to leave, but they don't tell you how to stay" (*Alain, Good News Training Centre, 2010*).

The experience of Good News was typical of the foster homes I surveyed, whether founded by Chinese or foreigners. Their situation showed the playing-out of state policies on unregistered NGOs on a local level. Hsia and White have reported that in the late 1980s, the central Ministry of Civil Affairs appeared to have adopted an informal "no recognition, yet no prohibition" approach to locally active foreign nonprofit groups in China, so long as their work was not "politically sensitive".[36] Guosheng Deng has researched how this "blind eye" approach to foreign groups was eventually extended, when the Ministry internally adopted the "three 'no[s]' policy"—no recognition, no banning, no intervention—in relation to unregistered NGOs generally.[37] For unregistered, independent *gu'er* homes like New Grace and Still Waters, this passivity created opportunities. The law was arguably unclear, so their work could be tolerated and even tacitly or overtly encouraged (depending on the particular officials involved); over time, they could build up legitimacy as providers of important services and resources, supplementing an overstretched and ineffective system of state welfare. But still their legal status was uncertain. The foster homes repeatedly related to me examples of local and provincial officials referring to their work as "illegal" or "not allowed", usually on the basis that only the government can care for Chinese orphans (this was more common for foreign-run foster homes but also happened to Chinese-run organisations on occasion).

Most of the foster homes I surveyed responded to this ambiguity by intentionally maintaining low visibility in China, although all had at least some dealings with local state officials (it was generally not possible for a home with more than a dozen or so children to operate completely under the radar). However, these interactions were not governed by formal laws or regulations. Rather, they were premised on unspoken norms and hidden rules, which could vary from place to place. As others have noted, the hidden rules that govern NGO activity tend to emerge at the local level in China, where "the state" consists of various officials who individually wield substantial discretion in choosing to support or interfere with local NGOs, and do not necessarily present a unified front.[38] As one foster home described it, "it all depends on who is in charge of your county—if he doesn't care, then you'll have no problems" (*Alain, Good News Training Centre, 2009*). Some foster homes had experienced disapproval in one location, only to be warmly welcomed by local officials on moving to a new location. Others had come under intense scrutiny in their early days, only to have earned the respect and support of state actors after years of building trust and doing visibly important work. Being transparent—open to unannounced visits and drop-ins by local police and Civil Affairs officials, willing to share files and open the accounting books—was considered very important in establishing this support and stability. Likewise, all of the foster homes were careful not to create controversy by overtly evangelising or emphasising the Christian nature of their work; although most were very open within their walls and with visitors about their religious motivations, the focus was much more on humanitarian work than the underlying "mission".[39] The homes also avoided drawing attention, domestically or internationally, to shortcomings in the state *gu'er* welfare system, criticising the policies and circumstances underlying abandonment (such as birth-planning restrictions and stigma against the disabled), or generally "embarrassing China" in any way. As one Chinese interviewee described the dynamic,

> orphanages are very emotive. Orphans are the most vulnerable people in China, and it's easy to see that public opinion could be very positive or negative. If something went wrong, it could be very, very negative—"What's the Chinese government doing, giving our kids to some foreigners? Why can't we take care of our own kids?" ... Any self-respecting country may have a problem explaining to its people why we cannot take care of our own kids.
>
> *(Austin Song, lawyer for New Grace Foster Home, 2010)*

As another foster home founder put it, "they worry that we're going to embarrass China by what we're doing, on an international basis, by showing the world that China is not doing its job looking after its children" (*Will Peters, founder of Autumn Rain Orphan Care, 2009*). Foster home websites tended to refer to "partnerships with the Chinese government" and emphasise the "best efforts" being made by China to care for its *gu'er*, while domestic fundraising efforts (if any) tended to be discreet: "We don't want the community to think the orphanage is not caring for their children. We don't want to bring them any shame, only positive recognition" (*Trisha, Wuzhong Foster Home, 2009*).

Homes that could abide by these norms and rules could achieve some degree of legitimacy in the eyes of both state and social actors, despite their quasi-legal status. To put it another way, although *legal* legitimacy, in the sense of being formally recognised by law, was not generally attainable, it was also not of central importance (other than for the aforementioned practical difficulties this caused). The foster homes tended to focus on other types of legitimacy—political, administrative, and social—rather than compliance with legal rules.[40] This aligns with Deng's findings on unregistered NGOs in China generally: that local officials tend to allow them to contribute to the local good without interference, so long as they do not pose an obvious threat to state interests.[41] Tam and Hasmath have noted a similar dynamic in relation to faith-based NGOs, finding that once an organisation "begins to deliver quality services and has proven to the state that it is a trustworthy organisation, the state will gradually loosen the reins and grant it further latitude to operate".[42]

As organisations were building up trust and latitude, they also experienced various forms of informal supervision by local state actors. For example, many foster homes spoke of receiving threats (variously referred to as "awkward hints", "being told off", or "scoldings") from local city officials and police officers, especially in their earlier years. These were generally interpreted as a way for officials to maintain "face" and demonstrate their authority. I witnessed a number of blustering but probably empty threats during my various stays at New Grace. On one occasion, David asked me to come upstairs and translate an apparently very heated argument going on between a man from the town offices and the home's Chinese staff manager. The official was irate that one of New Grace's nannies had been fired for striking a child, something that all staff were strictly forbidden to do as a condition of employment. He had come in to demand her reinstatement. The female staff manager humbly acknowledged his concerns, before sending him next door to drink *baijiu* (Chinese liquor) with the home's male chef and drivers, and that was the end of it. On another occasion, the foster home received notice from the local zoning authority that their main building was scheduled for demolition because it had been constructed in an industrial zone without planning permission. At the time of construction, there had been no way to apply for permission because the foster home was registered as a business. When the demolition notice arrived, "we panicked, we thought the bulldozers were coming down the road". When David sent his friend, an ethnically Chinese lawyer, to appeal to the town authorities, the lawyer was greeted with a barrage of threats and accusations of illegality (in relation to caring for *gu'er*). He also said that he knew the threats were empty: "I know enough about China to keep quiet and be humble". Eventually, the whole issue about the land use "just went away".

Conversely, most of the homes could give examples of visiting officials expressing informal or tacit approval of their unauthorised operations, at least once the nature of the work was understood: "Most [officials] know who we are and what we're doing, and they respect it. It's the ones who don't understand what we're doing and only know what the books say—they're the troublemakers" (*Tony, founder of Compassion Family Life House, 2009*); "They send us the message, 'OK, we approve, we'll allow you to do this, as long as you do what you say you are doing' " (*Zelda, Mustard Seed Creations, 2009*). For example, in the lead-up to the 2008 Olympics, a time of heightened police activity in China generally, a provincial-level police delegation arrived at New Grace and aggressively interrogated the staff on why foreigners were caring for Chinese orphans. The staff explained the mission and gave the group a tour, by the end of which the group's leader was offering to be a volunteer cook. In another episode, village officials arrived for an unannounced visit and demanded that all the *ayis* pass an exam to become qualified caregivers. When David expressed scepticism that his employees, most of whom had not finished primary school, would be able to pass an exam, he was given an answer sheet to distribute to the candidates. There were many such examples of foster homes building trust and rapport with local officials and leveraging that to benefit the children in their care. Another foster home was occasionally able to convince friends in the government to amend a child's official *hukou* record of birth date in order to increase their adoption prospects: "Over time, you play on this trust and ask them to take new risks—a new type of trust develops, and a tighter bond" (*Will Peters, founder of Autumn Rain Orphan Care, 2009*). Other areas where the foster homes felt comfortable pushing for leeway and a "blind eye" were in relation to soliciting donations in China (which is illegal for unregistered charities), taxation rates, and employment law, although as one foster home noted: "It's a tightrope we walk. You don't want to be too bold or too timid" (*Trisha, Wuzhong Foster Home, 2009*). The unspoken rules relating to evangelism and not embarrassing the government were uniformly regarded as lines not to be crossed.

In all, it seemed local officials were carrying out the same risk/benefit calculations as foster homes and state orphanages, with different results in different locations. Spires has pointed out that the tolerance of officials for illegal NGOs is "intimately linked to local-level politics", a finding supported by my data.[43] For example, when Prince of Peace made the move from Dongjian to its new location, this was in part because they found officials in the destination city to be relatively sophisticated, forward-thinking, and liberal, and so willing to work with the foster home, despite its foreign ties and lack of registration, for the sake of the employment and development prospects it represented: "this all accrues to the unspoken economy in the Party", as an American manager explained (*Mark, director of Prince of Peace, 2009*). Dongjian officials, by comparison, seemed more concerned that the number of "outsiders" caring for *gu'er* in the area would reflect poorly on local state welfare efforts.[44] My research participants emphasised the political risks to any official involved in closing an eye to the "illegal" nature of unregistered foster homes in their jurisdiction, caring for children from far-flung provinces: "If it's done well, it's a big plus.... The risk is if they work with an organisation that doesn't do it well" (*David, founder of New Grace Foster Home, 2009*); "foreign orphanages fly in the face of their sense of pride and control" (*Austin Song, lawyer for New Grace Foster Home, 2010*).

In this context of perceived vulnerability to local state discretion, some of the case study homes had actively procured higher-level political ties, such as with GONGOs, state orphanages, or friends in the central government, which were seen as protection in the event of things "getting nasty" with local state actors: "You need somebody somewhere willing to say, 'I know that guy—he won't give you any trouble'" (*Will Peters, founder of Autumn Rain Orphan Care, 2009*). For example, David of New Grace believed a major reason the foster home had not been hassled more often by local officials was because of the prominent display, in its foyer, of a letter from CH Tong, former governor of Hong Kong, commending "the people of [New Grace's township] for their work in caring for orphans". As David explained, "that letter in the foyer has without a doubt been an influence on the people who give us a hard time. Those sorts of things are unspoken ... but there's a difference" (*David, founder of New Grace Foster Home, 2010*).

Conclusion: ad hoc, chilled, and cautious development

It is difficult to assess the impact that the negotiated, extra-legal regulation of foster homes has had on private *gu'er* relief efforts. In one sense, the ambiguous regulatory landscape was productive, in that it created space for unauthorised organisations to make important contributions to child welfare. The foster homes introduced in this chapter were generally providing a very high quality of care, funded entirely by private donations and in many cases delivered by world-leading surgical teams or in hospitals abroad. Many were involved in impactful adoption advocacy in "receiving" countries such as the United States. But a child's access to those services and resources depended primarily on her home orphanage's willingness to partner with a foster home. No central-level authority had taken on responsibility for facilitating or coordinating the national movement of children to specialist foster homes. Instead, individual foster homes carved out their own roles in *gu'er* relief independently, in an uncoordinated and ad hoc way, by way of negotiations with interested state orphanage directors. The children who benefitted from foster home services were those whose state orphanages were willing to take a chance on unorthodox partnerships with organisations like New Grace and Still Waters (foreign-funded and religious groups, no less). They were not necessarily the children with the most pressing needs from the orphanages or regions in most need of NGO assistance. As one foster home manager described it,

> it's a messed-up system. There are tonnes of kids who need help, but there's no private organisation or NGO partnering with their particular orphanage.

> So often it's not which kids have the greatest needs, but who knows who—connections lead to access. There may be kids even in that same province without access to that care.

Moreover, the willingness and capacity of foster homes to try to influence state law and policy within China seemed to have been stifled by their lack of legal security. None of the homes were involved in any sort of political advocacy on the many pressing issues relating to their work—abandonment, quality of institutional care, legalisation of NGOs, and adoption. The prevailing sense was that the homes had earned for themselves a measure of leeway but could be reined in if they overstepped by drawing too much attention to themselves or to broader policy problems in China: "It's grace and favour. It's not law" (*Austin Song, lawyer for New Grace Foster Home, 2010*); "The law thing is a little bit, well, not solid. If there would be an incident, they would pull the law in to use it. But as long as everything is OK, they turn their eyes" (*Gail, director of Mustard Seed Creations, 2010*). This "chilling effect" of ambiguous regulatory policy has been described by Ashley and He in relation to unregistered NGOs generally, who have argued that "legal ambiguity combined with China's political climate seems to have shaped the overall agenda of China's grassroots NGOs to favor politically safe fields and politically prudent approaches".[45]

Whether this regulatory landscape had been deliberately shaped or not, it allowed state actors to unofficially but closely monitor and control foster homes, benefiting from their work but without incurring the expense or trouble of supervision. One founder described it as the government wanting to "have its cake and eat it too—it wants to let NGOs function in China, without legitimising them but while keeping control over them. They are walking a tightrope" (*Will Peters, Autumn Rain Orphan Care, 2009*). Another interviewee, the Chinese lawyer for New Grace, used the analogy of a parent adopting a curfew but consistently allowing their teenager to arrive home slightly past the set time but within reason, according to an unspoken degree of flexibility—but "it's very sensitive. They don't want to be *seen* as doing that" (*Austin Song, lawyer for New Grace Foster Home, 2009*). The director of Good News similarly speculated that local officials were "OK with being in the grey—it gives them the control to go either way" (*Alain, 2009*). These views echo that of NGO scholar Liu, who has described the regulation of Chinese charities as involving "underlying 'hidden' rules" that gradually come to replace law, "thereby further twisting the already problematic system, and increasing the difficulties in institutional reform and standardization of social administration".[46]

The hidden rules that characterised state-social interactions in the field impacted the scope and growth of this form of non-governmental *gu'er* welfare. On the one hand, the foster homes I visited had all survived for many years by being astute to the political climate and adopting protective strategies and networks. They had adapted to a system in which flexible, interpersonal relationships rather than formal rules/policies governed their work and in which social and political legitimacy carried more weight than legality. This had allowed them to take advantage of a vague regulatory environment to carry out work that had in some instances benefitted thousands of children over the years. As Keyser has pointed out, although the ambiguous legality of unregistered foster homes caused difficulties, "the very vagueness in the law on the protection of children as well as the ability to operate at the local level has also created opportunities".[47] However, both political acumen and a strong personal motivation were needed to persevere in the face of the many practical difficulties that being "half under the table" entailed: "There's an intangible hassle factor—we have to dance around all these hoops. It's a quiet sucking away of energy" (*Mark, director of Prince of Peace, 2009*). Many of my research participants expressed frustration with the vague, capricious, and negotiated nature of their interactions with state officials: "I live between lines that are moving constantly—it's a moving target. What is acceptable one day is not OK the next. You don't know where the line is so it's easy to cross it" (*Alana, founder/director of Red Thread Foster Home, 2009*). As Christians, the founders, directors, and managers of the foster homes were both motivated by faith, but also heavily reliant on their faith for the strength to face these moving lines. They uniformly expressed confidence that their work was protected by God and would continue in a manner and for a time as determined by providence, while acknowledging that being shut down (or, in the case of foreigners, asked to leave China) was always a possibility: "All of us could be stopped at any time from doing what we're doing" (*Vera, Loving Embrace Foundation, 2009*). Vulnerability was seen as an inevitable aspect of working in a contentious and unregulated field, with much more faith placed in divine protection than in the predictability of state policies and actions:

> This is the most frustrating feeling in China—you're never one hundred percent safe or on solid ground. This project, it's big, it's good, we've put so much into it. But in a week, they could bring us down. But that's also the beauty of China! Nothing is radical here. There's always room for negotiating.
>
> *(Alain, founder and CEO of Good News Training Centre, 2009)*

This was a sentiment I heard repeatedly—gratitude for the leeway that foster homes had been granted in practice and for what they had been able to achieve, despite changing laws and policies. Speaking in 2009, a Chinese staff member at Mustard Seed Foster Home said:

> Ten, fifteen, twenty years ago, you could do nothing of this sort—now, they are opening up a little.... They express approval of our work and even want to learn from us. There is more dialogue, and it is starting to open up. We are grateful for what we're able to do now.
>
> *(Zelda, Mustard Seed Creations, 2009)*

By the time of my next visit to Mustard Seed and the other Christian foster homes in this study, in 2017, the political terrain had shifted dramatically for *gu'er* welfare providers across China, as private orphanages and foster homes alike came under new scrutiny and restrictions in the wake of the Lankao tragedy and subsequent political developments.

Notes

1 See Chapter 2 at 39–41. *The Dying Rooms* was based in part on information gathered by researchers who had entered state orphanages under the guise of being international charity workers. This led to increased monitoring of foreign social groups after the film's release: Renee Yuen-Jan Hsia and Lynn T. White III, "Working amid Corporatism and Confusion: Foreign NGOs in China," *Nonprofit and Voluntary Sector Quarterly* 31, no. 3 (September 2002), 336.
2 Catherine H. Keyser, "The Role of the State and NGOs in Caring for At-Risk Children: The Case of Orphan Care," in *State and Society Responses to Social Welfare Needs in China: Serving the People*, eds. Jonathan Schwartz and Shawn Shieh (Abingdon: Routledge, 2009), 52–55.
3 For example, the British charity Care for Children set up a pilot project in Shanghai focused on training orphanage staff in setting up safe, supervised foster family programmes: Keyser, "The Role of the State and NGOs," 54.
4 Leslie K. Wang, *Outsourced Children: Orphanage Care and Adoption in Globalizing China* (Stanford: Stanford University Press, 2016), 16.
5 Xiaoyuan Shang, "Looking for Best Practice in Caring for Disabled Children: A Case of Socialized Foster Care in China," *Asia Pacific Journal of Social Work and Development* 22, no. 1–2 (March/June 2012); Xiaoyuan Shang and Karen R. Fisher, *Caring for Orphaned Children in China* (Lanham: Lexington, 2014), chapter 8. Johnson's research has also shed light on the extent of informal fostering practices in more rural parts of China: Kay Ann Johnson, *Wanting a Daughter, Needing a Son: Abandonment, Adoption, and Orphanage Care in China*, ed. Amy Klatzkin (St Paul, NM: Yeong & Yeong, 2004); Kay Ann Johnson, *China's Hidden Children: Abandonment, Adoption, and the Human Costs of the One-Child Policy* (Chicago: University of Chicago Press, 2016).
6 Anecdotal evidence from my research participants, and from Yoxall, suggests that in some cases children do not survive on returning to a state orphanage following surgery: James Wolf Yoxall, "Disparities Among the Orphans of China," *Southeast Review of Asian Studies* 29 (2007), 252.
7 For discussion of the issue of "ageing out" *gu'er*, see Chapter 6 at 139–140.
8 Wang, *Outsourced Children*, 19. See also Carsten Vala, "The State-Religion Relationship in Contemporary China: Corporatism with Hegemony," in *The Chinese Corporatist State: Adaptation, Survival and Resistance*, eds. Jennifer Hsu and Reza Hasmath (London: Routledge, 2012).
9 Wang, *Outsourced Children*, 99.
10 Wang, *Outsourced Children*, 89.
11 Wang, *Outsourced Children*, 78.
12 Tam and Hasmath's study of religious NGOs in modern China similarly found that most preferred to employ ethnic Chinese over Westerners, not only for pragmatic reasons such as language but also because "ethnic-Chinese-operated [religious NGOs] are perceived (whether correctly or not) to be trustworthy given their ethno-cultural affinity": Jonathan Tam and Reza Hasmath, "Navigating Uncertainty: The Survival Strategies of Religious NGOs in China," *Journal of Civil Society* 11, no. 3 (2015), 291.
13 Angela Ki Che Leung, "Relief Institutions for Children in Nineteenth-Century China," in *Chinese Views of Childhood*, ed. Anne Behnke Kinney (Honolulu: University of Hawai'i Press, 1995), 256–57; Paul A. Cohen, *China and Christianity: The Missionary*

Movement and the Growth of Chinese Antiforeignism, 1860–1870 (Cambridge: Harvard University Press, 1963), 78, 231.

14 Leung, "Relief Institutions for Children in Nineteenth-Century China," 256.

15 Xiaoyuan Shang, "Moving Towards a Multi-Level, Multi-Pillar System: Institutional Care in Two Chinese Cities," *Journal of Social Policy* 30 (2001), 262.

16 Hsia and White, "Working amid Corporatism and Confusion," 2002; Han Junkui, "International NGOs in China: Current Situation, Impacts and Response of the Chinese Government" in *NGOs in China and Europe*, ed. Yuwen Li (Farnham: Ashgate, 2011); Qiusha Ma, *Non-Governmental Organisations in Contemporary China: Paving the Way to Civil Society?* (London: Routledge, 2005), chapter 6.

17 Jeanne Wilson, "Coloured Revolutions: The View from Moscow and Beijing," *Journal of Communist Studies and Transition Politics* 25, no. 2–3 (2009).

18 Hsia and White, "Working amid Corporatism and Confusion," 336.

19 This is generally a less researched topic in China. Hsia and White reported in 2002 that there were around two hundred international NGOs in China but noted that this estimate did not include "small, Christian missionary groups that engage in small development and social service projects" (Hsia and White, "Working amid Corporatism and Confusion," 335n6).

20 Pseudonyms have been used to refer to these locations, to preserve anonymity.

21 Ministry of Civil Affairs, *Social Welfare Institutions Interim Measures* [*Shehui fuli jigou guanli zhanxiang banfa*], 30 December 1999. Available at www.mca.gov.cn/article/fw/bmzn/shfl/flfg/201804/20180400008415.shtml (retrieved 3 September 2018).

22 For a useful outline of the place and importance of the concept of *mianzi* (face) in Chinese culture, see Hsien Chin Hu, "The Chinese Concepts of 'Face,'" *American Anthropologist* 46, no. 1 (1944), 45.

23 Most of the foster homes were involved in the movement of children across provincial borders, from poorer provinces to more developed areas in close proximity to the country's best hospitals, meaning that such support would technically need to come from a central-level agency such as the Ministry of Civil Affairs, making securing a mother-in-law even more challenging. China's NGO rules provide that the region in which an NGO is permitted to carry out activities is determined and limited by the administrative level at which it is established—in other words, nationally active NGOs must be supervised by a central body. This is known as the rule against branching out. See, generally, Jillian S. Ashley and Pengyu He, "Opening One Eye and Closing the Other: The Legal and Regulatory Environment for 'Grassroots' NGOs in China Today," *Boston University International Law Journal* 26, no. 1 (Fall 2008).

24 As discussed in Chapter 5 at 125, until 2017 there were no laws providing for the recognition of foreign NGOs in China, other than as funds-disbursing "foundations" (*jijinhui*), a status that was in practice only available to a small number of politically powerful organisations such as the Ford and Gates Foundations. One unusual exception was New Grace Foster Home, which managed to register under the Foundation Regulation in 2011 due to the indirect influence of a high-level international diplomat, and only after many years of lobbying contacts in the Ministry of Civil Affairs.

25 Ministry of Civil Affairs, *Banning of Illegal NGOs Interim Measures* [*Qudi feifa minjian zuzhi zanxing banfa*], 10 April 2000. Available at www.lawinfochina.com/display.aspx?lib=law&id=4667&CGid= (retrieved 29 March 2019).

26 Guosheng Deng, "The Hidden Rules of Governing China's Unregistered NGOs: Management and Consequences," *The China Review* 10, no. 1 (2010), 192; Tina Qian and Nick Young, "Rule on Names Starts to Close Door to NGO 'Businesses,'" *China Development Brief* (15 April 2005) (on file with author).

27 Keyser, "The Role of the State and NGOs in Caring for At-Risk Children," 53.

28 Ashley and He, "Opening One Eye and Closing the Other," 83. See also Deng, "The Hidden Rules of Governing China's Unregistered NGOs," 59.

29 Government-organised NGOs, also known as "officially organised NGOs" as compared to "popular NGOs" or "top-down NGOs" as compared to "bottom-up NGOs", are "citizen-led efforts from organisations that are nominally independent but in fact are often established by and retain close ties with the state": Ashley and He, "Opening One Eye and Closing the Other," 32.

30 Anthony J. Spires, "Contingent Symbiosis and Civil Society in an Authoritarian State: Understanding the Survival of China's Grassroots NGOs," *American Journal of Sociology* 117, no. 1 (July 2011), 14.

31 Interview with Child Welfare Institution director, Shandong province, 21 September 2009 (on file with author).

32 As discussed below, the general confidence levels of private foster homes had changed by 2017, following the Lankao fire and enactment of the Foreign NGO Law: see Chapter 5 at 124–6.

33 See Chapter 2 at 42n106.

34 For a recent discussion of the reasons behind local government reluctance to shift away from institutional care and towards community-based care, see Karen R. Fisher, Xiaoyuan Shang, and Megan Blaxland, "Disability and Welfare Services," in *Handbook of Welfare in China*, eds. Beatriz Carrillo, Johanna Hood, and Paul Kadetz (Cheltenham: Edward Elgar, 2017), 255.

35 Yuwen Li, "Introduction: Challenges and Opportunities for NGOs in Different Parts of the World," in *NGOs in China and Europe: Comparisons and Contrasts: Comparisons and Contrasts*, ed. Yuwen Li (Farnham: Ashgate, 2011), 2.

36 Hsia and White, "Working amid Corporatism and Confusion," 338.

37 Deng, "The Hidden Rules of Governing China's Unregistered NGOs," 190–91.

38 Deng, "The Hidden Rules of Governing China's Unregistered NGOs," 191; Hsia and White, "Working amid Corporatism and Confusion," 340; Spires, "Contingent Symbiosis," 14 (noting that "understanding and support [for unregistered NGOs] come from individuals within the government, not "the government" more generally"). Hsu and Jiang similarly point out that "NGOs do not have relationships with 'the state' because there is no such thing as 'the state' in China. Instead, the Party-State is polymorphous, with fissures between the central and local governments, and competing agendas between different localities, departments and individual officials. Chinese NGOs build ties with particular state actors": Carolyn L. Hsu and Yuzhou Jiang, "An Institutional Approach to Chinese NGOs: State Alliance versus State Avoidance Resource Strategies," *The China Quarterly* (March 2015), 104.

39 Vala's research has similarly showed how local Chinese governments are open to religious NGOs, given the free, high-quality services they provide and that religious NGOs in China tend to focus more on humanitarian work than on evangelism: Vala, "The State-Religion Relationship in Contemporary China: Corporatism with Hegemony," 2012.

40 Bingzhong Gao, "The Question of Legitimacy of Social Organizations," *China Social Sciences* 2 (2000), translated in Junkui Han, "International NGOs in China: Current Situation, Impacts and Response of the Chinese Government," in *NGOs in China and Europe*, ed. Yuwen Li (Farnham: Ashgate, 2011), 35.

41 Deng, "The Hidden Rules of Governing China's Unregistered NGOs," 191.

42 Tam and Hasmath, "Navigating Uncertainty," 291.

43 Spires, "Contingent Symbiosis," 20.

44 See, generally, Spires, "Contingent Symbiosis," 20–21 (noting that successful NGO-government relations largely depend on "how or whether the particular government officials or agencies concerned are able to claim political credit for any good works the NGO performs in their jurisdictions. Conversely, officials are also concerned about any negative news that NGOs might expose about government performance failures").

45 Ashley and He, "Opening One Eye and Closing the Other," 83. See also Deng, "The Hidden Rules of Governing China's Unregistered NGOs," 198.

46 Liu Peifeng, "Development of Charities in China Since the Reform and Opening Up," in *NGOs in China and Europe: Comparisons and Contrasts*, ed. Yuwen Li (Farnham: Ashgate, 2011), 89.
47 Keyser, "The Role of the State and NGOs in Caring for At-Risk Children," 62.

Bibliography

Ashley, Jillian S., and Pengyu He. "Opening One Eye and Closing the Other: The Legal and Regulatory Environment for 'Grassroots' NGOs in China Today." *Boston University International Law Journal* 26, no. 1 (Fall 2008): 29–96.

Cohen, Paul A. *China and Christianity: The Missionary Movement and the Growth of Chinese Antiforeignism, 1860–1870*. Cambridge: Harvard University Press, 1963.

Fisher, Karen R., Xiaoyuan Shang, and Megan Blaxland. "Disability and Welfare Services." In *Handbook of Welfare in China*, edited by Beatriz Carrillo, Johanna Hood, and Paul Kadetz, 252–65. Cheltenham: Edward Elgar, 2017.

Gao, Bingzhong. "The Question of Legitimacy of Social Organizations." *China Social Sciences* 2 (2000). Translated in Junkui Han, "International NGOs in China: Current Situation, Impacts and Response of the Chinese Government." In *NGOs in China and Europe: Comparisons and Contrasts*, edited by Yuwen Li, 23–52. Farnham: Ashgate, 2011.

Han, Junkui. "International NGOs in China: Current Situation, Impacts and Response of the Chinese Government." In *NGOs in China and Europe: Comparisons and Contrasts*, edited by Yuwen Li, 23–52. Farnham: Ashgate, 2011.

High, Anna Jane. "China's Orphan Welfare System: Laws, Policies and Filled Gaps." *University of Pennsylvania East Asia Law Review* 8, no. 2 (2013): 127–76.

High, Anna Jane. "Grassroots NGO Regulation and China's Local Legal Culture." *Socio-Legal Review* 9, no. 2 (2013): 1–50.

High, Anna Jane. "'It's Grace and Favor, It's Not Law': Extra-Legal Regulation of Foreign Foster Homes in China." *University of Pennsylvania Asian Law Review* 12, no. 3 (Spring 2017): 357–405.

Hsia, Renee Yuen-Jan, and Lynn T. White III. "Working amid Corporatism and Confusion: Foreign NGOs in China." *Nonprofit and Voluntary Sector Quarterly* 31, no. 3 (September 2002): 329–51.

Hsu, Carolyn L., and Yuzhou Jiang. "An Institutional Approach to Chinese NGOs: State Alliance versus State Avoidance Resource Strategies." *The China Quarterly* (March 2015): 100–22.

Hu, Hsien Chin. "The Chinese Concepts of 'Face.'" *American Anthropologist* 46, no. 1 (1944): 45–64.

Johnson, Kay Ann. *China's Hidden Children: Abandonment, Adoption, and the Human Costs of the One-Child Policy*. Chicago: University of Chicago Press, 2016.

Johnson, Kay Ann. *Wanting a Daughter, Needing a Son: Abandonment, Adoption, and Orphanage Care in China*. Edited by Amy Klatzkin. St Paul, MN: Yeong & Yeong, 2004.

Keyser, Catherine H. "The Role of the State and NGOs in Caring for At-Risk Children: The Case of Orphan Care." In *State and Society Responses to Social Welfare Needs in China; Serving the People*, edited by Jonathan Schwartz and Shawn Shieh, 45–65. Abingdon: Routledge, 2009.

Leung, Angela Ki Che. "Relief Institutions for Children in Nineteenth-Century China." In

Chinese Views of Childhood, edited by Anne Behnke Kinney, 251–78. Honolulu: University of Hawai'i Press, 1995.

Li, Yuwen. "Introduction: Challenges and Opportunities for NGOs in Different Parts of the World." In *NGOs in China and Europe: Comparisons and Contrasts*, edited by Yuwen Li, 1–20. Farnham: Ashgate, 2011.

Liu, Peifeng. "Development of Charities in China since the Reform and Opening Up." In *NGOs in China and Europe: Comparisons and Contrasts*, edited by Yuwen Li, 71–94. Farnham: Ashgate, 2011.

Ma, Qiusha. *Non-Governmental Organisations in Contemporary China: Paving the Way to Civil Society?* London: Routledge, 2005.

Ministry of Civil Affairs. *Social Welfare Institutions Interim Measures* [*Shehui fuli jigou guanli zhanxiang banfa*], 30 December 1999. Available at www.mca.gov.cn/article/fw/bmzn/shfl/flfg/201804/20180400008415.shtml (retrieved 3 September 2018).

Ministry of Civil Affairs. *Banning of Illegal NGOs Interim Measures* [*Qudi feifa minjian zuzhi zanxing banfa*], 10 April 2000. Available at www.lawinfochina.com/display.aspx?lib=law&id=4667&CGid= (retrieved 29 March 2019).

Qian, Tina, and Nick Young. "Rule on Names Starts to Close Door to NGO 'Businesses.'" *China Development Brief* (15 April 2005) (on file with author).

Shang, Xiaoyuan. "Looking for Best Practice in Caring for Disabled Children: A Case of Socialized Foster Care in China." *Asia Pacific Journal of Social Work and Development* 22, no. 1–2 (March/June 2012): 127–38.

Shang, Xiaoyuan. "Moving Towards a Multi-Level, Multi-Pillar System: Institutional Care in Two Chinese Cities." *Journal of Social Policy* 30, no. 2 (2001): 259–81.

Shang, Xiaoyuan and Karen R. Fisher. *Caring for Orphaned Children in China.* Lanham: Lexington, 2014.

Spires, Anthony J. "Contingent Symbiosis and Civil Society in an Authoritarian State: Understanding the Survival of China's Grassroots NGOs." *American Journal of Sociology* 117, no. 1 (July 2011): 1–45.

Tam, Jonathan, and Reza Hasmath. "Navigating Uncertainty: The Survival Strategies of Religious NGOs in China." *Journal of Civil Society* 11, no. 3 (2015): 283–99.

Vala, Carsten. "The State-Religion Relationship in Contemporary China: Corporatism with Hegemony." In *The Chinese Corporatist State: Adaptation, Survival and Resistance*, edited by Jennifer Hsu and Reza Hasmath, 102–19. London: Routledge, 2012.

Wang, Leslie K. *Outsourced Children: Orphanage Care and Adoption in Globalizing China.* Stanford: Stanford University Press, 2016.

Wilson, Jeanne. "Coloured Revolutions: The View from Moscow and Beijing." *Journal of Communist Studies and Transition Politics* 25, no. 2–3 (2009): 369–95.

Yoxall, James Wolf. "Disparities Among the Orphans of China." *Southeast Review of Asian Studies* 29 (2007): 248–54.

5 Two eyes opening

The changing landscape of private orphan relief

Early in 2013, word spread among China's private orphanages and foster homes that a recent fire at an "illegal" orphanage in Lankao, Henan province might have ripple effects for private *gu'er* care providers. Mallory Williams, the American manager of Beijing-based foster home Sharon's Rose, decided not to take any chances. Her foster home specialised in congenital heart disease, caring for up to a dozen children at a time from state orphanages across China. At the time of the fire, her team of dedicated *ayis* had multiple Henan *gu'er* in their care, each with serious heart conditions. When Mallory heard word of the Henan fire, she was worried—previous experience had taught her that such high-profile events could make state orphanage directors wary of continuing unorthodox foster care arrangements, such as cooperating with distant, foreign-run foster homes like Sharon's Rose. But sending her *gu'er* back to their home orphanages in Henan, far away from their Beijing medical teams and the only caregivers they had ever known, was something she intended to avoid at all costs. Mallory rang the local Beijing hospital that had treated the Henan *gu'er*, explained her concerns to the hospital's chief cardiac surgeon, a long-time ally and supporter of Sharon's Rose, and requested that the children be readmitted to hospital that day as a precaution. In the days that followed, as three different Henan orphanages phoned to request that their fostered *gu'er* be immediately returned to Henan, Mallory was able to hold them off by telling them that the children in question were in hospital. She then had the surgeon send an official response on hospital letterhead: the babies were too ill to leave Beijing, due to recent heart surgery and their need for ongoing specialist care. In the end, Sharon's Rose Foster Home was able to keep its Henan *gu'er*, some for up to a year after the fire, until their adoptions were finalised and they left for "forever families" in America.

Four years to the month later, another event rocked China's welfare sector, when a journalist reported on a large number of unexplained deaths at a for-profit, all-ages welfare centre in Guangdong province. Again, the ripple effects of the scandal were felt across China, as various state orphanages in Guangdong decided to cancel foster care arrangements with foster homes across the country. Despite her best efforts, Mallory had to send four Guangdong *gu'er* back to their home orphanages.

By the time of my final fieldwork in mid-2017, the situation of China's private *gu'er* welfare providers had dramatically changed since a decade earlier. The Lankao fire and the Guangdong care home incident were two watershed moments for China child welfare policy. And two new key pieces of legislation had also recently passed—the 2016 Charity Law [*Cishan Fa*] and the 2017 Law on the Management of Foreign NGOs [*Jingwai Fei Zhengfu Zuzhi Jingnei Huodong Guanli Fa*]. This chapter discusses this series of developments, which collectively led to significant changes in the social, political, and legal landscape for private *gu'er* caregivers, and the effects of which are still unfolding today.

The Lankao fire

On a frigid winter morning in January 2013, a fire broke out at a residential apartment building in Lankao county, Henan province, killing seven *gu'er*. The home belonged to Yuan Lihai and was described in media reports as a "private orphan institution" (*minban gu'er suo*), known for taking in abandoned children from the area. At the time, there were eighteen *gu'er* living with Yuan. Most had severe disabilities. On the morning of the fire, Yuan had left to take the older children to school, leaving the babies and preschoolers home with the oldest of the group—this was Yuan Shen, a mentally impaired twenty-year-old with polio. When the fire broke out, neighbours called Yuan Lihai, who rushed home and joined the frantic effort to put out the fire. Only one of the children inside was saved. Yuan Shen died, alongside four boys and two girls under the age of five; the youngest was just seven months old. Yuan Lihai's remaining *gu'er* were taken into state custody. Yuan Lihai was taken in for police questioning but released almost immediately. Grief-stricken, she spoke to a reporter the next day, explaining that "the children were her heart" and that all she had wanted when she took them into her home was to give them a chance at life, a chance they may not have otherwise had as *gu'er* with disabilities.[1]

Yuan Lihai, who was in her late forties, was described in various news reports as "love mother" (*aixin mama*) to the *gu'er* in her care.[2] She had grown up in the area as the second of five children and had only a basic first-grade education. At the age of eight, she began working alongside her grandfather selling tea and soup at a stall by the gates of the Lankao County People's Hospital. She also did occasional odd jobs around the hospital, including arranging for the burials of deceased children for a small fee. In the course of her work, she often encountered parents who were unwilling or unable to care for their child due to the child's disability or illness. In 1989 she took in her first *gu'er*, a baby with a cleft lip who had been left at the hospital. Over time, she gained a reputation at the hospital and in the neighbourhood as someone willing to care for abandoned children with disabilities, and over the next thirty years she took in over one hundred such children. Some of these children grew up into adults capable of living independently, others were informally adopted by local families, and around 30 per cent died in her care. The strain of caring for dozens of children at any one time, with no training, education, or outside funding, was immense, and eventually Yuan Lihai's husband left. She persisted on her own for decades. Her neighbours described her as simple, unaffected, and a good person. Her relatives found it hard to understand why she took in so many children but supported her financially as they could when she most urgently needed help feeding so many hungry mouths.

Money had always been very tight for Yuan Lihai, and conditions at her makeshift orphanage were accordingly very basic (it is worth noting here that in 2013, Lankao was still officially designated a "poverty stricken" county, so the standard of living in the area generally was not high). Her children had slept crowded together in just a few beds and had worn secondhand clothing; post-fire media reports suggested that at least some of the *gu'er* previously in her care had died due to unsanitary conditions at the home. The children at Yuan's home became eligible for the national flat-rate "orphan allowance" (six hundred *yuan*, or about ninety US dollars, per month) when it was introduced in 2011, but because the makeshift orphanage was informal and unregistered, and Yuan had not legally adopted her charges, the allowance was not reaching them. Yuan did receive a small "subsistence allowance" of seventy *yuan* per child per month (about ten US dollars), but she relied largely on donations and her meagre street-stall income to provide for the *gu'er* in her care. Yuan had been open in previous media interviews about the high mortality rate at her home, which she attributed to being unable to afford food and health care.[3]

Yuan's "illegal" orphanage made national headlines after the fire, but the home had never been clandestine. Before the tragedy, Yuan's work had been well known and supported by the local community and had on occasion received favourable coverage in the local media.[4] There was no state orphanage in Lankao county, so sometimes foundlings had been brought to Yuan's home by the Lankao police themselves. The Lankao Civil Affairs Bureau (CAB) had publicly praised her as a loving and compassionate "love mother", despite the shortcomings and limitations of her care, of which they were apparently aware.[5] Yuan had previously been caring for her *gu'er* at a different location. About five years before the fire, that site was deemed unsafe by the CAB and shut down. Of the thirty-three *gu'er* in Yuan's care at the time, the CAB relocated around a dozen to state facilities in neighbouring counties but allowed the majority to continue living with Yuan, in part because of their emotional connection to her after years of calling her "mama" and in part because of the difficulty of finding orphanage placements.[6] The CAB also promised at the time that measures would be taken to protect the *gu'er* being raised by Yuan and to improve their quality of life, although it does not appear that any supervision or additional financial support was subsequently put in place.[7] Rather, the CAB adopted the legitimacy-focused "one eye open, one eye closed" approach that was so common when it came to private orphanages and foster homes across China. As the CAB admitted after the fire, its officials had been aware that Yuan was effectively running a private but unregistered and probably unlawful orphanage; they also admitted that she would not have qualified to legally adopt the children in her care and had not applied to do so. But being satisfied that her motives were genuine, they had chosen to take an attitude of acquiescence towards her work, which they described as a laudable act of "life-giving social responsibility".[8] As a trusted and legitimate "love mother", Yuan had been given a great deal of leeway in practice, despite her open noncompliance with law. Like the other care providers described in this book, her work was not legally authorised—reports later described her as a doer of "illegal good deeds" (*feifa xingshan*)[9] and a provider of "illegal love" (*weifa aixin*)[10]—but had never been forbidden in practice.

"Encourage love, strengthen supervision": repercussions of Lankao for "illegal love"

Two decades before the Lankao fire, China's state orphanages had been rocked by the "dying rooms" scandal. The Lankao fire had a similarly galvanising impact on China's private orphanage sector, at least in the immediate aftermath. At the local level, multiple Lankao officials were investigated and suspended for their failure to supervise Yuan's orphanage. County leaders acknowledged that the Lankao CAB had not fulfilled its responsibility to protect local *gu'er* and should have addressed regulatory loopholes and supervision gaps in Lankao orphan welfare. Beijing also rebuked Lankao county, issuing a stern clarification that *gu'er* are the responsibility of Civil Affairs, to be cared for in state orphanages or adopted into suitable families through the proper Civil Affairs channels.[11] This top-level criticism was accompanied by a wave of public concern for *gu'er* outside the state welfare system, with various newspaper editorials questioning why vulnerable children were being cared for in an unregulated private sector, without proper supervision by responsible government agencies. Importantly, there was also widespread acknowledgement of the importance of private charity as a supplement to overstretched government resources and a sense that the state should be tolerant of and indeed encourage citizen-led efforts to provide grassroots welfare services—as one editorial argued, "as a developing country, China needs to rely on the strength of society as a whole to care for vulnerable groups".[12] But the government was widely criticised for not providing enough supervision and financial support to professionalise those services. A *People's Daily* editorial warned that the seven deaths were only a small glimpse of a "neglected and obscured landscape" and should be treated as

> a reflection of the pain of China's grassroots charities. No matter the cause of the fire, Yuan was the children's de facto guardian, and did not fulfil her responsibilities. But we cannot put all responsibility for the deaths on Yuan. Without her, the fate of these children may have been even more bleak. Although China is a civilised society, when it comes to the care of abandoned babies, the response is still ad hoc, dependent on "good people" [*shanren*] and "benevolent hearts" [*shanxin*]. We provide our children with the necessities of life, but a happy and safe environment is still so often an unattained dream. … The improvement and professionalisation of private charity [*minban cishan*] is an urgent problem.[13]

The urgency of this problem was not news to my research participants or to researchers who were already familiar with the unregulated *gu'er* welfare sector. The Lankao fire was the realisation of a worst-case scenario, demonstrating the dangers of the state's ambivalent, "one eye closed" approach to unauthorised orphanages. As the fire brought national and international attention to the problem, the central government was forced to respond and to do so both quickly and humanely.

In light of the sheer scale of the problem, and the outpouring of support for Yuan Lihai as "love mother", it was not practically or politically feasible to respond by simply shutting down other private orphanages, reinstitutionalising thousands of children, and shoring up the state's ostensible orphanage monopoly. Rather than imposing a knee-jerk blanket ban, the central Ministry of Civil Affairs (MCA), in a formal Notice issued just two days after the fire, announced a national investigation into private *gu'er* institutions.[14] Four days after the fire, working groups were dispatched from Beijing to provinces across China to oversee the investigation. Local Civil Affairs bureaus were given one month to identify and evaluate private orphanages in their jurisdictions. These ranged from small home-based "love mothers" like Yuan Lihai to much larger, collective efforts by faith-based groups, such as St Martin's and Guanghui.[15] The Notice indicated that the previous "one eye closed" approach was to be replaced with formal regulation and increased financial support—as one Civil Affairs official remarked at a symposium held during the national inspection, "love should be encouraged and supervision must be strengthened" (*aixin ying guli, jianguan xu jiaqiang*).[16] As the Ministry expressly acknowledged, there were previously no conditions, rules, or safety measures in place for *gu'er* in private orphanages, and this needed to change.[17] Under the new plan, children in facilities deemed substandard were to be removed to state orphanages. Local Civil Affairs bureaus were also directed to severely crack down on anyone found to be profiting from *gu'er* relief work or treating *gu'er* "illegally". But private orphanages deemed suitable were to be permitted to continue providing care on the condition that they signed a cooperation agreement clarifying their rights and responsibilities, formalised their guardianship of *gu'er*, and were subject, moving forward, to MCA guidelines and ongoing state supervision—in effect, becoming "jointly established" with the Civil Affairs bureaucracy. In sum, the shift to welfare pluralism/privatisation that had been gradually and informally occurring even before the fire became more urgent and expressly sanctioned immediately thereafter.

The fire marked the beginning of a time of uncertainty and upheaval for private orphan caregivers like St Martin's and Guanghui. The response of Guanghui's Sister Yang was to form an alliance of sorts with other private orphanages across China. With the support of two high-profile registered NGOs, representatives from over forty faith-based "folk orphanages" (*minban shouyang jigou*)—run by Catholic, Protestant, Muslim, and Buddhist groups across China—met in October 2013 for a two-day conference. This was partly a defensive move. Sister Yang was aware that private orphanages were more vulnerable than ever to the discretion of local officials. The conference was a way to demonstrate the importance of private *gu'er* services and their commitment to professionalising and improving in line with new state law and policy, rather than in defiance of those rules. The organisers invited representatives from the MCA as well as experts in child welfare from Beijing universities and abroad. Importantly, the seminar speeches included an address by Xu Jianzhong, deputy director of the MCA Social Welfare and Charity Promotion Division, in which Xu affirmed the valuable contributions of private orphanages to *gu'er* relief.[18] He also emphasised the need to maximise child welfare pursuant to government policies and in cooperation with the state and noted the state's intention to systematise, standardise, and professionalise the sector. In response, orphanage representatives at the seminar independently formulated a private orphanage industry standard (*zilü changyishu*, literally "self-discipline proposal"). This included a declaration that private orphanages would voluntarily carry out orphan relief work "in accordance with national laws, regulations, and policies".[19]

For orphanages like Guanghui that had long been eager to partner with the state, the conference was an important step towards feeling acknowledged and appreciated by the state as legitimate and lawful contributors to Chinese child welfare. Even before the fire, Guanghui's relationship with local officials had been trending in this direction. Speaking in 2010, a long-term adviser to Guanghui described to me how he had seen the relationship between the sisters and local Civil Affairs officials evolve in recent years from one of enmity to one of cooperation: "There is more openness and less fear. And there is more freedom from the central government to tackle the problem in a different way, to find a way to cooperate instead of fighting" (*Charles Kramer, adviser to Guanghui, 2010*). This volunteer, like many of my research participants, attributed local officials' long-standing hesitance to formally recognise and support Guanghui to a fear of political reprisal from their higher-ups. But after Lankao, this became less of a factor, as recognition and support of private orphanages was for the first time expressly sanctioned by the highest levels of administration; importantly, in a follow-up 2014 Notice jointly issued by the MCA and Religious Affairs Bureau, China clarified that this in-principle approval extended to faith-based orphanages as permissible and legitimate *gu'er* care providers.[20]

In Guanghui's case, these policy developments translated to substantive changes. The orphanage passed its initial inspection and was one of the first to sign a foster care agreement with its local Civil Affairs bureau in accordance with the MCA Notice. The orphanage became subject to annual inspections by Civil Affairs but was able to maintain a large degree of independence, including as to its Catholic roots and identity. The children who were living at Guanghui in 2013 were permitted to stay—Sister Yang says this was in part because the government appreciated the emotional harm that removing them from their lifelong home would entail—but became "in the system", registered *gu'er*, benefiting from state programmes and eligible for formal adoption. The state became their legal guardian and Guanghui a legally recognised provider of foster care services. Speaking in 2017, Sister Yang said that her relationship with local officials had only continued to improve since the fire, to the point where they could joke together about the "quarrels" they had back in the 2000s, when Sister Yang was constantly knocking on doors to ask for recognition and support. The Guanghui children were finally subsidised by the state orphan allowance, which in 2017 was set at seven hundred *yuan* per month in their part of China.[21] Sister Yang attributed all of these developments to the fire, which was both a tragedy and an important catalyst for change. She felt that Guanghui had finally been acknowledged by the state, after decades of waiting. She was also understanding of why the wait took so long:

> I live by faith. Believing in God's providence requires patience. Governments change, change takes time, and we needed to wait patiently and be strong.... Policy [in China] often tends to lag behind social problems. So, we knew we had to wait but also to advocate for our children to the government in the meantime.

It is difficult to know to what extent Guanghui's positive experience post-Lankao is representative of the sector generally. Certainly, anecdotally there were many reports of private orphanages being shut down following the fire, and Professor Shang has expressed concern that in some instances, local governments may have chosen to reinstitutionalise *gu'er* not for safety reasons, but in order to "avoid public scrutiny of [unorthodox] foster care arrangements".[22] It is also likely that in some cases, private orphanages were disbanded for good reasons, such as legitimate concerns about care standards and practices. Although the removal of children from their lifelong homes should not be taken lightly, the Lankao fire had demonstrated that greater oversight and regulation of the sector were overdue, even if in some cases this might require disruptive actions. Other orphanages, including St Martin's, did not notice a substantive difference pre- and post-Lankao. Although various policies, standards, and notices relating to private orphanages followed from the initial 2013 Notice described above, the enforcement of these inevitably varied greatly from place to place, depending on the capacity and zeal of local officials. So, for example, while Guanghui became subject to annual inspections, St Martin's was visited just once soon after the fire, checked for electrical hazards and fire extinguishers, and largely left alone thereafter. As of 2017, the orphanage had not signed an official foster care agreement with its local Civil Affairs bureau, and its *gu'er* were still not receiving the national orphan allowance.[23] Whether this was due to St Martin's not being up to the standard required for formal Civil Affairs recognition, apathy and ambivalence on the part of local officials, or other reasons was unclear to me, and Sister Chen was extremely guarded when I probed on this point. What was clear was that the orphanage continued in a legal grey zone, tolerated but not formally recognised, not permitted but not forbidden. Sister Chen described her relationship with local officials as unchanged and "so so" (*yibanban*) and continued to rely on God's provision rather than state support: "If God is willing, then whether they support me or not, it's fine—this work will continue either way" (*Sister Chen, St Martin's, 2017*).

One of the biggest changes following the Lankao fire was a serious attempt to stop individuals and private orphanages from directly accepting abandoned children without first notifying, and receiving permission from, the state. A formal Notice banning the practice was issued in May of 2013.[24] If this rule is successfully enforced, then moving forward, abandoned *gu'er* should no longer end up being cared for by unregistered orphanages or "love mothers" but would instead be registered in the state system, issued a *hukou*, and sent to await adoption in a state-run or state-supervised facility or foster home. The extent to which the policy will be enforced in practice, particularly in more remote parts of China, remains to be seen. The very different experiences of St Martin's and Guanghui, in terms of their interactions with local Civil Affairs officials after the Lankao fire, was testament to the ongoing localised nature of state oversight (or otherwise) of private orphanages.

Cross-country foster care: upheaval and uncertainty

The Lankao fire brought all non-state *gu'er* caregivers into the spotlight. The ripple effects of the fire were felt not only by private orphanages like Guanghui caring for "outside the system" *gu'er* but also by the foster homes caring for *gu'er* from state orphanages, albeit less immediately. The call from Beijing for local Civil Affairs officials to pay closer attention to the welfare of *gu'er* in their jurisdictions apparently caused concern in some locations about the sheer numbers of children who had been fostered out of state orphanages, often for years at a time and to organisations located outside of the province and usually without ongoing supervision. As discussed in Chapter 4, such arrangements had typically not been formally authorised by Civil Affairs but were established instead on the basis of built-up trust with individual orphanage directors.[25] Some foster homes in Henan province were immediately asked to disband and return their children to their home state orphanages.[26] Foster homes outside of Henan, such as Sharon's Rose, soon came under pressure to return any Henan children to their home orphanages; this took the form of phone calls from state orphanage directors, most likely acting under instructions or pressure from their supervising Civil Affairs department. Some other provinces soon followed suit.

Years later, most of my foster home research participants could still vividly relate heartbreaking stories of having to send multiple babies and children back to Henan orphanages in the weeks and months after the Lankao fire. St Matthew's, an American-run home caring for boys who had aged off the adoption waiting list, had to take two teenagers back to their home orphanage in Zhengzhou, Henan, a place the boys had not seen for over a decade. The older of the two was able to move back a year later, when he turned eighteen, to attend a vocational school, and resumed living at St Matthew's on the weekends. One of the St Matthew's founders had tried to visit the younger boy a few times, but the visits had not gone well: "I've gone to visit, and he's not friendly to me at all … I think they [orphanage staff] told him we didn't want him" (*Bob, St Matthew's founder/director, 2017*).

One foster home in my sample was not immediately affected by the fire, despite caring for many children from Henan province. At the time of the fire, New Grace Foster Home was legally approved as a *gu'er* welfare provider. The organisation had unexpectedly received registration under the Foundation Regulation (*Jijinhui Guanli Tiaoli*) in 2011, after coming to the attention of a senior international diplomat (before 2011, the foster home, like so many others, was a commercially registered organisation, licensed to carry out "market research relating to orphanage and rest home equipment"). Its supervising unit was the central Ministry of Civil Affairs, the same agency with ultimate responsibility for China's system of child welfare and orphanages. The timing of New Grace's registration was fortunate. After the fire, none of New Grace's children were "recalled" because as a centrally registered NGO, the foster home had clear, formal authorisation to work at the national level, across provincial borders.[27] As founder and director David Dale explained in 2017,

> the advantage for us [of registration] is when things happen in China, the orphanages that work with us and send us babies know that we are registered properly with Civil Affairs. And so that gave us a level of credibility in the orphanages because they see that we are part of the same *danwei* [unit]. We're all under [the authority of] the same organisation.... The orphanage directors in a lot of other cases have been hesitant in giving babies to people because they're not registered. And so that's really allowed us to carry on through some of the problems—when they've had fires and things have happened which have caused a lot of kneejerk reactions with other orphanages. I don't think we've ever had problems because we are seen as an official organisation.

New Grace was in a minority of one in my sample. Most other foster homes had to send their Henan children "home" or move them to a registered care provider such as New Grace. But some were able to negotiate, as they had during previous periods of uncertainty. As described above, Sharon's Rose was able to avoid reinstitutionalising their Henan *gu'er* by preemptively checking them into hospital and enlisting a respected cardiac surgeon to plead their case. Still Waters, the Chinese-run foster home in Hebei that specialised in cerebral palsy, was also successful in holding onto their Henan *gu'er* (although they did lose three children to Inner Mongolia, which had followed Henan's suit in calling all of its fostered children back to the province). Still Waters initially came under pressure not only from Henan officials but also from their local Hebei-province Civil Affairs bureau, which asked them to submit a list of all their resident children and their home provinces. A short time later, the director of a Hebei state orphanage arrived, planning to remove the Hebei *gu'er* from Still Waters' care. However, he was soon convinced that the therapy programmes and facilities at the foster home were far superior to those available at any Hebei state orphanage and that it would not be in the children's best interests to move them. At his insistence, the Hebei children were allowed to remain at Still Waters. The foster home's leaders were likewise able to convince Henan officials that the Henan children should stay at Still Waters, a place that they had called home for most of their short lives: "We argued with them—the kids are not like furniture, you can move it here, send it back—they are humans. They have relationships. They already regard Still Waters as their home, they grew up here, some for ten years or more. It would be like a second abandonment to take them away" (*Grace, Chinese manager of Still Waters, 2017*). Other foster homes reported sending children back to Henan, only to receive more Henan *gu'er* to care for in subsequent years, after the initial hubbub of the fire had died down. In some cases, state orphanage directors evidently felt that sending children to specialist homes, even unregistered organisations in other provinces, was still a risk worth taking. As Mallory explained, "The orphanages are doing the best they can, and I've found some will break rules or do things under the radar because they know it's the only chance for these babies" (*Mallory Williams, American manager of Sharon's Rose Foster Home, 2017*).

At the time of my most recent trip to China, the memories of Lankao were fading, but another period of flux and negotiation was underway, this time due to a scandal in Guangdong province that had recently made national news. Guangdong officials had become nervous about foster care following a Beijing News exposé on a series of unexplained deaths—twenty within the first fifty days of 2017—at a private "care centre" (*tuoyang zhongxin*) in Shaoguan city, Xinfeng county.[28] The facility in question provided residential care for "vagrants and beggars". It was run by Lianxi Care Centre, a registered NGO founded by former state welfare employee Madam Luo. The investigation was sparked by the death of Lei Wenfeng, a fifteen-year-old autistic boy. According to Wenfeng's father, the teenager entered Lianxi's Shaoguan facility in late 2016 in good health and died weeks later from typhoid fever. Subsequently, a reporter from Beijing News discovered an alarmingly high mortality rate across all five of Lianxi's Guangdong facilities. These were collectively home to over seven hundred people, including foundlings, children with disabilities, and elderly. According to the report, residents in Shaoguan were living in appalling, prison-like conditions behind iron gates (the facility in question had formerly been a police detention centre); some were packed by the dozen into concrete rooms the size of a parking space, meaning pneumonia and other diseases were quick to spread. One employee told reporters that people would arrive in basically good health but quickly get sick due to poor sanitation in the centre. Children lived in a separate wing of the facility, in similarly poor conditions and with insufficient staff. According to a nurse in the children's unit, many of the children had severe disabilities like cerebral palsy and would routinely be tied up with ropes to keep them out of the way of the overstretched staff.

The Beijing News story was published on the twentieth day of March 2017. Within days, the responsible NGO was disbanded and its five facilities shut down, leaving authorities scrambling to find alternative housing for over seven hundred children and adults. One week later, the Ministry of Civil Affairs directed all local Civil Affairs bureaus across China to strengthen their oversight of welfare facilities and immediately terminate contracts with any found to be substandard. On the same day, Guangdong province announced that various city and county Party officials had been stood down and were facing disciplinary procedures for failure to supervise, and illegally profiting from, the centre; staff at the centre, including Madam Luo, were put under criminal investigation.[29] The Guangdong incident had once again highlighted the vulnerability of state officials who were found to have taken a "one eye open, one eye closed" approach to welfare pluralism, and most Guangdong state orphanage directors recalled children from foster homes in other provinces in direct response. Multiple foster homes in Guangdong were forced to close, and unregistered foster homes in other provinces with Guangdong *gu'er* once again came under increased pressure, to the point where some had to temporarily shut down. Unknown numbers of children were affected, including *gu'er* from more than half a dozen of the homes in my sample.

The months that followed the Lankao fire were a time of upheaval for foster homes, with those that did not have any NGO status most vulnerable and needing to negotiate day by day with their partner orphanages across China. But as the Guangdong incident showed, and as my research participants had noted even years before Lankao, seasons of upheaval, and sporadic restrictions on the movement of *gu'er*, were simply a fact of life for foster homes. The Henan and Guangdong "recalls" were unique only in that they were province-wide reversals, and therefore affected a very large number of foster homes and all at the same time. Foster homes had always been entirely dependent on the willingness of orphanage directors to foster their charges into the specialist homes and the willingness of local officials in a foster home's location to allow de facto orphanages to sprout up and continue. All of these relationships could be implicated in times of heightened activity around the issue of *gu'er* welfare—the lead-up to the Beijing Olympics, the Blue Sky Plan promulgation, the Lankao fire, and so on. Most of the larger foster homes could give examples of a state official in their town or county "getting nervous and causing trouble" or exerting pressure to move, disband, or return children. In this respect, the Lankao and Guangdong reversals were neither shocking nor unprecedented. As one of my research participants had noted in 2010: "The kids are not ours. At any moment, they can take the kids back, and they have done in the past" (*Eleanor Anders, foster home founder, 2009*).

"Living under question marks": new foreign NGO rules

When I visited China in the summer of 2017, a few months after the Guangdong incident, some of my research participants, who had welcomed me to stay at or visit their foster homes in 2009 and 2010, were no longer willing to meet in person. There was a stronger feeling of uncertainty in the air, for two reasons. First, there were rumours that in light of Lankao and Guangdong, the central government was planning to ban the interprovincial movement of *gu'er*, a move that could have drastic consequences for foster homes providing specialist care on a national scale (I return to this rumoured ban below). There had also been two recent and significant legislative developments—the enactment of the Foreign NGO Management Law (FNGO Law),[30] which came shortly after the passing of a long-awaited Charity Law.[31] During my conversations with foster homes about these new laws, I was often reminded of what was turning out to be a very prescient comment, made by a Shanghai-based foster home manager almost a decade earlier during my first block of fieldwork:

> Most of what we've accomplished could never have been done in our home country [USA]. And ten years from now, it may be impossible, because the government is just beginning to understand its responsibility to control NGOs.
>
> *(Vera, founder of Loving Embrace Foundation, 2009)*

In 2017, increased control of foreign-affiliated NGOs was the newest hurdle facing foster homes. Previously, there were no regulations allowing foreign NGOs to register in China, other than as a foreign funds–disbursing "foundation" (*jijinhui*) (approval for this was rarely granted in practice; as discussed above, New Grace Foster Home was an interesting exception).[32] In this respect, the new law represented an important clarification: foreign NGOs were permitted to operate in China but only if registered. The law required overseas NGOs that were active in China to be approved by the Ministry of Public Security, China's principal police and security authority, a department with a reputation for being "deeply suspicious" of non-profits.[33] It also gave the police broad search, seizure, and detention powers over any organisations receiving foreign funding. Given that all of the foster homes, and many of the private orphanages, interviewed for this study were dependent on donations channelled through foreign charities, the law appeared to formalise police oversight of private *gu'er* welfare, at least on paper.

New Grace Foster Home, as the only registered foreign NGO in my sample, was automatically reregistered with the Ministry of Public Security when the legislation took effect. When we spoke in 2017, founder David was not concerned about the new system of police oversight for foreign organisations because he felt it did not represent a significant change in practice in such an authoritarian context: "They've always had that power [to enter and search the seizures, review financial records]. If they want to do that, they'll do it.... It's one of those things where if you're not doing anything wrong, you don't have anything really to hide" (the same reasoning was used by the Standing Committee of the National People's Congress in its official response to the question of why only foreign, and not domestic, NGOs would be subject to police oversight).[34] But for the unregistered foreign foster homes, with a less secure status in China, the underlying spirit of the FNGO Law was worrying for two reasons. First, the "not permitted, not forbidden" approach had now been officially replaced: unless foreign NGOs received permission to work in China, they were now expressly banned by the new law. Second, the law's restrictive provisions, combined with the express grant of broad police powers, indicated that winds of deep scepticism and suspicion towards foreign involvement in Chinese civil society were once again blowing from Beijing.[35] In 2017, and like many of my other research participants, Mallory Williams of Sharon's Rose described this as the biggest challenge facing China's foster homes:

> The current political climate concerns me. It feels like at any moment they could say, "Sorry, you're closed. You're done". So that is concerning, in the sense that you feel like you're just living under question marks all the time. We're very respectful of the government, so if they tell us to send the babies back—well obviously we'll do whatever we can to ask permission, but at the end of the day, their rule is their rule, so we would send the babies back.

Localisation strategies

In all, the political climate for NGOs generally, and orphan relief workers specifically, seemed to be shifting more rapidly than usual in 2017. But even prior to the passing of the FNGO Law, many foreign-run foster homes had been pursuing various long-term strategies of localisation—such as transitioning to all-Chinese management and leadership—as a hedge against the uncertainty of working in a legal grey zone, with a view to ensuring their mission of serving *gu'er* could continue in the long term. These strategies were already evident when I first carried out fieldwork in 2009. As unofficial, quasi-legal welfare providers involved with the movement and treatment of large numbers of vulnerable children, foster homes had always been in a fraught position, especially those with foreign or church ties. Foreigners in the field were particularly aware that they could be asked to leave China at any time, were their work to become the subject of state disapprobation. The four largest foreign-run foster homes in my sample all shared a long-term vision of ultimately handing over operations to an entirely Chinese leadership team, in part due to this perceived vulnerability: "Our goal is that if we were kicked out, this could all continue. You have to hold everything lightly. Things change. You always keep in the back of your mind that we very well one day may not be here" (*Gail, founder/director of Mustard Seed Creations foster home, 2010*). Most of the foster homes were already employing mostly Chinese personnel at the highest management levels even prior to 2017. With the passing of the FNGO Law, there was an added sense of urgency to localise, and efforts to transition key leadership roles to local Chinese staff members had stepped up at many of the homes: "The FNGO Law really does restrict how much foreign NGOs can do now. So maybe this is God accelerating the process. It's caused me and other foreign staff to take a step back and not be so much in the forefront of everything" (*Robert Gilbertson, founder/director of Prince of Peace Village, 2017*). This type of "localisation" was also being embraced for ideological reasons: "It's the way missions are going, I think—looking for ministry to your own people. I think it's more effective" (*Cliff, volunteer coordinator for Prince of Peace Village, 2010*). Most of my

Western research participants spoke of seeing, over the course of their years in China, a growing sense of enthusiasm for charitable work, especially among young Chinese, and felt that it was appropriate for local missions such as foster homes to be directed by locals, as far as possible.

Localisation of donor base

In addition to transitioning to local leadership, most of the foster homes in my sample were also actively trying to increase their local donor base, where historically the lion's share of funding had been coming from overseas. Again, this strategy was both for pragmatic and ideological reasons. The FNGO Law had made it clear that organisations dependent on foreign funding could be subject, moving forward, to heightened state scrutiny as compared to local charities, so localisation was seen as a hedge against state interference. But even before the FNGO Law passed, there had been a general sense among my research participants that it was increasingly possible and appropriate for the main needs of China's vulnerable children to be met by Chinese donors, given the country's level of development and the rise of China's new middle class. In fact, this would seem to be a general sentiment underlying the FNGO Law, with its differential treatment of foreign charities as compared to domestic charities.[36] The latter are governed instead by China's Charity Law, which came into effect in September 2016. The Charity Law brought domestic charities under the jurisdiction not of the police but of the Ministry of Civil Affairs and was generally far less restrictive of domestic charities as compared to foreign NGOs. The Charity Law was cautiously welcomed by civil society scholars, not least because it expressly set out the government's "encouragement and support" for charitable activities, at least those that "represent the core values of socialism and promote the traditional morals of the Chinese nation".[37] Foreign-funded organisations, on the other hand, seemed to be viewed as presumptively problematic, subject to far more restrictions, police oversight, and higher hurdles to registration.

These two important pieces of legislation worked in tandem to incentivise organisations that had historically been foreign-funded to step up their efforts to increase their local donor bases. Historically, the bulk of funding for foreign foster homes in China had come from foreign sources, primarily churches and religious adoption advocacy groups in America. But with the Charity Law, the Chinese government appeared to be actively encouraging the emergence of an indigenous nonprofit sector, funded by private donors. There are various indications that this will be a successful effort. Apart from the Charity Law, other policy papers have similarly signalled the state is in favour of improved domestic philanthropy.[38] And researchers have noted that, since the Sichuan earthquake of 2008, Chinese society seems to have become more open to the concept of charitable giving outside of personal networks, with enthusiasm particularly strong among younger Chinese in their twenties and thirties—all of which bodes well for groups in China wishing to transition to a locally funded model.

Localisation of projects

Another common localisation strategy among the foreign foster homes was to pivot towards closer collaboration and partnership with recognised Chinese organisations. For example, many had set up, in addition to their main foster home site, targeted on-site partnerships with state orphanages. These projects were seen as less risky for orphanage directors in that they did not require children to be moved off-site, much less cross-country, and so could be more easily supervised. One of the foster homes I visited in 2017, Bethany Outreach, was planning to shortly close its Beijing unit in favour of focusing on one such on-site partnership. Their story is instructive—the home had found orphanage directors increasingly resistant to cross-country care arrangements in recent years, which had precipitated the transition to a targeted, on-site care model.

The Bethany Outreach foster home was established in 2003 by Jennifer Chan, a Chinese American Christian, after she heard about the work of Prince of Peace Village at a church for expatriates in Beijing. From the beginning, Jennifer's vision was that the home would be "Chinese, not foreign"—although she provided the funding, the home was managed by Lijing, a talented and humble Chinese woman who had previously volunteered at Prince of Peace. In total, Bethany Outreach had cared for over 130 children, whose photographs covered the walls in the home's living room. At the time of my visit, Bethany Outreach was caring for nine children. Their capacity was for twelve—Jennifer and Lijing had intentionally kept their home small, in part because the home was not registered and they did not want to attract too much attention in their high-density urban neighbourhood—but three children had recently been sent back to Guangdong after the care-centre scandal. On the day of my visit, Lijing had just been instructed by another state orphanage director to send four children back and was trying to negotiate for them to stay on until their impending adoptions.

In light of these types of challenges, Lijing and Jennifer had recently decided that it was time to pivot to a more stable care-delivery model. This had also been prompted in part by their experience returning children to a Guangdong state orphanage earlier that year—the women described feeling heartbroken to see rooms full of children being cared for by only one or two untrained nannies: "the situation was quite desperate". They spoke to the orphanage director and offered to provide on-the-ground assistance to the orphanage in the form of funding, training, and management. The director was initially "very resistant and fearful" of the idea but ultimately agreed to the plan. Lijing spoke of how foster homes in China were facing increasing challenges and restrictions and that a major "red flag" for local officials was the movement of children across provincial borders. She hoped to be able to impact a larger number of children by establishing a close partnership with just one willing and open state orphanage. Lijing and Jennifer expected that being "under the umbrella" of a recognised state institution would provide a measure of stability for Bethany Outreach in the face of changing rules and policies on private orphan welfare. At the same time, they assumed that Bethany Outreach could continue without registration, providing donations and services to the orphanage directly rather than running their own separate organisation: "Our desire is to empower them. We want them to have ownership of their orphanage. We want them to succeed" (*Jennifer Chan, founder of Bethany Outreach, 2017*).

Other foster homes had similarly pursued various types of agreements and arrangements with state orphanages, government-organised NGOs (GONGO), or hospitals, as a way of providing some measure of political cover in the face of changing times. As Ma has pointed out, partnering with recognised Chinese organisations is one of the easiest ways for foreign nonprofit groups in China to avoid bureaucratic obstacles of registration.[39] Compassion Family Life House, for example, had signed a memorandum of understanding with a sympathetic GONGO working in the medical field. The GONGO allowed Compassion to use its name to lawfully fundraise in China for the Compassion foster home project, charging an administrative fee of around 5 per cent on all funds raised. This arrangement had been a useful cover when state orphanage directors had called, as they did after both Lankao and Guangdong, to check on the legal status of the Compassion foster home—Compassion's response to the "are you registered" question was "we are a project under a registered GONGO". These types of arrangements allowed foster homes to come under the umbrella of a domestic, state-approved organisation, even though in practice they were independently managed and typically continued to be mostly foreign-funded.

The latest twist: new rules and closures

The impact of the FNGO Law on smaller organisations, such as foster homes and orphanages, was still unclear in 2017—at the time of my visit, the law had only been in place for six months—although it was certainly causing apprehension. Where previously even foreigners could get away with operating unregistered organisations in China, due in part to vague, ambiguous, and gap-filled laws, the rules had been clarified by the FNGO Law: foreign organisations now needed permission to carry out work in China, permission that had historically only been granted to a very small number of groups. Unregistered foster homes, like foreign-affiliated NGOs in China generally, were facing a difficult choice: try to register under the new law, risking closer state scrutiny of their work and the possibility of being asked to shut down; or try to lie low and avoid, as far as possible, interacting with state actors, other than trusted orphanage directors. In the past, as discussed in Chapter 4, the latter tactic had been very common. Foster homes had emerged in the grey zone between legal and illegal and had commonly been able to leverage the social legitimacy of their work to avoid any hassles or interference from state actors. The sense in 2017 was that this might not be a successful tactic moving forward, as with the new Charity and FNGO Laws, the state had signalled an intention to supervise civil society more closely. This, combined with increased scrutiny post-Lankao/Guangdong of unregistered caregiving arrangements, and rumours of an imminent crackdown on interprovincial foster care, had led to a sense of uncertainty for some of my research participants. But as discussed above, this was not the first period of heightened scrutiny and flux in the sector. The majority of my research participants remained optimistic that their *gu'er* relief work would be allowed to continue, regardless of the changing laws and policies coming out of Beijing and regardless of their unclear legal status—after all, that had always been the deal in the past.

It was not to be the deal moving forward. In October 2018, the Ministry of Civil Affairs issued updated *Measures on the Management of Child Welfare Institutions*, which came into effect in January 2019.[40] The Measures appear to ban interprovincial foster care, other than in exceptional circumstances, and have reportedly been applied as such.[41] By early 2019, six of the largest and oldest foster homes in my sample had received word from the Ministry of Civil Affairs, over the course of the previous eighteen months, that they would no longer be permitted to care for children from orphanages in other provinces. These homes were all highly visible, and widely respected, providing some of the best quality care available to *gu'er* in China. They also all had contingency plans in place in short order. For example, Good News Training Centre was permitted to register as an NGO, with a mandate to run a specialist training and therapy school for disabled children from local families. In this way, the organisation began shifting its focus "upstream", trying to keep families intact rather than serving children who have been abandoned. Prince of Peace, with its large, purpose-built, multimillion-dollar campus, likewise decided to register as a therapy centre and vocational training facility, working with a wider group of children with special needs, including some *gu'er* from state orphanages within their province, but mostly (non-abandoned) children from vulnerable families across China. New Grace was instructed to send its forty Beijing-based children back to their home orphanages but was advised by the Ministry of Civil Affairs that they would be permitted to continue running their on-site "special care units" at state orphanages across China and was encouraged to look for new ways to work with state orphanages in more rural areas of China in the future. Mustard Seed likewise planned to continue with its on-site orphanage projects, despite closure of their main foster care site.

It is difficult to say with certainty why these restrictions on foster care were put in place and to what extent they will be enforced in the future. Reportedly, children may still be permitted to leave their home provinces for temporary medical care in NGOs, as an "exceptional circumstance"—so Sharon's Rose, for example, the heart disease foster home introduced at the beginning of this chapter, has been allowed to continue fostering children from across China, at least for the time being. But the larger homes generally did not succeed in negotiating exemptions to the ban. It is possible that the Ministry of Civil Affairs intends to phase out all forms of cross-country foster care, or even all foster care to NGOs, so that *gu'er* are more closely supervised by the state. If that is the objective, then the closures could be seen as the result of a process that began with Lankao, as society questioned whether the state was adequately looking out for this vulnerable population, and Beijing clarified that *gu'er* should in principle be cared for in state institutions. The downside of restricting the foster home model is that it may become harder for humanitarians and NGOs to provide services to the *gu'er* population on an efficient, national scale. It is also possible that the closure of so many foster homes related in some way to broader political movements in China, such as new rules on foreign-funded NGO activity, or a desire to "localise" orphan relief and push foreigners out of the picture (rumours to this effect were already circulating prior to the most recent closures—that foreign-run foster homes in particular would soon be a thing of the past). Whatever the reasons behind them, the closure of so many high-quality foster homes suggests that the previous prioritisation of legitimacy over legality might not hold true moving forward.

Conclusion: changing roles and rules for private welfare providers

China's private *gu'er* welfare providers have faced numerous periods of uncertainty, tracing back to the first crackdown on volunteer groups following the "dying rooms" scandal. Despite the inherent unknowns of providing *gu'er* services in the face of changing laws, policies, and practices, hundreds of private orphanages and foster homes endured for years, sometimes decades. Previously, the state was largely missing from the field, at least as a facilitator or supervisor, except to the extent that certain hidden, unspoken norms had developed at the local level (as described in Chapters 3 and 4).

Generally, the lack of close supervision of private *gu'er* relief was not a concern raised by my research participants. Most of the orphanages and foster homes in my sample had expressed, at one point or another, a desire to simply be left alone by state actors: "If the Chinese government just gets out of our way, that's a big help" (*American director of Lydia's House [foster home], 2009*); "We just don't want to be under the government's thumb, telling us as to what we can and can't do" (*Ellie, founder of Compassion Family Life House*); "[we want to] make decisions solely on what ... is best for the organisation, [not] get caught up in government's planning and priorities" (*Will Peters, founder of Autumn Rain Orphan Care, 2010*). But there were two notable exceptions—Sister Yang of Guanghui, who had long been arguing that her *gu'er* were properly the responsibility of the state, and David of New Grace:

> The danger is there's no defined system or standard of care. So you end up with everyone doing what everyone thinks is right or best. And you have to ask yourself—are we really caring for the children well enough? I think we are. But that's just our judgment. That judgment should really be made by government, not us.
>
> *(David Dale, founder/director of New Grace Foster Home, 2009)*

The time of "everyone doing what everyone thinks is right or best" seems to be coming to an end, at least in theory. Since the Lankao fire, the state has been increasingly in the picture. For those who had been caring for "out of system" *gu'er*—from large Catholic orphanages to individual "love mothers"—the Lankao fire resulted in clearer rules as to care standards, procedures, and authorised providers, rules that required all *gu'er* to be brought "into the system". The dangers of the previous "one eye closed" approach to unauthorised private orphanages were highlighted by the tragedy, and as a result, local Civil Affairs officials were instructed to take more active responsibility for *gu'er* in their jurisdictions. To the extent these new rules are implemented, they should make the issue of *hukou*-less children in unregistered orphanages a thing of the past. But there are still question marks for caregivers like Sister Yang and Sister Chen—will the new rules and standards be enforced? Will the state provide meaningful, tangible help for grassroots orphanages such as their Catholic homes as they strive to professionalise and improve their services? When the memory of Lankao has faded, will there be appropriate enforcement of *gu'er* rights and appropriate intervention in cases of dangerous or neglectful orphanages?

There are question marks, too, over the future of foster care in China, particularly services offered by foreign-funded or foreign-run organisations. The long-standing model—of urban-based specialist homes providing free, high-quality care for needy *gu'er* from rural state orphanages—seems to have been largely banned in practice, at least for the time being. Some foster homes will no doubt attempt to carry on "under the radar", despite the latest wave of crackdowns. It is also possible that some foster homes will transition to a more medicalised model, focusing on providing short-term health care to larger numbers of children rather than long-term, family-style health-plus-foster care—this may be permissible under the new rules, depending on how they are applied. And some, like Bethany Outreach, New Grace, and Mustard Seed, will shift their focus to on-site partnerships, continuing the flow of private resources to *gu'er* in state orphanages, albeit on a more targeted, localised scale.[42] For the time being, the Ministry of Civil Affairs has indicated that such on-site collaborations will be supported (this would align with the urgent need, discussed in Chapter 2, for more training programmes and improved professionalism in the state orphanage sector).[43] And it may be that cross-country foster care to specialist homes will reemerge in the future, as policies and practices continue to change and negotiations between NGOs and state actors carry on.

Whether these developments will prove to be for the best for *gu'er* in China generally, and for the individual *gu'er* in private organisations who were immediately affected, is not yet known. To return to the point made by Sister Yang and David Dale, the state has ultimate moral responsibility for China's lonely children. Arguably the transition from "one eye closed" to "two eyes opening" signals that the state is taking that responsibility more seriously—by regulating NGO activity, requiring state orphanages to keep a closer eye on their charges, and setting and enforcing meaningful standards of care. As a result, private *gu'er* welfare providers, many of which have been providing high-quality, specialist services for decades, will need to renegotiate their roles and functions in China's welfare system.

With all of these question marks and changing rules, one thing is certain: implementation of new laws and policies will take time and will be mediated by the location and actors involved. Writing in the context of NGO regulation, Saich has previously observed "a significant gap between rhetoric and practice and between the expressed intent of the Party-State authorities, a system that is itself deeply conflicted, and what can actually be enforced for any significant period throughout the entire country".[44] As an ancient saying goes, in China "the mountains are high and the Emperor is far away" (*shan gao, huangdi yuan*). In a country as geographically and politically vast as China, it has historically been difficult to ensure regional compliance with central bureaucratic orders and authority—one Chinese foster home manager acknowledged this by wryly informing me that while "above there are policies, below there are counter-measures" (*shang you zhengce, xia you duice*) (*Carol, Good News Training Centre, 2017*). The negotiations and interactions between private orphanages and foster homes on the one hand and the state on the other were almost always happening at the local level, other than for the few who had been registered as national organisations. And at that local level, "the state" is made up of different branches, units, and people—with different priorities, agendas, personalities, and sympathies: "Even though they're officers, they're also human beings. They have a heart" (*Grace, manager of Still Waters Foster Home, 2017*); "Policy is one thing. Living together is another. Local government is made up of people's parents and friends" (*Charles Kramer, adviser to Guanghui, 2010*).[45] As such, the process of negotiating—for support, supervision, permission to forge new roles in orphan relief—will continue to be local, variable, and centrally important to the future of private *gu'er* welfare in China.

Notes

1 *People's Daily*, "Xinhua Interviews Yuan Lihai: I Just Wanted to Let the Children Have a Life," *people.cn*, 6 January 2013, http://politics.people.com.cn/GB/n/2013/0106/c70731-20104096.html (retrieved 8 August 2018).
2 Yi Wang and Qiao Chen, "Lankao Fire Orphanage Founder Controversy," *people.cn*, 5 January 2013, http://legal.people.com.cn/GB/n/2013/0105/c42510-20092018.html (retrieved 8 August 2018).
3 Wang and Chen, "Lankao Fire Orphanage Founder Controversy," 2013.
4 In the wake of the fire, online rumours accusing Yuan Lihai of selling children or profiting from their welfare payments blossomed, but these rumours were debunked by investigative journalists: Xingjun Zhang, "Lankao Civil Affairs Bureau: No Evidence that Yuan Profited from Adoption of Abandoned Babies," *people.cn*, 5 January 2013, http://politics.people.com.cn/GB/n/2013/0105/c14562-20098561.html (retrieved 8 August 2018).
5 Wang and Chen, "Lankao Fire Orphanage Founder Controversy," 2013.
6 Wang and Chen, "Lankao Fire Orphanage Founder Controversy," 2013.
7 *People's Daily*, "Lankao Shelter Adopted Over 100 Abandoned Babies in 20 Years – Were the Adoptions Proper?" *People's Daily*, 5 January 2013, http://society.people.com.cn/GB/n/2013/0105/c1008-20090924.html (retrieved 8 August 2018).
8 "Lawyer Explains Issues in Relation to Yuan Lihai Adoptions: Not Illegal to Adopt Orphans and Disabled Children," *chinesenews.com*, 17 January 2013, http://legal.

people.com.cn/GB/n/2013/0117/c188502-20239322.html (retrieved 8 August 2018); Chengdu Daily, "Scholar Predicts Yuan May Face Seven Year Sentence, Deputy County Chief Admits Lack of Supervision," 6 January 2013, http://legal.people.com.cn/GB/n/2013/0106/c42510-20102124.html (retrieved 8 August 2018).

9 Luo Xin, "Yuan Lihai Case: Maximum Penalty of Seven Years," *The Beijing News*, 12 January 2013, http://legal.people.com.cn/GB/n/2013/0112/c42510-20177296.html (retrieved 8 August 2018).

10 Wenjia Ma *et al.*, "Lankao, Henan: Yuan Released from Detention," *China National Radio*, 6 January 2013, http://politics.people.com.cn/GB/n/2013/0106/c70731-20105994.html (retrieved 8 August 2018).

11 Bo Chen, "Lankao Civil Affairs Bureau: Orphans Unsupported Due to Lack of Lawful Authority," *people.cn*, 5 January 2013, http://politics.people.com.cn/GB/n/2013/0105/c1001-20090477.html (retrieved 8 August 2018).

12 Mengyang Chen and Hang Chu, "Comment: Why is Liaoning's Yuan Lihai Facing Being Banned?" *people.cn*, 23 January 2013, http://cpc.people.com.cn/pinglun/GB/n/2013/0123/c78779-20299033.html (retrieved 19 November 2018).

13 *People's Daily*, "Abandoned Children's Deaths Reveal Charities' Pain," *people.cn*, 5 January 2013, http://politics.people.com.cn/GB/n/2013/0105/c70731-20089312.html (retrieved 8 August 2018) (freely translated).

14 Ministry of Civil Affairs, *Notice: Nationwide Investigation into the Situation of Individuals and Private Organizations Receiving Orphans* [*Tongzhi yaoqiu: dui geren he minban jigou shouliu gu'er qingkuang jinxing quanguo xingda paicha*], 6 January 2013. Available at www.mca.gov.cn/article/xw/mzyw/201301/20130115403510.shtml (retrieved 8 August 2018).

15 The term used by the Notice is *minban jigou shouliu gu'er*, literally "private organisations that take in orphans".

16 *People's Daily*, "Media Reports: Public Orphanages Lack Funds, Private Orphanages Lack Policies," *people.cn*, 11 January 2013, http://legal.people.com.cn/GB/n/2013/0111/c188502-20165512.html (retrieved 14 August 2018).

17 *People's Daily*, "Exclusive Interview with Ministry of Civil Affairs," *people.cn*, 10 January 2013, http://edu.people.com.cn/GB/n/2013/0110/c1053-20152107.html (retrieved 19 November 2018).

18 Xinde Review, *Chinese Non-Government Child Adoption Seminar* [*Zhongguo minjian ertong yangyu yantaohui*] (Shijiazhuang: *Xinde wenhua yanjiusuo* [Xinde Cultural Institute], 2014), 1 (on file with author).

19 Xinde Review, *Chinese Non-Government Child Adoption Seminar*, Annex 1: China Non-government Child Rearing Organisation Self-discipline Proposal [*Zhongguo minjian shouyang ertong jigou zilü changyi shu*], 169.

20 Ministry of Civil Affairs and Religious Affairs Bureau, *Notice: Regulating Activities Relating to Orphan and Abandoned Children by Religious Groups* [*Guanyu guifan zongjiao jie shouliu gu'er, qiying huodong de tongzhi*], 30 April 2014. Available at http://cccwa.mca.gov.cn/article/fgzc/zcwj/201504/20150400800423.shtml (retrieved 16 November, 2018).

21 Approximately one hundred US dollars.

22 Xiaoyuan Shang and Karen R. Fisher, *Caring for Orphaned Children in China* (Lanham: Lexington, 2014), 233.

23 It should be noted here that although the orphan allowance does not appear to be reaching all intended *gu'er*, entitlement to the allowance has been progressively widened over the years. Most recently, in 2016, the State Council expressly extended the orphan allowance to all children in distress, including de facto orphans and other vulnerable categories of children: Office of the State Council, *Opinion on Strengthening Work to Protect Vulnerable Children* [*Guowuyuan guanyu jiaqiang kunjing ertong baozhang gongzuo de yijian*], 13 June 2016. Available at www.gov.cn/zhengce/content/2016-06/16/content_5082800.htm (retrieved 16 January 2019).

24 Pan Yue, "Seven Ministries [Ministry of Civil Affairs, Development and Reform Committee, Ministry of Justice, Ministry of Public Security, Ministry of Finance, Health and Family Planning Commission and Bureau of Religion] Issue Notice Prohibiting the Private Admission and Handling of Abandoned Babies" [*qi buwei chutai tongzhi jinzhi size shouliu he chuli qiying*], Ministry of Public Security of the People's Republic of China, 19 June 2013, reported at www.mps.gov.cn/n2254314/n2254409/n2254456/c4221886/content.html (retrieved 10 January 2019). The full text of the Notice is available at www.mof.gov.cn/zhengwuxinxi/zhengcefabu/201306/t20130618_925460.htm (retrieved 16 January 2019).

25 See Chapter 4 at 106–7.

26 For example, the *Beijing Times* reported on Love House in Pingdingshan, Henan, an unregistered foster home which cared for *gu'er* from seven or eight Henan state orphanages and was given notice to return its eighteen *gu'er* on 14 January. Like many of my research participants, Love House had tried to register as a *gu'er* caregiver in the past but was told its work was not permitted: *Beijing Times*, "After Lankao Incident, Private Adopting Institutions Face Closure," *people.cn*, 17 January 2013, http://society.people.com.cn/GB/n/2013/0121/c136657-20265316.html (retrieved 19 November, 2018).

27 For discussion of the rule against "branching out" (locally registered NGOs working at a national level), see Chapter 4 at n23.

28 Zixing Liu *et al.*, "Xinfeng County's Lianxi Care Centre Investigation," *Beijing News*, 20 March 2017, www.bjnews.com.cn/feature/2017/03/20/437087.html (retrieved 8 August 2018).

29 Xinhua News, "Guangdong Seriously Investigating Persons Responsible for Lianxi Care Centre Issue," *xinhuanet.com*, 27 March 2017, www.xinhuanet.com/legal/2017-03/27/c_1120703548.htm (retrieved 8 August, 2018).

30 Law on the Management of Foreign NGO Domestic Activities [*Jingwai Fei Zhengfu Zuzhi Jingnei Huodong Guanli Fa*] 2017 (People's Republic of China).

31 Charity Law [*Cishan Fa*] 2016 (People's Republic of China).

32 Registration as a Foundation had only been granted to a small number of organisations, meaning the majority of foreign-funded NGOs in China had been operating in a legal grey zone, without legal status: Edward Wong, "Clampdown in China Restricts 7,000 Foreign Organisations," *New York Times*, 28 April 2016, www.nytimes.com/2016/04/29/world/asia/china-foreign-ngo-law.html?_r=0 (retrieved 2 November, 2018). See, further, Catherine H. Keyser, "The Role of the State and NGOs in Caring for At-Risk Children: The Case of Orphan Care," in *State and Society Responses to Social Welfare Needs in China: Serving the People*, eds. Jonathan Schwartz and Shawn Shieh (Abingdon: Routledge, 2009), 54 (reporting that since the enactment of the Foundation Regulation in 2004, anecdotally there was a window of only six months during which foreign NGO registration applications were accepted by the central MCA); Jillian S. Ashley and Pengyu He, "Opening One Eye and Closing the Other: The Legal and Regulatory Environment for 'Grassroots' NGOs in China Today," *Boston University International Law Journal* 26, no. 1 (Fall 2008), 75 (noting that the MCA appears to routinely stall review of foreign foundation applications); Guosheng Deng, "The Hidden Rules of Governing China's Unregistered NGOs: Management and Consequences," *The China Review* 10, no. 1 (2010), 189–90 (noting the difficulties faced by foreign foundations in registering under the Foundations Regulation).

33 "Why Do People in China Give So Little to Charity?" *The Economist*, 6 September 2018, www.economist.com/china/2018/09/06/why-do-people-in-china-give-so-little-to-charity (retrieved 3 November, 2018).

34 "There is an old saying: if you have any problems, go to the police; if you have done nothing wrong, you have nothing to fear" (*you kunnan zhao jingcha, bu weifa ni pa sha?*): National People's Congress, "Why are Foreign NGOs Supervised by Public

Security? Official Reply" [*jingwai fei zhengfu zuzhi daibiao jigou sheli weihe you gongan jiguan fuze? Guanfang huiying*], 28 April 2016. Available at http://npc.people.com.cn/n1/2016/0428/c14576-28312625.html (retrieved 3 November, 2018).

35 Wong, "Clampdown in China Restricts 7,000 Foreign Organisations," 2016.

36 Hsia and White have noted an "entrenched ... traditional official idea that the main needs of individuals should not be met by foreign relationships": Renee Yuen-Jan Hsia and Lynn T. White III, "Working amid Corporatism and Confusion: Foreign NGOs in China," *Nonprofit and Voluntary Sector Quarterly* 31, no. 3 (September 2002), 336.

37 Charity Law [*Cishan Fa*] 2016 (People's Republic of China), article 5 (translated by China Development Brief, available at www.chinadevelopmentbrief.cn/wp-content/uploads/2016/04/Charity-Law-CDB-Translation.pdf (retrieved 2 November, 2018)). The Law also makes it lawful for domestic nonprofit organisations to engage in public fundraising, while improving tax incentives and facilitating the establishment of charitable trusts.

38 See, generally, "Why Do People in China Give So Little to Charity?" *The Economist*, 2018 (noting relatively low charitable giving as compared to other countries, due in part to different cultural definition of charity and historic state aversion to charity, but that donations are growing, particularly in the 20s/30s demographic); Elaine Jeffreys, "Entrepreneurs, Celebrities and Charitable Foundations: Elite Philanthropy in China," in *Handbook of Welfare in China*, eds. Beatriz Carrillo, Johanna Hood, and Paul Kadetz (Cheltenham: Edward Elgar, 2017), 322 (noting top-level calls to grow China's philanthropic culture).

39 Qiusha Ma, *Non-Governmental Organisations in Contemporary China: Paving the Way to Civil Society?* (Abingdon: Routledge 2006), 194.

40 Ministry of Civil Affairs, "Measures on the Management of Child Welfare Institutions" [*Ertong fuli jigou guanli banfa*], 30 October 2018, reported at www.mca.gov.cn/article/gk/fg/shsw/201811/20181100012652.shtml (retrieved 28 January 2019).

41 The final Measures are somewhat less explicit on this point than the draft Measures, which were issued for public comment in February 2018 (Ministry of Civil Affairs, "Draft for Comment: Measures on the Management of Child Welfare Institutions" [*Ertong fuli jigou guanli banfa: Zhengqiu yijian gao*], 13 February 2018, reported at http://fgcx.bjcourt.gov.cn:4601/law?fn=dae002s757.txt (retrieved 25 February 2019)). Article 27 of the draft Measures set out an express ban on interprovincial foster care. Although this article was removed from the final Measures, Article 25 thereof could be interpreted as an implied ban on interprovincial foster care other than in exceptional circumstances.

42 When the closures took effect, Mustard Seed reported that one of their partner state orphanages had been overwhelmed by the return of over ninety children from foster homes across China and had already asked for help (the facility was caring for three children per bed even before the fostered *gu'er* were returned).

43 See Chapter 2 at 46n135.

44 Tony Saich, "Negotiating the State: The Development of Social Organizations in China," *The China Quarterly* 161 (2000), 125.

45 As Qian has pointed out in the context of studies of the religious sector in China, the commonsense notion that Chinese state actors are also ordinary people is often overlooked: Linliang Qian, "Everyday Religiosity in the State Sphere: Folk Beliefs and Practices in a Chinese State-run Orphanage," *China Information* 30, no. 1 (2016), 91.

Bibliography

Ashley, Jillian S., and Pengyu He. "Opening One Eye and Closing the Other: The Legal and Regulatory Environment for 'Grassroots' NGOs in China Today." *Boston University International Law Journal* 26, no. 1 (Fall 2008): 29–96.

Deng, Guosheng. "The Hidden Rules of Governing China's Unregistered NGOs: Management and Consequences." *The China Review* 10, no. 1 (2010): 183–206.

High, Anna Jane. "China's Orphan Welfare System: Laws, Policies and Filled Gaps." *University of Pennsylvania East Asia Law Review* 8, no. 2 (2013): 127–76.

High, Anna Jane. "Grassroots NGO Regulation and China's Local Legal Culture." *Socio-Legal Review* 9, no. 2 (2013): 1–50.

High, Anna Jane. "'It's Grace and Favor, It's Not Law': Extra-Legal Regulation of Foreign Foster Homes in China." *University of Pennsylvania Asian Law Review* 12, no. 3 (Spring 2017): 357–405.

Hsia, Renee Yuen-Jan, and Lynn T. White III. "Working amid Corporatism and Confusion: Foreign NGOs in China." *Nonprofit and Voluntary Sector Quarterly* 31, no. 3 (September 2002): 329–51.

Jeffreys, Elaine. "Entrepreneurs, Celebrities and Charitable Foundations: Elite Philanthropy in China." In *Handbook of Welfare in China*, edited by Beatriz Carrillo, Johanna Hood, and Paul Kadetz, 317–37. Cheltenham: Edward Elgar, 2017.

Keyser, Catherine H. "The Role of the State and NGOs in Caring for At-Risk Children: The Case of Orphan Care." In *State and Society Responses to Social Welfare Needs in China; Serving the People*, edited by Jonathan Schwartz and Shawn Shieh, 45–65. Abingdon: Routledge, 2009.

Ma, Qiusha. *Non-Governmental Organisations in Contemporary China: Paving the Way to Civil Society?* Abingdon: Routledge 2006.

Ministry of Civil Affairs. *Notice: Nationwide Investigation into the Situation of Individuals and Private Organizations Receiving Orphans* [*Tongzhi yaoqiu: dui geren he minban jigou shouliu gu'er qingkuang jinxing quanguo xingda paicha*], 6 January 2013. Available at www.mca.gov.cn/article/xw/mzyw/201301/20130115403510.shtml (retrieved 8 August 2018).

Ministry of Civil Affairs, and Religious Affairs Bureau. *Notice: Regulating Activities Relating to Orphan and Abandoned Children by Religious Groups* [*Guanyu guifan zongjiao jie shouliu gu'er, qiying huodong de tongzhi*], 30 April 2014. Available at http://cccwa.mca.gov.cn/article/fgzc/zcwj/201504/20150400800423.shtml (retrieved 16 November, 2018).

National People's Congress. "Why are Foreign NGOs Supervised by Public Security? Official Reply" [*jingwai fei zhengfu zuzhi daibiao jigou sheli weihe you gongan jiguan fuze? Guanfang huiying*], 28 April 2016. Available at http://npc.people.com.cn/n1/2016/0428/c14576-28312625.html (retrieved 3 November, 2018).

Office of the State Council. *Opinion on Strengthening Work to Protect Vulnerable Children* [*Guowuyuan guanyu jiaqiang kunjing ertong baozhang gongzuo de yijian*], 13 June 2016. Available at www.gov.cn/zhengce/content/2016-06/16/content_5082800.htm (retrieved 16 January 2019).

Qian, Linliang. "Everyday Religiosity in the State Sphere: Folk Beliefs and Practices in a Chinese State-run Orphanage." *China Information* 30, no. 1 (2016): 81–98.

Saich, Tony. "Negotiating the State: The Development of Social Organizations in China." *The China Quarterly* 161 (2000): 124–41.

Shang, Xiaoyuan, and Karen R. Fisher. *Caring for Orphaned Children in China*. Lanham: Lexington, 2014.

Xinde Review. *Chinese Non-Government Child Adoption Seminar* [*Zhongguo minjian ertong yangyu yantaohui*]. Shijiazhuang: *Xinde wenhua yanjiusuo* [Xinde Cultural Institute], 2014 (on file with author).

Yue, Pan. "Seven Ministries [Ministry of Civil Affairs, Development and Reform Committee, Ministry of Justice, Ministry of Public Security, Ministry of Finance, Health and Family Planning Commission and Bureau of Religion] Issue Notice Prohibiting the Private Admission and Handling of Abandoned Babies [*qi buwei chutai tongzhi jinzhi size shouliu he chuli qiying*]." Ministry of Public Security of the People's Republic of China, 19 June 2013, reported at www.mps.gov.cn/n2254314/n2254409/n2254456/c4221886/content.html (retrieved 10 January 2019).

6 Conclusion

Growing up and looking forward

When I returned to St Martin's in 2017, it had been seven years since my last visit. After running into Lina, I was reunited with the other girls who had lived with her in *jiating* number six. They all spontaneously addressed me as Anna *ayi* (auntie) rather than Anna *jiejie* (big sister) as they had previously. They had grown up, too, but they were all still living at St Martin's. This highlighted a problem facing many private orphanages: what arrangements to make for an ageing population of highly dependent teenagers and young adults. Unlike Lina, some of Sister Chen's former charges had gone on to gain some measure of independence outside the orphanage grounds, with ongoing support from Sister Chen and the wider church community. In 2010, Sister Chen had taken me to meet some of these young people. Our day started with a visit to a neighbouring hamlet to pick up some forty boxes of donated sugared fruit from their orchard to bring on our visits. Our next stop was a nearby church-owned dormitory, where a group of five teenage *gu'er* lived together and attended the local school, supported by the congregation. We then travelled one town over to have lunch with Fangfang, a woman in her early twenties with "split-hand" malformations who had recently got a temporary job in a restaurant. She seemed very excited to be making her own way in the world. We also visited a young blind woman in a wheelchair who lived and worked in a Christian-run massage parlour. Our last stop was an old persons' home (*lao'er yuan*) that had been founded by Sister Chen's church a year earlier, in part so that dependent St Martin's children would have somewhere to live when they aged out of the orphanage. The non-profit *lao'er yuan* was home to thirty elderly, childless men and women and four younger men who had grown up at St Martin's. One of these men was in his late twenties. Sister Chen introduced him to me as the same boy who in 1993 had been found at the age of ten in a rubbish pit with a high fever, the first of hundreds of children to be brought into Sister Chen's care.

The "ageing out" problem was a common concern raised by private orphanages and foster homes in interviews—how to provide appropriately segregated care for pre- and post-adolescents and how to avoid becoming hospices or aged-care homes as unadopted teenagers began to enter early adulthood. For example, Good News Training Centre invested enormous resources, with the assistance of experts from around the world, in giving its resident blind children the occupational therapy needed to live as independently as possible, whether they ended up joining a "forever family" or passing the cut-off age without a match. Adoption was always considered the best option, and the foster home worked closely with international adoption agencies to attempt to find matches for the Good News children, which was often facilitated by the strong ties between the home and supportive evangelical communities abroad. Each adoption was a cause for celebration, while acknowledging the grief involved as a child left one home for another. Other children, having passed the cut-off age without a match, went on to find different versions of community and belonging outside of adoption. When I last visited Good News, I met an enterprising young man who had lived at Good News for decades and who knew its French founders as *faguo mama, faguo baba* (French mama, French papa). He was unable to live on his own, due to intellectual disabilities, but had started running his own small business from Good News' front yard, selling ice-creams and cool drinks in the summertime to visitors and neighbours. At Prince of Peace Village, Wang Yong, also an "aged-out" *gu'er* with intellectual disabilities, had shown a keen interest in and eye for photography; when he was in his early twenties, he decided he was ready to leave Prince of Peace and wanted to return to his home province of Fuzhou, where he was welcomed back to his home state welfare institution and given the unofficial role of photographer for the organisation.

At Star Village, an orphanage for children with incarcerated parents, the question of "what next?" was one that founder Madam Leng regularly encouraged her charges to consider. She gave a monthly lecture to the children in her care entitled "*lu zai hefang*"—where is the path that should be taken? In the lecture, she tried to encourage the *gu'er* to hope for a better future than their parents and to take steps towards achieving independence and fulfilment on leaving their Star Village home. The children I met at Star Village, and at China's other orphanages and foster homes, were not voiceless and powerless objects of birth-planning policies, parental abandonment, and philanthropy (although the stories told in this book have been related in part to show the impact of those patterns on *gu'er* generally). They were growing up to navigate individual life choices and would no doubt continue to face disadvantage and discrimination of varying degrees and kinds even into adulthood. In recognition of this, Madam Leng attempted in her way to focus not just on putting a roof over their heads but also on their personal and moral development.

The "where is the way?" question was also relevant for the people and organisations involved in providing private *gu'er* relief in China. In the decades since Sister Chen took in the fevered boy from a rubbish pit, the social, political, and legal landscape for *gu'er* welfare has changed dramatically. Incidents like the Lankao fire brought heightened interest and scrutiny from society and the state alike, with increasing restrictions on direct admissions, cross-country foster care, and NGO operations generally. As oversight tightened, at least in certain places and in certain seasons, the humanitarian workers on the ground—those changing nappies and dressings, searching for funding, advocating for their children, devising care plans for their aged-out charges—needed to adapt. This chapter first considers the lessons that can be drawn from the narrative that has unfolded over the course of those decades. Although the private orphan relief sector is small and, in some ways, unique, the story of its growth and adaptation over the years is a useful illustration of many of the broader tensions and dynamics associated with civil society, welfare pluralism, law- and policy-making, and the status of children in China. In addition to looking back, this chapter also looks forward, to the future of child welfare, and private *gu'er* relief, in China. This is a sector that has always been in transition, a constantly moving target of analysis. Looking forward, this chapter considers the changes that are needed to best address the rights and interests of China's lonely children. How can private resources best be channelled to them? And how will the sector continue to grow and adapt in the face of shifting laws, policies, and practices?

"Utilitarian familism" through the church family

The story of private *gu'er* relief, as told in this book, is one strand of a bigger story, China's shift from a system of centralised state welfare to a pluralist system including non-government service providers. In the case of faith-based organisations—such as the church-funded orphanages and foster homes introduced here—this shift echoed the traditional Confucian "utilitarian familism" approach to welfare, in which the family, more than the state, was the foundation of welfare. Across China, people and groups, motivated by a world view that considers all people to be members of the family of God, reached out to provide for some of the most vulnerable members of that spiritual family, in response to biblical exhortations and visibly urgent local needs.

The standard of care provided by these makeshift orphanages and specialist foster homes varied enormously. But overall, the services provided by private orphanages and foster homes had improved noticeably over the course of my fieldwork, in line with the increased professionalisation of China's welfare system generally.[1] Most of the homes in my sample had a long organisational history, running for ten years or longer, and as a result had developed hands-on expertise and built up loyal and generous donor bases along the way. The improvements were most noticeable in the grassroots, locally funded Christian orphanages. In 2017, the living standards at Guanghui and St Martin's were a far cry from their earliest days, when food was scarce and bedrooms remained unheated through frigid winters. This was partly because regional living standards had improved, and largely because of an increase in donations. Western-style, arms-length *cishan* (charity), previously an unfamiliar concept in China, had begun to take root in Chinese society. Charity was no longer a maligned concept but rather had been "rehabilitated",[2] and a public donation culture was developing. At the same time, the growth of social media (especially WeChat, a ubiquitous app that provides a platform both for funding requests and bank transfers) had improved both the visibility of social problems and the ease of sending payments in response. For private orphanages and foster homes, these developments resulted in broader donor bases. Tech-savvy nuns were no longer solely dependent on their immediate communities for financial support and donations of goods. Likewise, foster homes that had traditionally relied on foreign donors were increasingly supported by wealthy, willing, and connected domestic donors.

There has also been growing recognition, in recent years, of the need to put in place effective national policies aimed at reducing the *gu'er* population by keeping birth families intact. Criminalisation of abandonment has not proven effective in this respect.[3] Instead, top-down policy changes are needed to support parents in the fulfilment of their parental duties, as well as bottom-up shifts in the cultural discourse on child rights, disability, and adoption. Given that disability seems to have overtaken sex as the most important risk factor for abandonment, the focus will need to be on supporting parents of children with costly medical needs and disabilities, and there have been promising developments to that end. Some regions of China have begun to discuss and implement policy initiatives such as free health checks for newborns, registration of special medical needs at birth, and free follow-up health care and therapy for children with special needs.[4] Further, in its 2016 *Opinion on Strengthening Child Protection*, the central government signalled its awareness of the pressures on families of children with special needs.[5] The Opinion, issued by China's chief administrative authority, called for free therapy and surgery to be available not only for *gu'er* through the existing orphanage-targeted Tomorrow Plan but also for children more generally; if implemented in China's poorest provinces, this is a move that will surely go a long way to reducing abandonment of children with costly medical needs.[6]

Importantly, the same Opinion also expressly acknowledged the importance of encouraging and supporting social forces as participants in child welfare, noting that charitable organisations should be cultivated and guided in basic standards and professionalisation. But in light of more recent political events in China, it remains unclear which types of organisations will be sanctioned and to what extent local and international "church families" will be able to continue contributing to welfare. The 2014 post-Lankao survey of private orphanages found that the majority were run by religious organisations, and my survey of foster homes likewise suggests that the majority are faith-motivated and funded largely or in part by foreign funds. However, with the passing of the Foreign NGO Law, Beijing appears to be tracking towards a more restrictive approach to the use of foreign funds in China, including for charitable purposes.[7] In addition, at the time of writing, there have been reports of a recent crackdown on unregistered churches and faith-groups in China, with organisations formerly tolerated by state authorities now subject to disbanding, church buildings demolished, and church leaders taken into custody.[8] Researchers say the crackdown may be the most restrictive since the Cultural Revolution and is "fuelled by government unease over the growing number of Christians and their potential links to the west".[9] Given the prevalence of both foreign and religious organisations in the field of private *gu'er* relief, the recent political scrutiny of both types raises questions as to the future of their associated *gu'er* missionary and service activities.

The negotiated legitimacy and legality of private orphan welfare

After the Lankao fire, Yuan Lihai was asked if she understood that she had been in noncompliance with child welfare formalities. She responded, “I am just a rural woman—of course I didn’t understand the laws on this. I simply saw children in desperate need, bundled them home, and tried to look after them”.[10] Time and again from my research participants, I heard this same story. People had seen a need and responded. They were not focused on legal processes and formalities, in large part because it was often hard to get a clear answer on what those formal rules were, and what would and would not be permitted in practice, and in large part because of the urgency of the problem before them. Caregivers were willing to sideline (admittedly vague) laws and technicalities for the sake of being able to do what they saw as being in the best interests of children. For example, when I asked Emma, the manager of a foreign foster home in Dongjian, whether her work was lawful, she responded,

> I don’t know what legal means here [in China]. I don’t know any of the laws. But I believe we are dedicated to caring for the ones that need us. We are simply helping out the orphanages that are not able to better care for the kids. And they’re allowing us to do that—so for that part, we are legal. And we’re not doing anything against the orphans.
>
> *(Emma, manager of Compassion Family Life House, 2017)*

Ivy, the Chinese manager of another of the original Dongjian foster homes, put it this way: “The children are my work. Government stuff is not my concern.... Legal or not legal is fine for me” (*Ivy, manager of Friendship Outreach, 2010*). Another of my research participants, an English expatriate in Shanghai who worked closely with grassroots private orphanages in the area, said of private *gu’er* relief generally—“We’re all doing this work illegally. We can’t think of legalities because if we do, the children would have died ... We do understand. We know we *can’t* do this work legally, but morally we *have* to do it” (*Nicki, volunteer coordinator for Rice Rescue, 2009*).

These caregivers had also found that by acting in the best interests of *gu’er*, it was possible to establish legitimacy in the eyes of donors, communities, and local authorities, regardless of legality or lack thereof. State actors were willing to turn a blind eye to formal laws and policies, so long as children were not in any obvious danger and so long as unspoken rules—against political activism, evangelism, embarrassing the state—were followed. By giving foster homes and orphanages the benefit of a blind eye, local authorities also stood to benefit from the flow of services and employment opportunities into their community, without needing to take on the expense or responsibility of providing *gu’er* welfare directly or supporting and funding private care providers. So, the “one eye closed”, legitimacy-trumps-legality approach was apparently widely considered to be mutually beneficial: “We are playing on the fact that their system [of state *gu'er* welfare] is not working. And if they were to insist on doing things the 'legal' way, we couldn't [provide these services], and they know it" (*Alain, founder/director of Good News Training Centre, 2009*). Private orphanages and foster homes were able to take advantage of a flexible and ambiguous regulatory landscape to carve out space for their work; the ambiguity of the legal landscape for *gu'er* relief was, in this sense, productive.

In his study of the survival of grassroots NGOs in China, Anthony Spires has described a situation of "contingent symbiosis", in which unauthorised NGOs can survive and are tolerated by an authoritarian state, provided they are addressing significant social needs (thereby relieving the state of welfare obligations), bringing political credit to state agents, and avoiding behaviour that risks drawing attention to state failings or crosses political lines.[11] The empirical findings in this book speak to Spires' contingent symbiosis framework as well as more general scholarship on state tolerance of "illegal" practices, scholarship that explores the blurred nature of lines between legal and illegal on the ground.[12] In the field of private *gu'er* welfare, at least before the turning point of the Lankao fire, registration was in practice limited to organisations with close government ties; the majority of non-governmental welfare organisations were unregistered and therefore unauthorised, ostensibly illegal but in practice widely tolerated.[13] This points to an important feature of modern Chinese civil society and legal culture: that legitimacy has frequently been prioritised over legality. My research has shown how formal laws were subordinated in practice to flexible, discretionary, and local understandings about an organisation's legitimacy as a care provider; to use Gao Binzhong's framework, organisations that could play by the rules, toe the line with local actors, and contribute to pressing welfare needs were regarded as socially and politically legitimate, including by state actors, despite their lack of legal legitimacy.[14] Likewise, most of my research subjects seemed to be far more preoccupied with being recognised (*chengren/renke*) by state actors as *legitimate* care providers than with being registered (*dengji/zhuce*) through state formalities as *legal* care providers (for example, questions about the latter were often treated as referring to the former).

Because of the emphasis on legitimacy, nonlegal norms or "hidden rules" were generally more important than (vague, ambiguous, or absent) legal rules in terms of determining who would be permitted to play what role in supplementing state welfare. At the time of my earliest fieldwork, most of my subjects considered the rules for unauthorised NGOs to be fairly predictable (although of course my sample had been filtered through a survivor bias) and felt confident in their ability to function in the absence of legally defined rules and relationships. There were recurring references in our conversations to game playing, trust building, and negotiating with state actors, all indications that law was subordinate in practice to other structures and processes. The dominant expectation was not that law would be impartially and consistently applied but rather that flexible norms would govern negotiated relations with paternalistic state actors, actors who wielded enormous discretionary power in practice. To borrow from Stephens' analysis of law in imperial China, the local mode of social control was more often "disciplinary/parental" than "adjudicative/legal".[15] This also accords with Hintzen's description of China as a culture in which individualised moral decisions are traditionally emphasised above generalised legal rules, and law is viewed as subordinate to the dictates of morality.[16] One of my research subjects echoed Hintzen in describing the law in China as "elastic—we operate within the scope of this elastic legal structure. Law is not rigid, it is tempered by humanity" (*Mr Gao, assistant manager of Star Village, 2009*).

My research subjects also acknowledged that the "rules of the game" were subject to change and depended greatly on the individual state actors involved—as one foster home founder put it, "I live between lines that are moving constantly" (*Alana, Red Thread Foster Home, 2009*). The contours of legitimacy were negotiable and flexible, not clearly defined or static. These negotiations were mostly taking place at the local level and therefore the meaning of "illegal-but-legitimate" was closely linked to local-level dynamics, priorities, and politics and varied from place to place.[17] The contours of legitimacy could also change over time, due to other externalities—such as changing central laws and policies and shifts in the broader political climate (for example, local officials tended to be stricter towards unauthorised care providers during periods of political upheaval, such as after the Lankao fire). This intersection of localism with top-down events highlights another of Spires' points: that different levels of government can have different sets of concerns, which can come into conflict.[18] As a result of all of these negotiations, externalities, and conflicts, there was always a degree of uncertainty as to the future of their organisations—would today's illegal-but-legitimate care provider still be considered legitimate and tolerable tomorrow?—and therefore the future of the children who called these places home.

Although the "one eye closed" approach seemingly created opportunities for caregivers to work, it also created organisational risks, challenges, and uncertainty for the orphanages and foster homes, as described throughout this book—for example, relating to *hukou*, financing, child entitlements, donations, and standards of care. There were also risks for state actors turning a blind eye to unauthorised caregivers. This political risk materialised for the Lankao officials who lost their jobs in the wake of the fire for failing to appropriately supervise and support "love mother" Yuan Lihai. As for the children in unauthorised homes, it is impossible to generalise as to the impact of the "one eye closed" approach to their welfare. A great many lives have been bettered, if not saved, by "love mamas", private orphanages, and foster homes; there were also many children in private homes who missed out on their state entitlements as *gu'er*, including access to adoption, health care, and education. And as the Lankao case demonstrated, self-governance, good intentions, and a willingness to work to the point of exhaustion were not always enough to ensure child safety and welfare.

This case study of private *gu'er* welfare also adds an interesting data-point to Spires' contingent symbiosis framework: with the Lankao fire, a local crisis drew national attention to an unauthorised-but-tolerated sector, leading to a top-down intervention. Importantly, the state response to Yuan's work as "love mama", and to the private orphanages it subsequently surveyed, confirmed that "illegal" groups could be considered legitimate, even by the central government. The Ministry of Civil Affairs did not attempt to deny the social legitimacy of Yuan's work.[19] But it did signal an intention to begin redefining the relationship between state authorities and private *gu'er* caregivers. Since Lankao, the state approach to private *gu'er* relief has shifted, becoming more focused on clear standards, rules, and policies; the same could be said of the state's approach to foreign NGOs, since the Foreign NGO Law was passed, and of foster care, since the recent move to restrict interprovincial foster care. Where previously, in practice, legality was of less importance than legitimacy, the state has now signalled an intention to use law and policy to standardise and regulate the sector. Seen in this light, these recent shifts speak to a much bigger and ongoing debate in Chinese legal scholarship: the extent to which China is transitioning to some form of rule of law. In the field of private *gu'er* relief, at least, there has been a change in emphasis, from legitimacy to legality—the rules seem to have changed, at least on paper (the implementation of these rules will continue to be heavily mediated by time and place as local officials decide to what extent they are willing and able to implement new central laws and policies). Practically speaking, the state generally appears to be tracking towards a regulatory landscape that allows the resources of private organisations to continue to be mobilised to supplement state welfare but ensures that those organisations are subject to tighter oversight, and effectively absorbed into the periphery of the state's enormous bureaucracy, and thereby required to comply with the priorities and agendas set by government. This mirrors the approach of the Chinese state to NGOs generally—as Zheng and Fewsmith have noted, China's model of close NGO supervision is one that effectively appropriates organisations as " 'helping hands', rather than autonomous organisations".[20]

Rhetoric shift: from child welfare to child rights

Around ten days after the Lankao fire, it was reported that two *gu'er* in a state orphanage in Hengdong county, Hunan province, had recently passed away. Fu Li was a ten-year-old boy with cerebral palsy and kidney problems. A care worker had noticed he was in distress and called a doctor to come from the nearby hospital, but Fu Li could not be saved. The next day, three-year-old Fu Lishui, a girl with congenital heart disease, cerebral palsy, and cleft lip and palate, was also found in distress, her face pale and short of breath. The same doctor attempted cardiac compression, but Fu Lishui also passed away. Despite overall improvements in recent years, deaths in China's state orphanages remain common, given the disabilities and medical needs that often characterise the population; so, although Fu Li and Fu Lishui's lives were important and inherently valuable, their deaths were also unremarkable. But coinciding with the Lankao tragedy, they did not go unnoticed. A local reporter rushed to the orphanage to investigate whether negligence had in any way contributed to the deaths, interviewing staff members as well as the doctor who had tried to revive the children. The journalist reported that the orphanage workers were facing immense pressure and challenges and found there were some worrying aspects to health care at the orphanage that may have been at play but concluded that the deaths were primarily due to preexisting medical conditions.[21]

The report on Fu Li and Fu Lishui's deaths was one of many news items in the weeks following Lankao to highlight the rights of *gu'er* to adequate care. This period of renewed national focus on *gu'er* welfare and rights was arguably also indicative of a broader shift that had been taking place in China even before Lankao: from focusing on child welfare towards viewing children as rights-holders. The distinction between child welfare and child rights may sound subtle but is not simply a question of semantics. Rights are entitlements premised on human dignity, demands that correlate to state duties, rather than requests that rely on state benevolence and mercy. As Sanford Fox has argued, unless premised on child rights, child welfare will be "dependent on a supply of kindness and concern that both past and present demonstrate is too often in short supply".[22] In other words, children's rights are an essential foundation of child welfare, as they empower a vulnerable population to "compel advancement of their welfare by the assertion of rights".[23]

China has a long history of concern for child welfare. China sees itself as a culture with a strong tradition of "loving the young".[24] This aspiration—of special regard for children and child protection—was reflected in one of the first statutes of the People's Republic, the 1950 Marriage Law [*Hunyin Fa*], which enshrined the duty of parents to protect and rear their children. Since then, China has continued to "[claim] a high degree of concern for the wellbeing of children".[25] But child welfare in China has not historically been premised on the idea of children as rights-holders. Confucianism, which still strongly influences modern Chinese culture, sees the family as the basic organising unit of society, not the individual. Accordingly, obligation and interdependence are emphasised over rights and individualism. In the Confucian world order, children are conceptually not independent but are rather embedded in and belonging to the family unit, valued for their future potential to continue familial relations and fulfil relational obligations. As a result, role-based duties of filial piety, respect, and care for elders traditionally precede and dominate any idea of children's rights.

In this cultural context, there has been a noteworthy shift in Chinese law, society, and politics over the past few decades towards "rights talk", with the Chinese Communist Party "increasingly appropriat[ing] a language of human rights and rule of law, not only about minors, but also about the citizenry as a whole".[26] China published its first white paper on human rights in the 1990s. Since then, China has firmly adopted at least the language and rhetoric of human rights on the international stage, including through participation in various human rights treaties and institutions. These include the United Nations Convention on the Rights of the Child (which was co-sponsored by China when it was introduced), an instrument that recognises the special vulnerability of minors and their corresponding fundamental entitlements.[27] It should be noted that the state-sanctioned notion of rights in China is not necessarily congruent with Western democratic norms, in that China tends to review rights as "revocable privileges conferred by the state rather than as "natural" prerogatives possessed by each individual".[28] But even domestically, at least in the field of child welfare, the concept of "rights and interests" (*quanli liyi*, or *quanyi* for short) has become both a subject of growing public discourse and a legislative priority, institutionalised in a number of social protection laws—for example, the 1991 Law on the Protection of Minors [*Weichengnianren Baohu Fa*], which was significantly amended in 2006 in order to better reflect the Convention on the Rights of the Child.[29] Orna Naftali has argued that the Law embodied a new way of thinking about children and child rights by acknowledging that minors "are not ancillary to their families but constitute a separate social group that is entitled not only to protection but also to respect as human beings".[30] She ties this to the emergence of a new child rights discourse which "casts children as 'subjects' rather than 'objects' and as 'independent persons' rather than mere 'appendages' to their families, society or the nation".[31] This shift is one important thread in an ongoing human rights story—Tony Saich has argued that since 2003, under slogans such as "putting people first" (*yirenweiben*) and "building a harmonious society" (*guojian hexie shehui*), combined with Xi Jinping's more recent "China dream" and accompanying welfare policies, "the glimmers of a rights-based consciousness in assessing access to public goods and services" have become increasingly apparent in China.[32]

The extent to which this growing consciousness of children as subjects with rights, rather than objects of welfare measures, will translate to meaningful advances in child welfare outcomes is an ongoing question. The discourse of child rights in China is still often in tension with other cultural narratives, including about disability and the role of children in the family unit. Further, the implementation and funding of welfare initiatives is still largely decentralised in China, dependent on local governments, meaning that central welfare targets and policies can have very different impacts in different locations.[33] But the rhetoric shift may prove to be a useful advocacy tool, given China's concern with presenting as a rights-respecting state. Further, since Lankao, there have been various indications of a transition from a child welfare system focused on basic survival to a more holistic, rights-based approach to the well-being of all minors as equal Chinese citizens, entitled to active state protection. Most notably, in its 2016 *Opinion on Strengthening Child Protection*, the State Council called for a comprehensive approach to the protection of child rights and interests, noting that children are the "hope of families and the future of the nation".[34] Unlike previous policy instruments, the 2016 Opinion acknowledged that children can face vulnerability even within the family setting and called for an expanded child protection mechanism that addresses parental abuse, thereby recognising that child rights may in certain cases trump even parental autonomy.[35] The Opinion also pledged to use state channels to properly resettle any children who have lost their parents, echoing the 2013 post-Lankao Notice and indicating a continued commitment to actively taking responsibility for *gu'er* as wards of the state. Importantly, the Opinion is just one of many policies and funding programmes directed at children through which China has acknowledged the special vulnerability of children without families and identified *gu'er* as a target population for welfare services.[36]

The duty to embrace a pluralist approach to *gu'er* relief

The realisation of children's rights, particularly the socioeconomic rights implicated by abandonment (such as to health care, education, identity, and an adequate standard of living), will necessarily be a gradual process, constrained by the availability of resources. Since the 1990s, when China began to shift away from a welfare statism model, the Chinese government has recognised the social and political need to create at least some space for non-government actors and resources to contribute to the enormous welfare needs of its growing population. Recent economic events in China have further implicated the state's ability to provide for all of the needs of its population.[37] In a context of growing rights-consciousness, this has in turn highlighted the rights-based duty of the state to utilise *all* available resources towards progressively meeting those needs—including those of the third sector. This duty was recognised, respectfully and with humility, by Sister Chen of St Martin's, when we spoke in 2017: "If the government does not have the capacity to take over private [*gu'er*] organisations, they should provide support and ensure they are safe places. I think this is what the government needs to do". In short, the state's responsibility and expressed commitment to caring for all *gu'er* as rights-holders must translate into active promotion and facilitation of welfare pluralism.

Related to this, an important aspect of child rights is the underlying interest of equality—ensuring that as the socioeconomic rights of children are progressively realised, this is done, as far as possible, with regard to equality of access. Taken together, the stories told in this book demonstrate how the provision of non-government resources and services to Chinese *gu'er* has often happened in an uncoordinated and disorganised way, resulting in unequal access to those resources and services. There was no central agency or department with responsibility for coordinating the movement of children from state orphanages to privately funded, specialist foster homes to ensure that the neediest children and orphanages were benefiting from the available private resources. Likewise, at least until the Lankao fire, there were no systems in place to ensure that *gu'er* in private orphanages were receiving their full state entitlements, given access to adequate care standards, or waitlisted for formal, state-regulated adoption. In these ways, the flow of resources, both state and private, to China's *gu'er* was unsystematic and dependent largely on location and chance. This inequality mirrored and reinforced the inherent inequality of welfare provision in China generally, which Saich has noted has historically depended more on place of birth or residence than on a notion of citizenship-based entitlement.[38]

As China continues to focus on the protection and fulfilment of child rights, including the right to equality, it will be important to embrace welfare pluralism and work towards achieving an "enabling legal and political environment for NGOs as an independent social force".[39] Such an environment has historically been lacking in China, given the state's "contradictory ideas" about NGOs, which have long been seen as both an important source of social services and a potential threat to state policy and stability.[40] In the field of *gu'er* welfare, these contradictory ideas, combined with a decentralised and underfunded local Civil Affairs bureaucracy, would appear to have been a major factor behind the local "one eye closed" approach to unauthorised care providers. And as discussed above, while such a flexible and discretionary approach created space for humanitarians to pitch in to the enormous task of *gu'er* relief as they saw fit, it was also not conducive to long-term security and growth and did not adequately safeguard against substandard care, neglect, or mismanagement.

Improving the supervision of non-governmental orphan welfare will take time, as post-Lankao experience has shown. The flurry of central directives and state notices after Lankao generally indicated approval, at the highest level, of private welfare efforts—at least *native* private welfare efforts—but put the onus on local governments to inspect and supervise the sector. To do this, and to take meaningful responsibility for the children in local private homes such as Guanghui and St Martin's, minimum care and safety standards for private orphanages need to be clearly articulated, and local governments need to be adequately trained, funded, and staffed in order to enforce those standards, with support from higher levels of government.[41] Given the fragmented and decentralised nature of the Chinese state bureaucracy, this will be challenging, and overstretched local officials may continue to adopt a "blind eye" approach in some cases. There is no sign as yet of a central agency with a clear mandate to supervise social efforts to protect *gu'er* and to support local officials in their oversight duties.[42] More generally, the system for discovering, reporting, and transferring *gu'er* to appropriate alternative care providers needs to be strengthened, alongside the development of a robust mechanism for removing children from abusive or neglectful environments. These are long-term policy changes, which will require continued re-conceptualisation of the role of the state—from sole benevolent provider to facilitator and supervisor of a professionalised third sector. As Shang and Fisher have noted, also in the context of *gu'er* welfare,

> [g]overnment responsibility does not necessarily mean direct government provision.... However, relying on ... community carers does not absolve the government of responsibility to properly resource, regulate, and monitor them to ensure that they meet the rights of the orphans and other family members, and follow international good practice.[43]

Recently, as discussed in Chapter 5, a decision appears to have been made that taking responsibility to regulate community *gu'er* carers requires restricting the national movement of *gu'er*, other than for medical treatment. As a result, the foster home model introduced in this book may soon be a thing of the past. In some respects, this move is not surprising—facilitating and supervising the sector would be complicated. The complexity relates in part to China's restrictive NGO laws and policies, which frown upon local or provincial NGOs being involved in national activities.[44] The foster home sector was also dominated by foreign-affiliated organisations, organisations that were subject to increased scrutiny generally with the passing of the FNGO Law. Many of these homes were recognised as national leaders in care standards and certain medical specialties and had access to some of the world's best medical teams, as well as millions of dollars of international funding. Ideally, these types of high-quality, NGO-state partnerships will be allowed to continue, at least in the form of on-site initiatives such as New Grace's special care units. Setting up a central agency to sanction, oversee, and standardise these partnerships could be a useful way of encouraging more such partnerships to develop, given that NGO contributions here could cross multiple disciplines (medical, educational, disability rights, child protection). Such central facilitation would also ensure that the "half under the table" approach described in this book does not carry over to new forms of welfare delivery. It is also conceivable that in time, with the proper supervision, the model of national foster care catering to special subpopulations of *gu'er* could be revived. Unfortunately, early indications are that the new legal and political environment for foreign-affiliated NGOs will be rather more restrictive than enabling, which may further stifle the use of private resources to protect *gu'er* rights and interests. Given the state's duty to utilise all available resources to realise the rights of its children, a strong argument can be made that *gu'er* in private and state orphanages should not be cut off from international NGOs and actors due to unnecessary restrictions on foreign funding; that would be an unfortunate return to the "big government, small society" days of the early PRC, when state orphanages were banned from collaborating with NGOs for political reasons, resulting in the interests of *gu'er* being subordinated to political considerations.

Conclusion: *"Lu Zai Hefang"*, where is the way?

Just as domestic *baoying hui* (societies for the preservation of babies) and foreign missionary groups responded to *gu'er* needs in imperial China, and as networks of informal adoptive parents emerged in modern China to take in vulnerable children, so private orphanages and foster homes have played a quiet but important role in caring for *gu'er* in response to the deficiencies of welfare statism. Across China, church groups, mission workers, and enterprising individuals devised different means of catering to the needs of local *gu'er*. Although their methods, standards, and shortcomings varied, there was generally a clear trend towards improved services and professionalisation over the course of my research.

Returning to Madam Leng's question for her *gu'er*, as a question that is also relevant for the private orphan welfare sector: the way forward is uncertain. Generally, China has continued to track towards greater openness to pluralism in this area of welfare, coupled with increased regulation and oversight of the sector, the drawbacks and dangers of the previous "one eye closed" approach having been brought into sharp relief by the Lankao and Guangdong events. But the state's approach to regulating private *gu'er* welfare has also been largely reactive and localised, rather than considered and coordinated. For my research participants, this has meant continued uncertainty about their future role in caring for lonely children and in many cases a continuing renegotiation of those roles at the local level, in the wake of national events and top-down shifts in law and policy. This uncertainty has been particularly pronounced in the case of organisations receiving foreign funding, organisations connected to unofficial church groups, and organisations involved with the interprovincial movement of children.

On my last trip to China in 2017, there were many signs that the field of private *gu'er* welfare was heading in new directions. At Guanghui, since becoming Civil Affairs–approved and supervised following the Lankao overhaul, *gu'er* admittance rates had dropped off, as the local standard of living had improved. This had allowed the sisters of Guanghui to shift their focus to therapy and education initiatives for children with disabilities, with a view to supporting parents and preventing abandonment. The importance of these upstream measures, in light of the misunderstanding that often surrounds disability even in modern China, was illustrated by a poignant story I heard from one of the volunteer physiotherapists at Guanghui:

> One day I was told that a mother had arrived with her ten-year-old daughter, who had cerebral palsy, wanting to give her up. I went to meet her, and as soon as the mother explained to me that she wanted to leave her child with us, because she couldn't take care of her anymore, the little girl started crying—just as you would expect from a child who knows she is being deserted. She understood what her mother was saying. And the mother, until this point, had no idea that her ten-year-old daughter could understand her. I was able to show her, over time, using alternative ways of communicating, what her daughter was capable of.
>
> *(Giulia, Guanghui Children's Home, 2010)*

Sister Yang's hope was that abandonment would one day be a thing of the past in her community, that eventually most local families would be able to remain intact, and that Guanghui would no longer be needed as an orphanage. Likewise, at St Martin's, the local abandonment rate seemed to have dropped in recent years, which was a cause for relief, and a state orphanage had been constructed nearby; for Sister Chen, this had allowed her to shift her focus to elder care. She considered this to be the more pressing issue in her community and had redirected much of her energy and resources towards expanding the church's aged-care facility for childless elders.

Foster homes that had worked directly with state orphanages for years, in some cases for decades, were facing a similar transition to alternative care models, a transition that is still unfolding. For example, Good News Training Centre has shifted its focus from *gu'er* in state orphanages to providing support to children who might otherwise be at risk of abandonment. The organisation's loyal donor base will continue to channel funds, both from China and abroad, but those funds will now be used for tuition subsidies and teacher salaries, rather than for medical expenses and nanny wages.

Generally, all of the caregivers were looking forward to a future in which families are better supported, treatment for children with disabilities is more freely available, and institutional care for *gu'er* is no longer needed. As these changes unfold, abandonment rates drop, and the population of children in alternative care changes, the participation of civil society in child welfare will remain important. In new ways, then, the ability of non-state actors to cultivate legitimacy, navigate shifting norms, and adapt to an ever-changing political context will continue to be crucial to the fate of China's lonely children.

Notes

1 Karen R. Fisher, Xiaoyuan Shang, and Megan Blaxland, "Review Article: Human Rights Based Social Policies – Challenges for China," *Social Policy and Society* 10, no. 1 (2010), 71.

2 Carolyn L. Hsu, "'Rehabilitating Charity' in China: The Case of Project Hope and the Rise of Non-Profit Organizations," *Journal of Civil Society* 4, no. 2 (September 2008); Elaine Jeffreys, "Entrepreneurs, Celebrities and Charitable Foundations: Elite Philanthropy in China," in *Handbook of Welfare in China*, eds. Beatriz Carrillo, Johanna Hood, and Paul Kadetz (Cheltenham: Edward Elgar, 2017), 320.

3 See Chapter 2 at 28n11.

4 Xiaoyuan Shang and Karen R. Fisher, *Caring for Orphaned Children in China* (Lanham: Lexington, 2014), 231.

5 Office of the State Council, *Opinion on Strengthening Work to Protect Vulnerable Children* [*Guowuyuan guanyu jiaqiang kunjing ertong baozhang gongzuo de yijian*], 13 June 2016, www.gov.cn/zhengce/content/2016-06/16/content_5082800.htm (retrieved 16 January 2019).

6 There is an interesting parallel between such proposals for abandonment prevention measures in modern China, and the emergence of gentry-led *baoying hui* (societies for the preservation of babies) in post-Taiping China. Many *baoying hui* focused not only on supporting orphanages but also on "outdoor relief"—the term referred to giving financial support in the form of monthly rice and cash stipends to needy parents of newborns, as a preventative measure against abandonment and infanticide. These stipends were funded by donations from society and were probably fairly widespread by the mid-1800s. See, generally, Angela Ki Che Leung, "Relief Institutions for Children in Nineteenth-Century China," in *Chinese Views of Childhood*, ed. Anne Behnke Kinney (Honolulu: University of Hawai'i Press, 1995), 253–64.

7 See Chapter 5 at 124–6.

8 Benjamin Haas, "'We are Scared, but we have Jesus': China and its War on Christianity," *Guardian*, 28 September 2018, www.theguardian.com/world/2018/sep/28/we-are-scared-but-we-have-jesus-china-and-its-war-on-christianity (retrieved 3 November 2018); Javier C. Hernández, "As China Cracks Down on Churches, Christians Declare 'We Will Not Forfeit Our Faith,'" *New York Times*, December 26, 2018, www.nytimes.com/2018/12/25/world/asia/china-christmas-church-crackdown.html (retrieved 24 January, 2018).

9 Lily Kuo, "In China, They're Closing Churches, Jailing Pastors—And Even Rewriting Scripture," *Guardian*, 13 January 2019, www.theguardian.com/world/2019/jan/13/china-christians-religious-persecution-translation-bible (retrieved 18 January 2019).

10 Xingjun Zhang, "'Lankao does not have a Child Welfare Institution, Civil Affairs Bureau Often Helped Me'—Conversation with Yuan Lihai" (6 January 2013) *XinhuaNet* www.people.com.cn/GB/24hour/n/2013/0106/c25408-20109071.html (retrieved 24 January 2019).

11 Anthony J. Spires, "Contingent Symbiosis and Civil Society in an Authoritarian State: Understanding the Survival of China's Grassroots NGOs," *American Journal of Sociology* 117, no. 1 (July 2011).

12 See, for example, Josiah Heyman, ed., *States and Illegal Practices* (Oxford: Bloomsbury, 1999).

13 Yuwen Li has argued that to treat the millions of unregistered NGOs in China as existing illegally is "obviously unsustainable" ("Introduction: Challenges and Opportunities for NGOs in Different Parts of the World," in *NGOs in China and Europe: Comparisons and Contrasts*, ed. Yuwen Li (Farnham: Ashgate, 2011), 3. Whether it makes sense to refer to groups that are openly tolerated by the state as "illegal" relates to the well-worn legal anthropological debate on what is properly termed "law"; the term is commonly used both narrowly, to refer to state-enforceable law, and more broadly, in reference to "socially enforced binding rules", depending on "what one is trying to emphasise for analysis" (Sally Falk Moore, "Law and Social Change: The Semi-Autonomous Social Field as an Appropriate Subject of Study," *Law and Society Review* 7, no. 4 (Summer 1973), 745).

14 Professor Gao deconstructs legitimacy into four types: political, administrative, legal, and social, concepts which Han Junkui notes have a "strong interpretative power for Chinese social organisations": Bingzhong Gao, "The Question of Legitimacy of Social Organizations," *China Social Sciences* 2 (2000), translated in Junkui Han, "International NGOs in China: Current Situation, Impacts and Response of the Chinese Government," in *NGOs in China and Europe: Comparisons and Contrasts*, ed. Yuwen Li (Farnham: Ashgate, 2011), 34–35.

15 Thomas B. Stephens, *Order and Discipline in China: The Shanghai Mixed Court 1911–27* (Seattle: University of Washington Press, 1992).

16 Geor Hintzen, "The Place of Law in the PRC's Culture," *Cultural Dynamics* 11, no. 2 (1999).

17 See, also, Spires, arguing that tolerance for illegal NGOs in China is closely linked to local-level politics ("Contingent Symbiosis and Civil Society in an Authoritarian State," 19–20).

18 Spires, "Contingent Symbiosis and Civil Society in an Authoritarian State," 13.

19 Spires has noted that "the social legitimacy of NGO services" in China is "virtually unchallenged": "Contingent Symbiosis and Civil Society in an Authoritarian State," 32.

20 Yongnian Zheng and Joseph Fewsmith, *China's Opening Society: The Non-State Sector and Governance* (Abingdon: Routledge, 2008), 3. See discussion in Chapter 1 at 10.

21 Wenjie Ding, "Two Abandoned Children with Disabilities Died One Day Apart at Hunan Hengdong Welfare Institution," *xinhuanet.com*, 16 January 2013, http://politics.people.com.cn/GB/n/2013/0116/c1026-20221883.html (retrieved 9 August 2018).

22 Sanford J. Fox, "Remarks for the Opening Session of the Beijing International Conference on the Protection of Children's Rights," *British Columbia International and Comparative Law Review* 13 (1990), 52.

23 Fox, "Remarks for the Opening Session of the Beijing International Conference," 51.

24 Ronald C. Keith, "Legislating Women's and Children's 'Rights and Interests' in the PRC," *The China Quarterly* 149 (March 1997), 43. On whether it is appropriate to study a country of China's size and complexity as a unit of legal culture, see Michael Palmer, "Rethinking Children's Rights and Interests?: Economic Reform, Social Protection and Legal Culture in Post-Mao China," *Journal of Comparative Law* 5, no. 2

(2010): 261 (noting that overall China is a unitary and fairly centralised state, with a strong sense of cultural unity, continuity, and uniformity).

25 Palmer, "Rethinking Children's Rights and Interests," 261.

26 Orna Naftali, "Empowering the Child: Children's Rights, Citizenship and the State in Contemporary China," *The China Journal* 61 (2009), 102.

27 Convention on the Rights of the Child, 20 Nov., 1989, 1577 U.N.T.S. 3. Available at www.refworld.org/docid/3ae6b38f0.html (retrieved 17 January 2019).

28 Naftali, "Empowering the Child," 103.

29 Palmer, "Rethinking Children's Rights and Interests," 262.

30 Naftali, "Empowering the Child," 83. See, further, Palmer, "Rethinking Children's Rights and Interests," 260, noting that China has sought to institutionalise the concept of children's rights over the last twenty years.

31 Naftali, "Empowering the Child," 81. Fisher, Shang, and Blaxland have likewise argued that China's welfare system is moving towards a human rights-based system: "Review Article: Human Rights Based Social Policies," 2010.

32 Tony Saich, "The Politics of Welfare Policy: Towards Social Citizenship?" in *Handbook of Welfare in China*, eds. Beatriz Carrillo, Johanna Hood, and Paul Kadetz (Cheltenham: Edward Elgar, 2017), 95.

33 Saich, "The Politics of Welfare Policy," 81.

34 State Council, *Opinion on Strengthening the Work of Protecting Vulnerable Children* [*Jiaqiang kunjing ertong baozhang gongzuo de yijian*], 2016.

35 Until recently, the focus of alternative care (i.e. arrangements for children who do not live with their birth parents) in China, as in most developing countries, has mostly been on children without families rather than children at risk from their guardians. Accordingly, China does not have a developed child protection system in place to investigate and address cases of suspected abuse or neglect. According to Fang Zhao *et al.*, China's first case of parental custody deprivation only occurred in July 2014 and received nationwide attention. There is a strong cultural presumption of parental autonomy in China, which research suggests has contributed to a reluctance to revoke parental guardianship, other than in extreme cases. See, generally, Fang Zhao, Juha Erkki Antero Hämäläinen, and Honglin L. Chen, "Child Protection in China: Changing Policies and Reactions from the Field of Social Work," *International Journal of Social Welfare* 26, no. 4 (October 2017); Xiaoyuan Shang and Ilan Katz, "Missing Elements in the Protection of Children: Three Cases from China," *Journal of Social Service Research* 40, no. 4 (2014).

36 Other key policy developments discussed elsewhere in this book include the Blue Sky Plan (Chapter 2 at 42n106), the Tomorrow Plan (Chapter 2 at 42n101), and the post-Lankao national investigation into private orphan relief (Chapter 5 at n14). Also relevant are the 2011–2020 National Child Development Programme, which sets out priorities and targets for child welfare over the current ten-year period (China Centre for Children's Welfare and Adoption, *China Child Development Programme (2011–2020)* [*Zhongguo ertong fazhan gangyao*] http://cccwa.mca.gov.cn/article/fgzc/zcwj/201504/20150400800428.shtml (retrieved 10 July 2018)); and the 2018 Measures on the Management of Child Welfare Institutions, which sets out updated standards for state-run orphanages and welfare homes (Ministry of Civil Affairs, "Measures on the Management of Child Welfare Institutions" [*Ertong fuli jigou guanli banfa*], 30 October 2018, reported at www.mca.gov.cn/article/gk/fg/shsw/201811/20181100012652.shtml (retrieved 28 January 2019)).

37 Jennifer Y. J. Hsu and Reza Hasmath, "Chinese NGOs as Welfare Providers: Challenges and Constraints," in *Handbook of Welfare in China*, eds. Beatriz Carrillo, Johanna Hood, and Paul Kadetz (Cheltenham: Edward Elgar, 2017), 299.

38 Saich, "The Politics of Welfare Policy," 2017. See, further, Shang and Fisher, *Caring for Orphaned Children in China*, 237, discussing the decentralised nature of funding and administration of alternative care in China and the resulting differences in levels

of financial support, quality control, and management of alternative care systems across China, "from full support and participation in some eastern areas, to government neglect of responsibilities for children's rights in some poorer areas. As a result, child outcomes also differ".

39 Li, "Challenges and Opportunities for NGOs," 19.

40 Li, "Challenges and Opportunities for NGOs," 2.

41 For a discussion of the difficulties faced by local officials in interpreting and implementing social policies in China generally, in part due to the lack of enforceable regulations, see Megan Blaxland, Xiaoyuan Shang, and Karen R. Fisher, "Introduction: People Oriented: A New Stage of Social Welfare Development in China," *Journal of Social Service Research* 40, no. 4 (2014), 510.

42 Currently, responsibility for child welfare and protection policies is distributed across numerous agencies: Shang and Fisher, *Caring for Orphaned Children in China*, 42; Catherine H. Keyser, "The Role of the State and NGOs in Caring for At-Risk Children: The Case of Orphan Care," in *State and Society Responses to Social Welfare Needs in China: Serving the People*, eds. Jonathan Schwartz and Shawn Shieh (Abingdon: Routledge, 2009), 47. Both Guanghui and St Martin's reported being pushed back and forth from Civil Affairs to the Religion Bureau, when looking for state support/supervision, as a result.

43 Shang and Fisher, *Caring for Orphaned Children in China*, 238.

44 See Chapter 4 at n23.

Bibliography

Blaxland, Megan, Xiaoyuan Shang, and Karen R. Fisher. "Introduction: People Oriented: A New Stage of Social Welfare Development in China." *Journal of Social Service Research* 40, no. 4 (2014): 508–19.

China Centre for Children's Welfare and Adoption. *China Child Development Programme (2011–2020)* [*Zhongguo ertong fazhan gangyao*]. Available at http://cccwa.mca.gov.cn/article/fgzc/zcwj/201504/20150400800428.shtml (retrieved 10 July 2018).

Fisher, Karen R., Xiaoyuan Shang, and Megan Blaxland. "Review Article: Human Rights Based Social Policies—Challenges for China." *Social Policy and Society* 10, no. 1 (2010): 71–77.

Fox, Sanford J. "Remarks for the Opening Session of the Beijing International Conference on the Protection of Children's Rights." *British Columbia International and Comparative Law Review* 13 (1990): 47–52.

Gao, Bingzhong. "The Question of Legitimacy of Social Organizations." *China Social Sciences* 2 (2000). Translated in Han Junkui, "International NGOs in China: Current Situation, Impacts and Response of the Chinese Government." In *NGOs in China and Europe: Comparisons and Contrasts*, edited by Yuwen Li, 23–52. Farnham: Ashgate, 2011.

Heyman, Josiah, ed. *States and Illegal Practices*. Oxford: Bloomsbury, 1999.

High, Anna Jane. "China's Orphan Welfare System: Laws, Policies and Filled Gaps." *University of Pennsylvania East Asia Law Review* 8, no. 2 (2013): 127–76.

High, Anna Jane. "Grassroots NGO Regulation and China's Local Legal Culture." *Socio-Legal Review* 9, no. 2 (2013): 1–50.

High, Anna Jane. "'It's Grace and Favor, It's Not Law': Extra-Legal Regulation of Foreign Foster Homes in China." *University of Pennsylvania Asian Law Review* 12, no. 3 (Spring 2017): 357–405.

Hintzen, Geor. "The Place of Law in the PRC's Culture." *Cultural Dynamics* 11, no. 2 (1999): 167–92.

Hsu, Carolyn L. "'Rehabilitating Charity' in China: The Case of Project Hope and the Rise of Non-Profit Organizations." *Journal of Civil Society* 4, no. 2 (September 2008): 81–96.

Hsu, Jennifer Y. J., and Reza Hasmath. "Chinese NGOs as Welfare Providers: Challenges and Constraints." In *Handbook of Welfare in China*, edited by Beatriz Carrillo, Johanna Hood, and Paul Kadetz, 299–316. Cheltenham: Edward Elgar, 2017.

Jeffreys, Elaine. "Entrepreneurs, Celebrities and Charitable Foundations: Elite Philanthropy in China." In *Handbook of Welfare in China*, edited by Beatriz Carrillo, Johanna Hood, and Paul Kadetz, 317–37. Cheltenham: Edward Elgar, 2017.

Johnson, Kay Ann, Huang Banhan, and Wang Liyao. "Infant Abandonment and Adoption in China." *Population and Development Review* 24, no. 3 (September 1998): 469–510.

Keith, Ronald C. "Legislating Women's and Children's 'Rights and Interests' in the PRC." *The China Quarterly* 149 (March 1997): 29–55.

Keyser, Catherine H. "The Role of the State and NGOs in Caring for At-Risk Children: The Case of Orphan Care." In *State and Society Responses to Social Welfare Needs in China; Serving the People*, edited by Jonathan Schwartz and Shawn Shieh, 45–65. Abingdon: Routledge, 2009.

Leung, Angela Ki Che. "Relief Institutions for Children in Nineteenth-Century China." In *Chinese Views of Childhood*, edited by Anne Behnke Kinney, 251–78. Honolulu: University of Hawai'i Press, 1995.

Li, Haiyan, Xiaoyuan Shang, and Jianpeng Cheng. "An Analysis of Reasons Behind the Abandonment of Orphans and Disabled Children in Beijing (*Beijingshi Gucan Ertong Bei Yiqide Yuanyin Fenxi*)." *Beijing Social Sciences* 4 (2004): 164–68.

Li, Yuwen. "Introduction: Challenges and Opportunities for NGOs in Different Parts of the World." In *NGOs in China and Europe: Comparisons and Contrasts*, edited by Yuwen Li, 1–20. Farnham: Ashgate, 2011.

Ministry of Civil Affairs. *Measures on the Management of Child Welfare Institutions* [*Ertong fuli jigou guanli banfa*], 30 October 2018. Available at www.mca.gov.cn/article/gk/fg/shsw/201811/20181100012652.shtml (retrieved 28 January 2019).

Moore, Sally Falk. "Law and Social Change: The Semi-Autonomous Social Field as an Appropriate Subject of Study." *Law and Society Review* 7, no. 4 (Summer 1973): 719–46.

Naftali, Orna. "Empowering the Child: Children's Rights, Citizenship and the State in Contemporary China." *The China Journal* 61 (2009): 79–103.

Office of the State Council. *Opinion on Strengthening Work to Protect Vulnerable Children* [*Guowuyuan guanyu jiaqiang kunjing ertong baozhang gongzuo de yijian*], 13 June 2016. Available at www.gov.cn/zhengce/content/2016-06/16/content_5082800.htm (retrieved 16 January 2019).

Palmer, Michael. "Rethinking Children's Rights and Interests?: Economic Reform, Social Protection and Legal Culture in Post-Mao China." *Journal of Comparative Law* 5, no. 2 (2010): 260–80.

Saich, Tony. "The Politics of Welfare Policy: Towards Social Citizenship?" In *Handbook of Welfare in China*, edited by Beatriz Carrillo, Johanna Hood, and Paul Kadetz, 81–97. Cheltenham: Edward Elgar, 2017.

Shang, Xiaoyuan, and Karen R. Fisher. *Caring for Orphaned Children in China*. Lanham: Lexington, 2014.

Shang, Xiaoyuan, and Ilan Katz. "Missing Elements in the Protection of Children: Three Cases from China." *Journal of Social Service Research* 40, no. 4 (2014): 545–59.

Spires, Anthony J. "Contingent Symbiosis and Civil Society in an Authoritarian State: Understanding the Survival of China's Grassroots NGOs." *American Journal of Sociology* 117, no. 1 (July 2011): 1–45.

Stephens, Thomas B. *Order and Discipline in China: The Shanghai Mixed Court 1911–27*. Seattle: University of Washington Press, 1992.

Zhao, Fang, Juha Erkki Antero Hämäläinen, and Honglin L. Chen. "Child Protection in China: Changing Policies and Reactions from the Field of Social Work." *International Journal of Social Welfare* 26, no. 4 (October 2017): 329–39.

Zheng, Yongnian, and Joseph Fewsmith. *China's Opening Society: The Non-State Sector and Governance*. Abingdon: Routledge, 2008.

Index

For Product Safety Concerns and Information please contact our EU
representative GPSR@taylorandfrancis.com
Taylor & Francis Verlag GmbH, Kaufingerstraße 24, 80331 München, Germany

www.ingramcontent.com/pod-product-compliance
Ingram Content Group UK Ltd.
Pitfield, Milton Keynes, MK11 3LW, UK
UKHW022123190926
475702UK00013B/1620

9781032091396